IN SEARCH OF THE RIVER JORDAN

In Search of the River Jordan

A Story of Palestine, Israel and the Struggle for Water

James Fergusson

YALE UNIVERSITY PRESS
NEW HAVEN AND LONDON

For Milo

For information about this and other Yale University Press publications, please contact:
U.S. Office: sales.press@yale.edu   yalebooks.com
Europe Office: sales@yaleup.co.uk   yalebooks.co.uk

Set in Adobe Caslon Pro regular by IDSUK (DataConnection) Ltd
Printed in Great Britain by TJ Books, Padstow, Cornwall

Library of Congress Control Number: 2023930267

ISBN 978-0-300-24415-1

A catalogue record for this book is available from the British Library.

10 9 8 7 6 5 4 3 2 1

Contents

CONTENTS

Illustrations

1. *Joshua Passing the River Jordan with the Ark of the Covenant*, by Benjamin West, 1800. Abbus Archive Images / Alamy Stock Photo.
2. The Madaba map, *c.* sixth century. Valery Voennyy / Alamy Stock Photo.
3. The lower Jordan, near Alumot. Photograph by the author.
4. Qasr al-Yahud, West Bank, April 2019. Shutterstock.
5. Aerial image of the Jordan River gorge, close to the Dead Sea. Shutterstock.
6. An abandoned jetty on the Dead Sea coast. © Marco Zorzanello.
7. Palestinians throw shoes at an effigy depicting Arthur Balfour during a protest in the West Bank city of Bethlehem, November 2017. Reuters / Alamy Stock Photo.
8. Yasser Fahmi. Photograph by the author.
9. The *Mukata'a*, Yasser Arafat's mausoleum in Ramallah. Photograph by the author.
10. Rawabi. Photograph by the author.
11. Israel's National Water Carrier in the Galilee. Israel Images / Alamy Stock Photo.
12. Irrigated fields near Beit She'an in the Harod Valley. Photograph by the author.

13. A worker at the Sorek desalination plant in Palmachim, near Rishon LeZion, Israel, November 2021. Xinhua / Alamy Stock Photo.
14. Crowds of tourists on the beach at Tel Aviv, Israel, April 2008. Robert Harding / Alamy Stock Photo.
15. Gazans fleeing IDF tear gas at a border demonstration. Photograph by the author.
16. The Gaza Strip, April 2019. Claudia Weinmann / Alamy Stock Photo.

Israel-Palestine

⎯⎯⎯⎯⎯ *National Water Carrier*

0   50 kms

0   30 miles

Litani

▲ *Mt Hermon*

LEBANON

Hasbani

Banias

• Majdal Shams

Dan

Hula Valley

▲ *Mt Bental*

Golan Heights
(disputed area)

• Katzrin

S Y R I A

Sea of Galilee

Tabgha

Sapir Pumping Station

Haifa

Tiberias

Ginegar

Degania

Yarmouk

Nazareth

Naharayim

• Dara'a

Tel Megiddo

Harod

Umm al-Fahm

Beit She'an

Zaatari Refugee Camp

M e d i t e r r a n e a n

Jenin

Bardala

S e a

W E S T

Qalqilya

Nablus

Yanoun

Zarqa

Rosh HaAyin

Azzun
Atma

Jiftlik

Zubeidat

Tel Aviv

Shiloh

Jalud

Jaffa

Rawabi

B A N K

Rishon Lezion

Al-Auja

• Amman

Sorek Desalination Plant

Ramallah

Allenby Bridge

Jericho

Ashdod

Jerusalem ■ Abu Dis

Qasr el-Yahud **(baptism site)**

Nitzan

Battir

Ashkelon

Erez Checkpoint

Bethlehem

Dead Sea

Gaza City

Sderot

• Hebron

GAZA STRIP

Khan Yunis

• Nir Oz

Rafah

Beersheba

Hatzerim

Mitzpe Revivim

Ashalim Solar Array

J O R D A N

Kadesh Barnea

Shivta

Sde Boker

Hatseva

Mitzpe Ramon

N e g e v

D e s e r t

A r a v a V a l l e y

E G Y P T

S i n a i

D e s e r t

Ketura **(Arava Institute)**

Gulf of Aqaba Eilat

Aqaba

Jordan

Introduction

M Y PATH TO the River Jordan was not straight.

I first saw it up close in 1987 when, as a callow student back-packing around the region, I ambled onto the Allenby Bridge that connects Israeli-occupied Palestine with Jordan, the country that takes its name from the river that delineates its north-western edge. The old wooden structure has been replaced now and pedestrians are not encour-aged to linger in the military border zone, but in those gentler, pre-intifada days it was possible to take more time. My guidebook said the Jordan was the most important, indeed the only large river in this notoriously dry part of the world. So I was struck, as everyone is, by how little actual water it contained.

The streambed was an expanse of smelly mud from which grew a few clumps of reeds. The river itself was a dirty brown ditch narrow enough to jump across. I thought, could this really be the holy water of biblical fame, in which John baptised Jesus, a river once so powerful that it had to be stayed by the hand of God before the tribes of Israel could cross into their Promised Land? Where had all the water gone?

Almost thirty years went by before I returned to it, but I never forgot the empty river I had seen. I became a journalist, a foreign correspondent

1

reporting from North Africa, Afghanistan, Somalia, where I observed how often water scarcity – or more accurately, the inequitable distribution of that finite and diminishing natural resource – was a driver or multiplier of violent conflict. I became so fascinated by this paradigm that in 2013 I took a Master's degree in hydrogeology, and wrote a thesis on the political consequences of the collapse of the aquifer beneath the Yemeni capital, Sana'a.

It was as a mature student that I learned how the pioneering founders of Israel had dammed the Jordan's feeder lake, the Sea of Galilee, as long ago as the 1930s, to the obvious detriment of Palestinian Arabs through whose territory the river once naturally flowed. Since the 1960s, billions of gallons of water have been extracted from the lake, and pumped west and then south via a cleverly constructed canal, the National Water Carrier, to the crowded heartlands of Israel. Neighbouring Arab countries also bore responsibility for the river's depletion, by extracting water from its upper tributaries. But it was Israel who did it first and, when the National Water Carrier came online, extracted by far the most.

The most obvious and best-known environmental cost is the catastrophic shrinkage of the river's natural terminus, the famous Dead Sea, which is now just 48 kilometres long, 32 kilometres shorter than half a century ago. The lowest point on the surface of the earth, 436 metres below sea level, is still going down by about a metre per year.[1] The purloining of the Jordan, I discovered, was just one part of Israel's bid for regional water hegemony. Since 1995, under the supposedly interim arrangements of the Oslo Peace Accords, Israel has almost entirely prevented West Bank Palestinians from exploiting their other major natural water resource – the mountain aquifer beneath their feet – while continuing to do so themselves.

The Israel–Palestine dispute over land and sovereignty is the longest and most intractable in the Middle East and, perhaps, the most infamous symbol of discord between the West and the Muslim world. What role does water inequality play? The statistics are certainly suggestive. Israelis enjoy an average of 240 litres of fresh water per capita per day, while Palestinians have access to an average of 72 litres. In some parts of the Occupied Territories, where a great many communities are not even connected to the mains, availability is as low as 25 litres per capita per day,[2] well below the basic minimum of 50 litres a day that the World Health Organization recommends, and perilously close to the absolute minimum of 20 litres that it says 'should be assured to take care of basic hygiene needs and basic food hygiene'.

Palestinians, as well as critics abroad, accuse Israel of 'weaponizing' water. Israel, they say, deliberately restricts supply in order to dominate them, turning it into another cruel but effective tool of the occupation. The British Professor of International Relations Jan Selby calls this 'the other Israel–Palestine conflict'.[3] The Israelis deny this: they insist that they comply with the water allocation requirements of the Oslo Accords, and even exceed them in some instances. Yet there is no question that Palestinians still do not have enough water, while the River Jordan remains a reproachful trickle of its former self.

Palestinian water stress, and the suffering that attends it, is greatest in the Gaza Strip, the enclave of more than 2 million people on the Mediterranean coast abutting Egypt. Ever since the virulently anti-Israel Hamas party seized power there in 2007, the Strip, with varying degrees of support from Cairo, has been blockaded by the Israeli military. The Strip's traditional water source, the coastal aquifer, has been ruined by years of over-extraction, a crisis compounded by Hamas mismanagement. As the water table dropped below sea level, the Mediterranean leached in, rendering 97 per cent of the municipal supply too salty to drink. Just as seriously, Gazans lack the power to treat their sewage, which sinks back into the aquifer, making it even more undrinkable; or else it is pumped directly into the sea, contaminating every beach.

Gazans live in isolation from their compatriots in the West Bank, thanks to Israel's blockade, the effects of which are made much worse by Palestinian politics. Gaza was administered until 2007 by the Palestinian Authority, the 'interim self-government' known as the PA, which was set up with Israel's agreement at Oslo. Dominated by the late Yasser Arafat's Fatah party, the PA continues to run the West Bank from Ramallah in uneasy cooperation with their Israeli occupiers, has never given up what it sees as its right to control Gaza, and has tried ever since to undermine Hamas by denying it the money, fuel and clean water it needs to run Gaza properly. In consequence, the enclave has become so water-stressed that in 2015, the United Nations (UN) repeated an old warning that it could become literally 'unliveable' within five years. Gaza was at risk of an epidemic even before the 2020 outbreak of coronavirus.

The scale of the problem, this gross disparity of access to water, is most clearly visible along the border fence that separates Gaza from Israel. In aerial photographs, the farmland on the Israeli side is a picture of order and scientific efficiency.[4] Hamlets nestle in a patchwork of huge green fields, all perfectly irrigated. Some of the fields are round and resemble pie charts, with segments of different colour where crops have been planted in rotation. The water that irrigates this region is brought there by the National Water Carrier, which terminates close by. It is the apotheosis of the famous ambition of Israel's first prime minister, David Ben-Gurion, to 'make the desert bloom'.

The dominant colour on the Palestinian side, by contrast, is concrete grey. Chaotic tendrils of urban development stretch from the coast all the way to the fence, where a few fields cling on. These fields, the supposed breadbasket of 2 million people, are the size of postage stamps, and they are mostly dun-coloured; none has the lush hue of the mega-fields to the east.

How and why did this happen – and with what dire sociopolitical consequences? More to the point, what are the prospects of restoring some semblance of water equality – and what might such a restoration imply for the future of Israel-Palestine? In a world where populations everywhere are climbing, and natural resources of all types are under more pressure from humanity than ever before, these questions feel significant. This book is an attempt to answer them, based on several research trips that began in 2017.

My findings are not necessarily a narrative of despair. Israel, importantly, no longer depends as it once did on natural water. Since 2005 the country has built five huge coastal desalination plants, with more due to open soon. These days as much as 80 per cent of its domestic water is manufactured: one of the highest proportions of any country in the world. In fact, Israel produces so much water that it now has a surplus, an extraordinary achievement, given its location in one of the most drought-stricken regions on the planet.[5]

In the jargon of hydrologists, water supply here is no longer a 'zero-sum game'. The country is a world leader not only in desalination but also in wastewater recycling and irrigation techniques. Perhaps most astonishingly of all, Israel is preparing to refill the Sea of Galilee with desalinated water

from the coast, a project that could undo decades of environmental degradation along the Jordan river, and even mitigate the future effect of climate
change. Israel's water technology is genuinely dazzling – and it has the
potential, at least, to do great good throughout the region.

This book is hardly another liberal polemic against Zionism, therefore.
On the contrary, I found much to admire and celebrate in Israel: not just
ingenuity and technological capability, but the pluck and energetic self-belief
of its people, and their inspiring, pioneering spirit. In any case, I have long felt
a connection to the place; enough of one, at any rate, to make me care about
Israel, and want it to succeed as a state. This has less to do with my own slight
Jewish heritage – a maternal great grandfather, Max Michaelis, originally
from Eisfeld in central Germany – than from the fact that my great-great-
great-uncle on my father's side was Arthur Balfour, British foreign secretary
and prime minister, whose famous (or infamous) Declaration of 1917 granted
British support for the establishment of a Jewish 'national home' in Palestine.
The Declaration was the first public expression of support for this idea by any
major foreign power – and it proved a critical boost, if not precisely the start
whistle, for the entire Zionist project.

I have spent much of my journalistic career immersed in Muslim countries and causes, but my upbringing predisposed me towards Israel. Balfour's
enthusiasm for Zionism was shared by his biographer, his niece, who passed
it to her daughter, my grandmother Frances, who in turn passed it to me.
Frances and I coincidentally shared a birthday, 2 November, which by
further coincidence is the day the Balfour Declaration was signed in 1917.
Each year as a young boy, I would receive a card in my grandmother's spidery
arthritic hand that read something like:

November 2nd. Very important day!!!
* Your birthday
* My birthday
* Birth of the state of Israel

As an adult, however, I of course did not look on Israel with the starry
eyes of my youth. Balfour's support for a Jewish homeland came with the

important condition that 'nothing shall be done which may prejudice the civil ... rights of the existing non-Jewish communities in Palestine'. Yet Israel has repeatedly broken that condition, not least in its obligation, as military occupiers of the West Bank, to ensure that all the Palestinians who live there have access to enough clean and affordable water – which the United Nations says is a fundamental human right. What would Balfour make of that if he were alive today? What, more importantly, do modern Israelis think?

Modern Israel certainly troubles me. Under the long-term, stop-start premiership of the mercurial Binyamin Netanyahu, the character and future direction of the country have been put in question. The Likud party leader's coalition government, widely held to be the most right-wing in Israel's history, was squeezed from power in 2021, but made an astonishing come-back at the end of 2022, following the country's fifth general election in four years. Netanyahu's legacy runs deep. Jerusalem and Tel Aviv are still spectacularly diverging, the former increasingly dominated by the religious orthodox, the latter by the liberal Zionist left. The feverish politics I witnessed as I conducted my field research, above all in the epic election year of 2019, felt at times like a battle for the country's soul.

On my first trip there as a twenty-year-old in 1987, I was accompanied by a Jewish girlfriend from London, who in those days was a keen Zionist, fiercely proud of Israel's progress and swaggering military prowess. Some of her fervour must have rubbed off on me, because I remember buying one of those tub-thumping T-shirts, still for sale in tourist markets today, that read 'Uzi Does It' in celebration of Israel's famous submachine gun. The Allenby Bridge, the farthest east we went on our holiday tour, felt like the edge of civilization; to my girlfriend, the heavily guarded border must have seemed like the ice wall in *Game of Thrones*, beyond which dwelt only barbarians and evil.

Two years later, however, I stood on the Allenby Bridge again, this time at the end of a long road trip with an American friend through Egypt, the Sinai and Jordan. Approaching the border from the other side felt very different. Now I understood and indeed empathized with the Arab sense of outrage at the overbearing Israeli border guards. Who were these interlopers, I spluttered to myself, to behave so arrogantly in what is so patently an Arab, Muslim land?

I had to check myself. I saw that the guards, the bridge, and the empty river beneath it, were all as they had been before. Only my perspective had changed; yet this was enough to invert my response. It was an experience that I still privately call 'Allenby Bridge syndrome', and I have never forgotten the lesson I drew from it: when considering Israel-Palestine, *everything* depends on which end of the telescope you look through. It is therefore vital to try to look through both ends before pronouncing any kind of judgement. And that is the principle I have tried to apply in this book.

My first idea was to hike the length of the Jordan, perhaps by heading upstream from its Dead Sea terminus to its source, 250 kilometres to the north in the Anti-Lebanon Mountains: a closely defined, solo expedition that would form the spine of a classic travel narrative. So far as I could discover, no one had written about the river in this way for years; perhaps not since the 1840s, when a swashbuckling American naval officer named Lynch attempted the journey downstream by boat. I imagined myself armed with an Old Testament-style stick to fend off dogs (or maybe wolves), passing from village to village, befriending local Arabs and Jews and recording their ancient riparian stories. I could get close to nature, and camp out at night on the riverbank beneath the stars.

It was fantasy, of course. I soon learned that the banks of the lower Jordan, the river's most politically contentious and interesting section that gives the West Bank its name, have been a 'closed military zone' since the war of 1967, a sensitive international border almost wholly off-limits to the public.

I found other ways, eventually, to approach its depleted waters, but ultimately the river proved no more than an intellectual starting point for an inquiry into the much broader Israel-Palestine water question. The dispute over water resource is so closely connected to the old struggle for territory and statehood that it cannot usefully be considered in isolation from it. The issue also has a strong international dimension, equally impossible to ignore. History, theology, geography, geology: there is probably no end to the rabbit holes an author can tumble down when writing about water in the Middle

East. I felt compelled to read around the subject, and did so voraciously. I travelled, likewise, wherever I could in the region, as opportunity arose. Developing a bigger picture in this piecemeal way has its drawbacks. My approach led me on many detours which, while always interesting, often turned out to be false leads, like the promising pieces of a jigsaw that don't immediately fit.

My ground research was conducted in stops and starts over three years, in legs of a journey that were not always sequential or geographically contiguous. I travelled on foot, by car, and once even by motorbike, up the Jordan Valley. I was usually alone, although sometimes accompanied by local guides. On one memorable occasion, I stayed with my wife and four young children in an illegal Israeli settlement in the Samarian Hills, in lodgings booked through an online holiday rental website.

The resulting narrative does not begin anywhere near the Jordan, as I first planned, but in Gaza. The Strip has by far the worst water crisis in the region. It also presents the greatest domestic security threat to Israel, a threat that could become existential should an epidemic, waterborne or otherwise, be allowed to get out of hand there. Gaza still feels like a catastrophe in waiting, an urgent news story of global import if or when it breaks. I was driven by primitive journalistic impulse to examine this notorious place first, from the Palestinian point of view.

As I discovered, Gazan anger and frustration go far beyond the homemade missiles that are sporadically lobbed across the border at Israel. From March 2018, under the direction of Hamas, tens of thousands of Gazans gathered most Fridays at the border fence to hurl stones, or worse, at the Israeli soldiers on the other side, who responded with tear gas and bullets. The demonstration I attended was a very long way indeed from the gentle river ramble I once envisioned. Hundreds of fence-demonstrators have been killed since 2018, and thousands injured. How desperate does one have to be to risk death in a futile political protest? And to what extent is the violence driven by the scarcity of clean water; what does that UN word 'unliveable' really mean?

From Gaza my narrative proceeds to the West Bank, the other Palestinian polity, beginning in the lower Jordan Valley, which in 2019 was under

renewed threat of formal Israeli annexation by Netanyahu, then in full elec-
tioneering mode. After the Jordan Valley I proceeded to Ramallah, looking
for a better understanding of the seemingly endless conflict over Israel-
Palestine's land and resources, and in particular, of the failure of the Oslo
Peace Accords of 1993–5, from which so many of Palestine's present troubles stem. From Ramallah I began to explore the interior of the West Bank,
from Bethlehem to Jenin, and many places in between. My findings form
the first half of the book.

The second half is dedicated to my travels in Israel, a journey that begins
in Jerusalem, continues to the Sea of Galilee via Armageddon, and from
there to the source of the Jordan in the Golan Heights on the borders of
Syria and Lebanon. From the Golan I turned south to pick up and trace the
130-kilometre course of the National Water Carrier, passing through the
conurbation around Tel Aviv, and onwards to the empty spaces of the Negev
desert as far as the border with Egypt.

Later, when I traced my wanderings on a map chronologically, the line I
drew looked like a tangle of string: an appropriate metaphor, no doubt, for
a subject as convoluted as mine. However, my journey as presented does
have a broadly circular shape, since it ends almost where it begins, near the
terminus of the National Water Carrier on the Israeli side of the border
with Gaza. Like my circuit of the region, the Israel-Palestine water question
keeps returning to the future of that desperate place.

The 50:50 structure of the book, covering Palestine in the first half and
Israel in the second, is designed to help save it from Allenby Bridge
syndrome; because my ill opinion of the occupation hardened as I travelled
around Gaza and the West Bank, as I knew it might. The bullied and
dispossessed Bedouin I encountered, the arrogance and casual cruelty of so
many Israeli conscripts, the outrageous posturing of certain settlers: who
could not but be appalled?

In many places, water did indeed appear to have been weaponized. In the
West Bank, I saw for myself how Israeli settlers have appropriated springs,
sunk multiple wells, planted vineyards and constructed indoor swimming
pools, all with the apparent approval of the authorities, while Bedouin Arabs
have their portable toilets confiscated and the narrowest of water pipes

destroyed. Water, it seemed to me, fuelled the motor of the settlement programme, which the UN has serially condemned as illegal under international law. The settlers' continuing advance is still eroding the viability of an independent Palestine, and thus the 'two-state solution' that has underpinned all Western peacemaking efforts of the last half-century.

My progress down the canalised spine of Israel provided a kind of corrective. The water engineers and officials I interviewed along the way were not monsters. Few, if any of them, approved of the settlers' hardcore tactics. They all wanted peace, and to fix things with their technology. There is enough water to go around, they insist – if only a political settlement can be reached.

To reiterate: my book does not aim to ascribe blame. Finger-pointing has never led anywhere useful in Israel-Palestine; and in any case, both sides do bear some responsibility for the impasse in the peace process. Nevertheless, I became convinced as I travelled that it is for Israel, not Palestine, to initiate the change required to break the old deadlock. The dispute is not a contest between equals, if indeed it ever was. Israel has more money, more firepower, more friends abroad, and greater capacity than Palestine. The onus is surely on Israel to try to end it.

A fairer allocation of water resource, whether natural or manufactured, might make an excellent start. Water provision is not just a humanitarian requirement, after all, but is also critical to Israel's own long-term security interests. Nature, in its way, also demands that water resources be shared, because subterranean aquifers are no respecters of political borders, any more than tidal flow in the sea. A regional hydrological system cannot be sliced down the middle. Not for nothing does Eran Feitelson, a senior geographer at Jerusalem's Hebrew University, describe Israel and Palestine as being 'like a Siamese twin with one shared organ'.[6] Since water already forms such a connection between the nations, then perhaps a bold 'new deal' on water, struck as far as possible in isolation from the bitter partisanship of the region, could be the foundation of a wider peace based on equality before the law and the upholding of human and civil rights. It is wishful thinking, perhaps; but why not dream of such a thing?

For now, however, the tragic dialogue of the deaf recorded in these pages, between Palestinians demanding their rights and Israelis promising prosperity through technology instead, chunters madly on. As I write this, the BBC is reporting yet another flare-up over Gaza, where the Israeli air force yesterday assassinated a militant leader in his home. The response wasn't long in coming: YouTube today is carrying dashcam footage of a rocket exploding on an Israeli motorway junction.[7] Sirens are wailing across Tel Aviv, and *Haaretz* is running a photograph of confused-looking tourists on the beachfront, beneath the headline 'Sunny, with a chance of missiles'.

The mysteriously empty river I first puzzled over thirty years ago once again seems the most apt and eloquent symbol of a relationship gone terribly wrong.

PART I

PALESTINE

CHAPTER ONE

Gaza

The People Must Burst

Through billowing clouds of tear gas they stumble, a coughing stretcher party with streaming eyes. The crowd opens to let them through like the parting of the waters in the Bible. I glimpse a knee, smashed to a crimson pulp, and then the contorted face of its owner, a boy of perhaps fourteen years old. The crowd closes up again as though this is normal – which it is. The boy is the third teenager I have seen shot in ten minutes. A young man with a black-and-white anarchist mask attached, nightmarishly, to the back of his head, resumes with his slingshot, hurling a rock with astonishing force towards Israel. The border fence is barely 100 metres away, the khaki helmets of the Israeli Defense Forces, the IDF, clearly visible through the gaps in the Palestinian smokescreen, a wall of oily black pluming from heaps of fiercely burning tyres.

And I think: I shouldn't be here. I had come to Gaza to investigate the enclave's water crisis, and had spent the week as planned, interviewing hydrologists and civic officials in Gaza City, and inspecting desalination plants and sewage outfalls along the beaches. Attending the demonstration was a last-minute decision, and I am unprepared. There are a few other journalists present, doing crouching pieces to camera with their backs to the flames, and none of them, I note uneasily, is without a helmet and flak jacket.

15

My companion, Samir, is a stringer for an Arab TV news channel who has covered two dozen of these demos, and has developed a keen eye for danger. 'You must keep looking up,' he says. 'You must be ready to run.'

Sure enough, the smoke-stained sky is suddenly streaked white with tear gas, the contrails arcing over us like the ribs of a great black umbrella – and we all run, the front ranks falling back among the onlookers to the rear, retching, spluttering, their sooty faces shining with snot and tears. I see two men hauling back an unconscious third one, his head webbed with blood from the gash of a falling canister. An old woman in black, an Arab Florence Nightingale, squirts water in the faces of anyone she can get close enough to with a laundry sprayer.

'Look up! Look up!' warns Samir again.

The salvo has mostly fallen short, and the prevailing wind has carried most of the gas away, but now the Israelis deploy a quadcopter drone which skims far beyond us and releases a dozen more canisters that will surely catch us all.

Hamas, the Islamist rulers of Gaza, call this weekly ritual 'the Great March of Return', as though simple force of numbers might actually succeed in reversing the 'Nakba', the Arab 'catastrophe' of 1948 when, following the first Arab-Israeli war, some 700,000 Palestinians, almost 85 per cent of the Arab population of what was to become Israel,[1] were driven from or fled their ancestral lands beyond the border fence. Hundreds of Arab villages were taken over or destroyed. The young demonstrators here are mostly the grandchildren or even great grandchildren of people who once lived all over what is now north and central Israel. Three quarters of Gaza's population, some 1.4 million people, are classified or identify themselves as refugees.[2] The rage on display today is the product of decades of humiliating failure to address their plight. The fence itself is a kind of monument to the failure of the Arab-Israeli peace process that has been moribund for more than twenty years.

The turnout at the fence today is larger than usual: 20,000 people at least. Hamas and their Islamist offshoot organizations, of which there are many in Gaza, have been exhorting the people to demonstrate all week. I had seen for myself the convoys of pick-up trucks moving slowly through the streets of Gaza City, with loudspeakers mounted on their cabs blaring anti-Israel propaganda. Firebrand sheikhs have played their part, too. There are more than a thousand mosques in the Strip, 90 per cent of them supervised by the government. Many of the demonstrators today have arrived straight from Friday prayers, aboard buses laid on for the occasion by the mosque committees.

Events begin to speed up. There is a popping noise from the fence; Samir and I instinctively duck as a bullet ricochets off something and whizzes overhead, a *peeeow* sound from a cowboy movie. The crowd may be large, but the feeling of safety its size offers is an illusion. The bullets the IDF are shooting are not all of the rubber kind. Perhaps none of them are. All the people here are risking their lives. Samir, muttering and dragging me back by my sleeve, points at a teenage girl who has collapsed close by on our left, the tyre she has just been pushing still tottering to a halt. She disappears beneath another squad of willing first-aiders who bear her away to the back.

Samir has skilfully steered me away from where the tear-gas cloud is thickest, so we are not badly affected by it – just a slight smarting of the eyes, and a constricted throat with a lingering bitter chemical taste. The gas eventually clears, and as the crowd reforms I realise with astonishment that the deadly game of Grandmother's Footsteps is to continue as though nothing has happened. A vendor cheerily reclaims a rickety cigarette cart abandoned a few moments previously. Someone else picks up the actual tyre the shot girl was rolling, and pushes it onwards to the fire.

The snipers generally aim for the knees, in line with what Israel's Ministry of Defense calls a policy of 'restraint', a description that is, at best, relative. *Haaretz*, the left-leaning Israeli daily, later interviewed a sniper named 'Eden' who boasted of shooting '42 knees in one day'.[3] Eden also freely acknowledged that even proficient snipers sometimes miss their targets, and kill by mistake. A bullet through the legs can easily be fatal if it hits the femoral artery; while ordnance fired over the heads of a dense crowd has to come down somewhere. Some 200 people have been shot dead so far in these year-long demonstrations, and 6,000 more have been seriously injured.

Yet the demonstrations continue. Even those previously shot are not necessarily deterred from coming back. Some, indeed, are clearly sporting their wounds as a badge of honour. The leg of one protestor hopping away from the tear gas is held together with a shiny metal brace, the bolts protruding from either side. Another has lost his legs altogether, and is attending today in a wheelchair.

Samir and I stop by a group of smoke-smudged youths resting cross-legged on the ground. I ask to photograph them, and they instantly coalesce into a starburst of teeth and victory signs. The hands and jumper of the lad at the centre are caked with red: the blood, he proudly explains, of a 'martyr' he has just helped carry from the field. 'I too have suffered, see?' he adds, pulling down the waist of his shorts to reveal a healed bullet wound on his hip.

For the Israeli soldiers on the other side, heavily armed but nevertheless vastly outnumbered, the people's persistence must be frightening. There is a panicky urgency in the way their command vehicle races up and down the line, pausing at the hotspots to launch yet more rounds of tear gas from the mortar mounted on its cab. The fence itself is also not as strong as it looks, because at one stage a group of boys succeeds in breaching it. One of them tries to set fire to the side of a sniper post, although the fire quickly goes out. Another briefly appears sitting astride the fence, rocking and facing back towards Gaza waving a Palestinian flag, to roars of approval.

'That's suicide,' murmurs Samir, 'he'll be shot, for sure.' Yet he is not. Five minutes later I see the boy again, jubilantly towing a tangle of barbed wire and metal that his gang have torn down, a trophy for all to see.

Like the 'separation barrier' that divides Israel from the West Bank, the border fence is a work in progress, and is still being reinforced. High above the smoke, two tall derricks loom: mobile rigs that are said to be engaged on the construction of a subterranean wall designed to deter Hamas tunnellers. The depth and design of this new wall, which will eventually run the whole 65-kilometre length of the border and is costing Israeli taxpayers millions, is a closely guarded military secret. In Gaza, it is rumoured that foreign engineers have been invited to tender a design for a barrier reaching down to an extraordinary 90 metres. The Israelis already control all the enclave's borders, airspace and coastal waters. If the rumour is true, Gaza's containment will soon be absolute.

High above, a cluster of brightly coloured balloons drifts eastwards, their tails lashed around what looks like a firecracker: an incendiary bomb, designed to ignite the fields beyond. An IDF sniper promptly shoots it down, and the onlookers, impressed by the marksmanship, unexpectedly cheer. I wonder nervously where these vertical bullets are going to fall. There is a commotion off to our right as someone else gets shot. I give Samir a look and he nods his agreement: it is time to retreat. By the end of the day, seven Palestinians will be dead, including two boys aged twelve and fourteen, and over five hundred will be injured, ninety of them by gunfire.[4]

The atmosphere further back is bizarrely festive. The protest site, a dusty field on the edge of town, has become semi-permanent, complete with a barnlike marquee. Beneath bunting that snaps in the hot and salty onshore breeze, two dozen white-shirted young men are performing a traditional *dabke* dance, hopping in a circle with their arms joined, before an audience that whoops and claps in time to the high-energy jangling music.

The dance is followed by rabble-rousing speeches by Gazan politicians. All the rhetoric is fiery. Hamas, originally an offshoot of the Muslim Brotherhood in Egypt, are still self-declared jihadists who, despite a recent softening in their position, sought the 'obliteration' of Israel from the moment they founded their party in 1988. Khalid Abu Helal, head of Al-Ahrar, a militant Fatah splinter group allied to Hamas, speaks to the audience, stressing the need for Palestinian unity. Then the Hamas deputy, Khalil al-Hayya, explains why the March of Return must continue. The front row of the audience nods in solemn agreement, a line of old dignitaries in snow-white *thobe* who clasp the handles of their walking sticks with bony hands. The speeches, though, seem like window-dressing to the main event. The crowds outside mostly stream back and forth without stopping.

Hawkers sell smoothies and pretzels. A long queue waits in front of an ice-cream van. I spot a young family who are quite clearly here for a picnic, the mother proudly bearing a smart wicker basket, three tiny daughters toddling behind in order of size, as vulnerable as ducklings in their pristine matching hijabs. I watch them step to the side of the road to make way for a wailing ambulance, one of several that are ferrying casualties from the front line in a loop.

Protest days, Samir says, are always like this. The demonstrations, he explains, are the best party of the Gaza week these days, no question. Because in this enclave where three out of four people are refugees, where the average age is eighteen, where youth unemployment runs at almost 70 per cent, where escape is impossible, and where even the sea is too filthy to swim in, what else is there for the young to do?

'The people here are all poor people,' Samir says. 'People with jobs, with a future – they do not come to these demonstrations. Only people with nothing. Because they have nothing to lose.'

Historians like to debate when the fortunes of Palestine's Arabs began to take a downward turn, but 1917 was undoubtedly a pivotal year; the moment, arguably, that events leading to the present disaster in Gaza were first set in train. It was in that year that the British General, Edmund 'Bloody Bull' Allenby – the builder of the bridge over the River Jordan – defeated and expelled Palestine's Ottoman overlords, ending four centuries of almost unbroken Ottoman Muslim control. His victory was accompanied, in November 1917, by the Balfour Declaration, with its fateful promise of British support for the establishment of a Jewish 'national home', and then by a period of British rule under a mandate from the UN.

The 'Yishuv', as the Jewish settler community was known in Mandate Palestine, rapidly expanded, their numbers greatly swelled by migrants fleeing persecution in Bolshevik Russia and, later, the unfolding Holocaust in Nazi-dominated Europe. Simmering Arab resentment at these new competitors for land and resources boiled over into 'The Great Revolt' of 1936–9, which was mercilessly crushed by the British. Mandate rule ended in 1948: the year of the first Arab-Israeli war, the Nakba, and the establishment of Israel.

The next opportunity to push back came in 1967, when Israel fought the Six Day War with an Egyptian-led coalition of five Arab nations. This was a nervous moment for the Jewish nation. The late Chief Rabbi of Britain, Jonathan Sacks, recalled that it seemed as though the 'unthinkable' – a second Holocaust – was about to take place.[5] Instead, the Israelis spectacularly triumphed and expanded the territory under their control by driving Egypt out of Gaza, and Jordan from the West Bank; territory they have occupied ever since. Arabs refer to the Six Day War as the *Naksa*, or 'setback'. It wasn't their last: an Arab coalition was narrowly beaten again in the Yom Kippur War of 1973.

Until 1967, the international community viewed the conflict in the region primarily as a competition for land and resources between Israel and the Arab world. The Palestinians, per se, were considered the victims of circumstance, unluckily caught up in the middle of it all; their plight was treated as a humanitarian rather than a political issue. That soon changed with the emergence of the PLO, Yasser Arafat's underground Palestine Liberation Organization. Founded in 1964, the PLO sought to throw off the yoke of Israeli occupation by unconventional military means, including violence aimed at Israeli civilians. Although the PLO has enjoyed observer status at the United Nations since 1974, it was not until 1991 that the United States and Israel dropped their appellation of the PLO as a terrorist organization.

The First Palestinian Intifada, or uprising, lasted for almost six years, from 1987 to 1993, and resulted in cooperation with the Israeli peace camp, and the internationally-brokered Oslo Peace Accords. Oslo was an interim agreement that was supposed to lead to Palestinian statehood, the implementation of the fabled 'two state solution' that might yet lead to peaceful coexistence in the region. But a summit at Camp David in 2000 failed to produce the promised 'Final Status' between the two sides, which triggered a second uprising, the Al-Aqsa Intifada, a far bloodier affair that was defined by Islamist rhetoric and suicide bombs. This time, Israel's peace camp did not participate. By the time Al-Aqsa ended in 2005, an estimated 3,000 Palestinians and a thousand Israelis had lost their lives.

Israel's response, from 2000 on, was to build a security fence around the insurgency, both along its border with the West Bank and around Gaza. If the threat could not be neutralized, Israel reasoned, it could at least be contained. Gaza was further isolated in 2005, when Israel unilaterally 'disengaged' from the Strip, pulling back its military and even forcing some 9,000 Israeli settlers, who had lived there since 1967, to abandon their homes and move back over the border. Gaza was left in the hands of the PA until 2007, when Hamas Islamists ousted them from power, whereupon Israel's containment strategy turned into a full-on blockade.

Thousands of Palestinians who once depended on jobs in Israel were no longer permitted to commute there. The southern border with Egypt was also eventually sealed. In consequence, Gaza's 2 million inhabitants have now been shut off from the world for almost an entire generation. Their isolation has been punctured four times by war, in 2008, 2012, 2014 and 2021. Israeli military operations aimed at Hamas have caused the death or injury of thousands of civilians; and the blockade continues as before.

British Prime Minister David Cameron once described Gaza as a 'prison camp', a remark that sparked trouble on the diplomatic circuit at the time,[6] although it did not seem inaccurate to me. Indeed, Gaza felt like a prison camp from the moment I arrived, a week before the demonstration I attended.

The heavily fortified border post at Erez, the only way in or out of the Strip, is a huge building of steel and glass, as sterile as an airport terminal. Built to handle thousands of people, it was eerily empty on the day I passed through it, and so quiet that my footsteps echoed on the concourse. A few thousand carefully vetted Gazans are normally permitted to commute each day to labouring jobs in Israel, but that permission had temporarily been withdrawn, as it very often is, in response to the latest salvo of cross-border rockets. The usual security arrangements had not been relaxed, however. Hidden cameras and watchers behind a bank of one-way mirrors recorded my self-conscious progress through the chicanes and steel turnstiles. A dead-eyed official, a young woman in fatigues behind bulletproof glass, looked longer than necessary at the press visa in my passport, the fruit of weeks of careful negotiation with the Government Press Office in Jerusalem.

Released at last from this uncomfortable scrutiny, I passed through to a different world. The border post on the Palestinian side was a kiosk fronted by an open-sided shack. Flies buzzed above a fetid pool where the toilet block overflowed. Bored taxi drivers sat around waiting for customers, scratching their bellies in the stupefying heat.

As I had been warned, this border post was run not by the ruling Hamas party but by officials from the PA, who doggedly continue to check passports as they did before they were ousted from power in 2007. New arrivals must go through the process twice, first with the PA, then with their hated rivals Hamas, whose officials occupy another border post exactly 1 kilometre further down the road. This second border post, with which the first did not in any way communicate, was revealingly worse. I trudged across a sand dune to a decrepit Portakabin, where a half-asleep militiaman turned my letter of introduction around and around in his meaty hands, with the bafflement of the properly illiterate. There were no queues, yet the whole entry procedure took more than an hour: an excellent practical first lesson in the administrative chaos that has blighted the lives of a generation of Gazans. It was a relief to be rescued by a driver sent by my main contact in Gaza, Ahmad Yaqubi, the retired General Director of the Palestinian Water Authority, the PWA.

Ahmad was an affable man, an Egypt-educated hydro-engineer who had worked in his younger days on water infrastructure projects in Kuwait and Libya. I had played up my degree in hydrogeology, so that he welcomed me almost as a peer, so warmly in fact that I felt a bit of a fraud. But he didn't mind at all when I explained that I was more of a journalist than a scientist. Interest in Gaza's plight shown by anyone from outside was welcome, he said. His experience and status made him a reassuring companion in Gaza City, which was a bewildering and sinister place for a new arrival like me, and I knew I was lucky to have found him.

I checked into the Al-Deira, a mud-brick hotel on the seafront traditionally favoured by foreign correspondents, although there were few guests of any kind staying here now. Gaza was once full of casino hotels that were very popular with tourists from Egypt – until 1967, Gaza was occupied and run by Egypt, as a kind of puppet state of Cairo – but the tourist industry collapsed following the Six Day War. It seemed as though the Al-Deira had been waiting for customers ever since. In the upstairs lobby, I found a neglected antique record player, complete with a 1973 Tamla Motown LP by The Temptations; the album was entitled, futuristically, *1990*. The hotel restaurant felt cavernous, empty apart from a dozen bored waiters who lurked in the shadows at the back. Despite the stultifying heat, the ceiling fans in the restaurant were still because there was no power. I was to grow used to that. Throughout my stay in Gaza, municipal electricity supply was limited to just four hours a day, and was usually only switched on after dark. The hotel had its own generator, but management preferred not to start it up unless they had to, in order to conserve precious fuel.

Ahmad led me to a table by an open sliding window, where at least a faint hot salty breeze blew. The windows looked over a grubby beach where in 2014, beneath the gaze of foreign journalists sitting where we were now installed, four schoolboys were killed by a shell from an Israeli gunboat. Beyond it lay a scruffy fishing harbour, all that remains of Gaza's once magnificent port. A better clue to the city's illustrious mercantile past survives in its name: Gaza was once the centre of a flourishing textile industry, whose most celebrated export, a type of woven silk called *ghazzi*, is remembered in the modern English word *gauze*.

Ahmad ordered a pot of tea, and began to brief me on Gaza's myriad water supply problems.

The nub of it was that Gaza's primary source of fresh water, the coastal aquifer, was too small to support the number of people who live in Gaza, and was now exhausted. He explained that it contained enough water to sustainably supply about 600,000 people, but that Gaza's growing population now numbered more than 2 million. The crisis had been made exponentially worse by the blockade, which restricted alternative sources of water and increased Gaza's reliance on the aquifer, even as its population grew. For the last several years already, Gazans had been extracting water from the aquifer at roughly twice the rate that nature was able to replenish it, with inevitable results: as the water table sank, saline water intruded from the sea. As Ahmad reminded me, it is the first principle of hydrogeology, an indisputable law of physics, that water always finds its way. The salt had wrecked the aquifer, probably permanently, since there was no realistic prospect of flushing it out again.

Some Israelis blame Gaza's overcrowding on poor family planning. Gaza's population growth, certainly, is one of the fastest in the world; the UN predicts that at the present rate, Gazans could number 3.1 million by 2030, and an astonishing 4.7 million by 2050.[7] Yet the root cause of the crowding is not a lack of contraception, but the Nakba that first drove the base population to seek refuge in the Strip, compounded by decades of subsequent conflict, and now the blockade that keeps their descendants here. For centuries, Arabs had lived in natural equilibrium with the groundwater beneath their feet, but the displacement of so many of them had pushed the balance completely out of kilter. Without the conflict, Gaza's millions would still be spread across the land of Palestine, and the coastal aquifer would not be so overburdened. Meanwhile, the springs and wells that formerly served their ancient villages have of course been requisitioned by Israel.

In the early years following the Nakba, no one much worried about the sustainability of the Gaza aquifer. The population boom is a relatively recent phenomenon; as late as 1967, the population stood at a manageable-sounding 400,000. No one then was predicting the kind of numbers that the UN warns about now. Domestic consumption, however, was not the main culprit in those days. The naturally nutrient-rich soil of the Strip has always attracted farmers. Even before 1967, groundwater was being extracted for agricultural purposes at a rate faster than nature could replace it; and the over-extraction accelerated after 1967, following Israel's occupation.

There were twenty-one Israeli settlements in Gaza until Ariel Sharon ordered them out in 2005, and each settler disposed of twenty times the amount of water allocated to the Arab farmers of the Strip.[8] The community included 166 large Israeli farms; their produce, which included flowers, was worth US$120 million a year to Israel, accounting for 15 per cent of all Israeli agricultural exports, including 60 per cent of all cherry tomatoes and herbs.[9] In short, if the Gaza aquifer was now wrecked by decades of over-extraction, it was very probably not only Palestinians who were responbile.

Ahmad said that no one knew precisely how much water was now being extracted, because regulation of the water sector was so lax under Hamas, if it existed at all. There are 250 large municipal wells in Gaza, but also another 300 wells of similar size operated by privateers, three quarters of whom do so without a licence. There are, in addition, at least 4,000 smaller domestic wells that are not even registered with the authorities. 'There is no question that in Gaza we are in deep trouble,' he said.

The obvious remedy, he went on, was to desalinate, as the Israelis did up the coast. But desalination requires a lot of power, which Gaza cannot generate because it lacks the fuel, thanks to the blockade and the feud between Hamas and the PA. Not even foreigners have been able to surmount this obstacle. Down the coast at Khan Younis, a state-of-the-art seawater desalination plant had recently opened, at a cost of US$10 million provided by the European Union. It was designed in its first phase to provide drinking water for 75,000 people, but the shortage of power meant that it was operating at one sixth of its capacity. 'Not even a Rolls Royce works without petrol,' Ahmad observed glumly.

Gaza, in any case, only has one power plant, which was designed to generate a maximum of 140 megawatts when it opened in 2002. Yet even this is about half what the enclave now actually requires at peak times. Shortages of fuel and spare parts, furthermore, mean that the plant has never operated at maximum capacity. It certainly did not help that Israel had twice bombed the plant, in 2006 and again in 2014, and had since obstructed importation of the material needed to repair it, particularly pipes, on the grounds that militants could convert these into mortar tubes.

Restrictions on such 'dual use' material, as the IDF classifies it, are a major bugbear in Gaza, where stories of bureaucratic obstruction are common currency. An official at the World Bank, Adnan Ghosheh, later told me how an application for a small forklift truck for the PWA was blocked by the IDF for five years, even though forklift trucks at the time were in fact available on the open market in Gaza. Ahmad recounted how the engineers at the EU desalination plant at Khan Younis wanted to circumvent the shortage of municipal power by generating their own with solar panels, for which a patch of land had already been acquired. Yet the land stood empty still, for want of vital connecting cables, the import of which had – once again – been halted by the IDF, citing 'security reasons'. 'We don't exactly know why. It's not as if cables can be converted into weapons. The situation is very confused.'

The external challenges Ahmad's sector faced were real, although in his opinion as a water management professional, they had also been exacerbated by Hamas's mismanagement. He explained that the Palestinian Water Authority for which he worked was a child of the Oslo Peace Accords. As such it answered exclusively to Ramallah, which automatically made it suspect in Hamas's eyes. When Hamas took power in 2007, therefore, all seventy of the PWA's local staff were fired and replaced with party loyalists.

'It was a disaster,' he recalled. 'The Hamas people had no experience of water sector management, and we had all the contacts with international aid organizations. In fact, organizations like USAID simply *couldn't* give dollars to Hamas.'

Hamas soon realised their mistake, and began to negotiate the return of key PWA workers, one by one, although many of the old guard remained loyal to Ramallah and refused. The quarrel was still unresolved. Arrangements in the Water Authority office in the city were consequently Kafkaesque. Ahmad described how the staff sat in different parts of the building according to political affiliation, with one half of the team barely speaking to the other, and every decision liable to be questioned and countermanded. Gaza's water sector would be difficult to administer even in normal times, but the rivalry and suspicion the feud engendered made it next to impossible.

The following morning Ahmad took me by car to look at a sewage outfall at Al-Shati Camp in the middle of town – as good a place to start my tour as any, he said. I gazed out at the city traffic, still stupefied by the heat and dust. Twenty-four hours previously I had been in the air-conditioned glitz of central Tel Aviv. Now I was stuck in a jam of beaten-up Toyotas, which honked as they inched their way between grimy apartment blocks.

We came eventually to a city square where squads of armed young men were parading in time to martial music blaring from speakers: a funeral ceremony, organized by one of the many jihadist factions that operate in Gaza in uncertain alliance with Hamas. 'Stupid kids', said Ahmad, unimpressed by the youthful fervour on display.

I, however, shrank back in my seat. The black flags they were flying, along with their ninja-style keffiyehs, suggested they were members of the Iran-backed, internationally designated terrorist organization, Islamic Jihad. Ahmad said that one of their number had been killed – although you could tell they would say martyred – while trying to sneak over the border into Israel the previous night.

The narrow beach at Al-Shati was an environmental disaster zone. A rocky breakwater had partially disappeared beneath tons of plastic rubbish, discarded there by the residents of the slums across the road. A greenish trickle flowed amongst the detritus, fanning across a strip of sand stained a dark oily grey: 'All shit', according to Ahmad. A group of small children was playing in the surf, nevertheless. There were also two fishermen, hawking shore crabs from a makeshift stall on the side of the road. The reek of this place, a heady mix of sewage and rotten shellfish, did not make me think of food. Inshore crab-fishing was, I supposed, a safer occupation than the open ocean kind. Gazan trawlers that strayed more than 3 nautical miles offshore risked being shelled by Israeli gunboats.

Ahmad took me to another outfall, on a beach half an hour's drive away, to the south of Gaza City. The pipe here was much bigger, a proper gusher. For hundreds of metres around, the effluent the pipe emitted had tinged the sea a whitish-yellow colour, forming foamy globules all along the tideline. A few refugees were living nearby in shacks knocked up from driftwood and bits of old carpet: an embryonic shantytown in the dunes. Ahmad said that people like this typically survived on one daily meal of tomatoes and salt. Further back, hanging between a series of posts, I noticed what I took to be drying fishing nets, but which turned out to be for the trapping of *fir*, or quail, an old Gazan tradition. These migratory birds once made landfall here in their thousands, exhausted from their passage across the Mediterranean. It was September, usually the high season for the *fir*-trappers. The nets, however, were all empty. Thanks to over-trapping, few quail plied the route from northern Europe any more. The poverty on this beach was the worst I saw in Gaza – and the ruination of nature was its emergent theme.

We followed the outfall pipe inland to its source, a treatment plant on the edge of the Wadi Gaza, the largest of all the natural watercourses that flow into the Strip from Israel. There was, however, no water to be seen in the wadi, just a reedy bog where two or three egrets skulked, up to their spindly knees in mud.

We smelled the treatment plant before we saw it: an aerobic lagoon the size of a football pitch, covered in white polythene. The engineer in charge, Nihad al-Khatib, welcomed us into his little control room, where he sat at an empty desk and fiddled with a biro. The switches for the plant's machinery were housed in a row of glass and metal cupboards on the wall behind him, but the lights were all dark, their purposeful hum replaced by the sound of bluebottles head-butting the window.

'There isn't much for me to do here, to be honest,' he confided. 'The treatment process in the sedimentation ponds requires continuous oxygen. If the stirrers stop for even half an hour, the system takes a month to recover.

We have our own generators, but we don't have the fuel to run them for twenty hours a day. Without power, it is hopeless.'

The plant, he said, was designed to treat 10,000 cubic metres of sewage a day when it was built in 2011. The designers, however, had underestimated the effect of a public policy introduced at about the same time, the decommissioning of private cesspits in Gaza City. They had also not foreseen the accelerated degradation of the Strip's infrastructure brought about by the blockade or the 2014 war. For whatever reason, Engineer Khatib's plant now had to deal with 25,000 cubic metres of sewage a day. The lagoon through the window was literally bursting at the seams. He had no choice but to use what electricity was available to pump the sewage untreated into the sea. His treatment plant, furthermore, was only one among many in the Gaza Strip, which overall is depositing an estimated 90,000 cubic metres of raw sewage, enough to fill 36 Olympic swimming pools, into the Mediterranean every day.[10]

The sewage disposal problem was clearly critical, but it was also an issue that mostly only preoccupied water managers like Ahmad. Ordinary Gazans naturally worried much more about the front end of the supply chain – the lack of potable water in household taps – although as I soon discovered, the two issues were very closely connected.

The following day I was taken by an official from Oxfam to the very north of the Strip to visit one of Gaza's eight refugee camps, Jabaliya, a place long associated with resistance. In 1987, an IDF truck collided with a civilian car and killed its four occupants, three of whom were from Jabaliya. Some locals suspected the collision was deliberate. The protests that followed mushroomed into the First Intifada, an uprising that spread across the whole of Palestine and lasted for almost six years.

Jabaliya, I found, was not a camp in the usual sense of the word. The Israel–Palestine conflict is so old that most of its residents have lived here for generations. Their original tents and shacks were replaced long ago by permanent structures, so that Jabaliya today is almost indistinguishable from any poor Arab town.

I was taken to meet Hussein and Sana'a Lubad, who live with five of their eight children in a two-room concrete blockhouse down a dusty alleyway too narrow for cars. Sana'a, in a voluminous embroidered *thobe* and a flowery blue head shawl, greeted me in her tiny courtyard, the family's de facto living room. Without electricity for a fan, she said, the interior of the building was unbearably hot during the day. It was sweltering even outside in the courtyard, where we sat on camp chairs in the paltry shade of a shrivelled vine. The heat, however, was not her greatest concern. 'As a mother, I spend two-thirds of my time thinking about water supply,' she told me.

She had lived in the house for twelve years. To begin with, she recalled, the tap water was fine to drink, but in 2013 it began to taste 'bitter'. It was also sometimes 'tea-coloured' – the result, they suspected in Jabaliya, of contamination from one of the neighbourhood's six decrepit sewage collection ponds. 'The children got sick with diarrhoea, and it gave you skin rashes,' she remembered.

Eventually, in 2016, the municipal supply broke down altogether – and it wasn't repaired. The Water Authority told the residents that they lacked the resources to fix the system, which might well have been true. Because governance is so weak in this refugee society, an estimated 80 per cent of Gazans either cannot or do not pay any water rates, which means that the Water Authority is permanently cash-strapped; although Sana'a was unsure if that was the real reason.

'Who knows?' she shrugged. 'Sometimes Hamas prefers not to mend such things. They think that the people will blame their suffering on the PA in Ramallah, or else on the Israelis, and that this will make them support Hamas more.'

For whatever reason, from 2016 Sana'a was forced to buy all her domestic water from private well operators who delivered it by tanker. The deliveries, however, were unreliable, and the water quality extremely variable. 'One of the suppliers has a good desalination system, but the others are unlicensed cowboys who sell untreated well water,' she said.

Sana'a's life had become easier since Oxfam sank an emergency well in the neighbourhood, along with a small, solar-powered desalination system. 'I know we are lucky. I know many people without access to any well.' The Oxfam well, in fact, served no more than 1,200 households in a camp that was home to tens of thousands.

Sana'a's impoverished, donor-dependent lifestyle was certainly unenviable. Her husband, a part-time taxi driver, made an average of fifteen shekels (US$4) a day. She herself once worked as a janitor in a school run by UNRWA, the United Nations Relief and Works Agency, on which her family also relied for food. But she had recently been laid off, a disaster that she blamed on Donald Trump, who had just cancelled all US funding of the agency, on the grounds that it was complicit with Hamas and was perpetuating the refugee 'problem'.

The World Bank warned in 2018 that Gaza's economy was 'imploding'. Sana'a's experience illustrated what that meant in practice. Life here was not just financially impoverished. Lassitude born of desperation hung over Jabaliya like a cloud. 'The real problem,' she said thoughtfully, 'is boredom. Especially for women. Every day I think: please, someone, get me out of here.'

She couldn't afford to take her children on day trips. 'It would cost a hundred shekels [US$30]. That's quite impossible,' she said. 'We do sometimes go to the beach, but I am too frightened of the dirty water to let the children swim. We just sit on the sand and look at the sea.'

When I asked if she, or perhaps her older children, ever attended the weekly fence demonstrations, she looked uneasily at my accompanying Oxfam official and changed the subject. 'You ask me about water. I would say: we can cope. We Palestinians have experienced worse things, and we are tough. But our water problems do contribute to an overall frustration and depression here. We are so tired by our situation – the lack of water, the lack of electricity, the lack of jobs: everything.'

I wondered if it was really true that she spent two-thirds of her life worrying about water supply. My visit to her house was arranged not by me but by Oxfam, who had a new well they wanted to show off, and who had taken foreign journalists to meet the Lubads before. One afternoon some days later, however, plodding along the sultry corniche towards my hotel, I fell into step with a lifeguard and his two young children, the elder a seven-year-old who restlessly circled us on a BMX bike.

Gaza's golden beaches, said the lifeguard, should have been one of the Strip's greatest assets, a magnet for sun-seeking tourists, just as they were up the coast at Tel Aviv. But, he complained, there were no tourists and few local swimmers in Gaza these days, and therefore little lifeguarding for him to do. 'Some days the water is clear, but mostly it is full of sewage,' he said. 'Today it is half and half.'

The state of the beaches seemed genuinely to pain him. He said he had been a swimmer all his life; he used to surf, too, in winter, when the waves could reach 6 metres. Just then his phone rang, a crisis call from his wife at home. 'Ay,' he tutted as he finished. 'She's been waiting in all day for a tanker delivery, but it hasn't come, yet again. We have no water at home. I have to go and find some somehow.' And he peeled off towards the city centre, his fractious children in tow.

Refugee camps like Jabaliya were the grim public face that Gaza showed to the world, but as time went by I began to see that there was another side to the Strip, and above all to Gaza City. Parts of it, to be sure, were as sad and impoverished as anything I had seen in the Middle East. Here and there I found buildings and, sometimes, whole neighbourhoods that had been reduced to rubble by Israeli airstrikes and ground offensives over the years. Yet the spirit of the city seemed far from snuffed out.

In the centre of town one evening, I found myself in a grand boulevard of ten-storey buildings, the centre of which was laid to lawns shaded by palm trees. The grass, it was true, was brown for lack of watering, and the palm fronds were ragged and limp. The pavements, furthermore, were not exactly teeming with shoppers. Yet on the top floor of one of the buildings, I found a bustling café full of smartly dressed young men and women, smiling and laughing together: evidence of a kind of social life that I had thought did not exist in Gaza. The customers sat at tables by sliding glass windows through which a soft sea breeze blew. Tuxedoed waiters whizzed about, serving alcohol-free cocktails and replenishing hookah pipes. This cheerful scene looked quite the opposite of 'unliveable', that gloomy prediction put forward by the UN.

The customers belonged to social stratum very different to the impoverished masses that made up the bulk of the crowd at the weekly fence demonstration. On the other hand, they did not look especially prosperous, either. Ascribing middle-class 'normality' to Gaza, I was aware, is a propaganda trick once practised by the IDF, who in 2013 published a photograph of a 'sparkling, new' shopping mall with a description of Gazans 'out in force . . . doing their shopping in pristine grocery stores and markets heaving with fresh produce'. It was a clunking attempt by the IDF to play down the effects of its siege, because no such shopping mall exists in Gaza; the photograph later proved to be a stock image of a mall in Calcutta.[11]

Prosperity, however, was not quite the point. I admired the determination of this café crowd to carry on with life, and their refusal to give up on its small pleasures. Thoughts of the abominable siege, the endless conflict, the immense Palestinian suffering it continued to cause: all seemed to have been left firmly in the coatroom as they came in. I sat down at a window table of my own; and as I gazed down on the shadowy streets below, I felt an unexpected flash of optimism. The city's physical infrastructure was tired and battered, but perhaps enough of it was intact for it to thrive again one day, if a political settlement could ever be reached. In the meantime – at least in this moment, from the vantage point of my café table – Israel's bombs and barriers seemed unlikely ever to subjugate the Strip's greatest potential asset, the energy and resourcefulness of its young.

The blockade had fostered a kind of Blitz Spirit among everyone in Gaza, a culture of make-do-and-mend that defied the shrill politics and dreary stagnation of their daily lives. The cars of the city, to give another example, are generally old, because the import of new ones is restricted; and they often bear the signs of bodged repairs, because spare parts are unavailable. In town, I had seen donkey carts piled with scrap, or fruit and vegetables – a relatively new phenomenon in Gaza, I was told. Ten years ago, the drivers of these carts would perhaps have been at the wheel of a van. Yet although the city's car fleet is undoubtedly diminishing, enough of them are still running to form the occasional traffic jam. Gaza reminded me a little of Havana, another city that responded to years of crippling blockade by fixing rather than scrapping their cars as they aged; vehicles that eventually became so old that some have since become valuable classics.

Not every sewage treatment plant was in as dire a state as the one I saw by Wadi Gaza, as I found when I visited the recently opened Northern Gaza Emergency Sewage Treatment plant, known as NGEST, a 'flagship intervention project' of the international community. Built using Swedish technology, it had cost tens of millions of dollars to build, all paid for through the World Bank. The engineer in charge was an Italian contract worker called Paolo; his lieutenants were locals, bright young chemistry graduates from one of Gaza's three universities.

'All site visitors must wear a helmet and a hi-viz vest', said a sign. NGEST appeared an oasis of modernity in a land being dragged back to mediaeval times. The plant dealt with the effluent of four urban communities in northern Gaza, including that of the Lubad family in Jabaliya. The project, which took thirteen years to complete, was spurred forward by an incident in 2007 when the wall of an old sewage lagoon in nearby Beit Lahia collapsed, releasing a tidal wave of filth that drowned five people. The old system, built in the 1970s, was designed to serve 50,000 people. By the time of the collapse, it was serving 190,000. NGEST was now serving 360,000.[12]

The engineers at NGEST were well used to foreign visitors. I was led smoothly around the gantries above the sand filtration ponds, some of them already so clean that they had carp swimming in them. The treated sewage was piped back underground to a depth of 90 metres, where in winter it helped to recharge the aquifer; in summer it was extracted again via fourteen recovery wells, and used for irrigation.

Electricity supply was seldom a problem here, according to Paolo, because, he said, NGEST received 'special treatment' from Hamas. In future, he added, it was possible that Israel would supply a direct connection from their national grid, although talks on that topic had so far led nowhere. As a stopgap, NGEST was planning to reduce its dependence on municipal supply by installing its own dedicated solar power plant.

NGEST did face other challenges. One of them was the plant's location, less than 500 metres from the border fence. In May 2018, Paolo recalled, a demonstration there got out of hand. 'They came over the fences. It was a like a river of people, sheltering from the gunfire. We were forced to shut the plant down'.

Even this prestigious international project, furthermore, was hampered by the IDF's arcane import restrictions. Israel's attitude was deeply ambiguous. On one hand, the plant's construction, completed in 2018, had required large amounts of piping that fell into the IDF's dual-use 'restricted' category. The plant's very existence therefore showed that Israel broadly approved of it, because the IDF had allowed the import rules to be bent. On the other hand, the import rules still applied, now that the plant was up and running. Paolo said he had been waiting for six months for some chemicals needed for the analysis of water quality, and he had no idea when they might arrive.

Paolo said that he had no human interaction with the Israeli border officials: no meetings, no phone calls. The only communication was by formal emails to and from COGAT, the Israeli Defense Ministry's notoriously bureaucratic Co-ordinator of Government Activities in the Territories, which controls the movement of all goods and people through Erez. It remained Paolo's strong impression that Israel tolerated rather than encouraged the foreigners' initiative – and he found this puzzling, because it was common knowledge that Gaza's sewage was a public health hazard for them, too. 'The IDF know very well that it is a strategic issue for them. The smell at Erez is terrible'.

Many local watercourses, notably the Wadi Hanoun, flow northwards across the border. For years, they have carried untreated sewage from the crowded northern end of the Strip into Israel, forcing the local authorities there to treat it at their own considerable expense.[13] As Paolo observed, Gazan overspill continues to be a problem on the Israeli side, but at least NGEST helped to mitigate it. Why was Israel not more supportive of the project?

Israel's policy on Gaza felt incoherent throughout the Strip, though perhaps nowhere more so than in this matter of unwanted human effluent, which exposed the limits – or perhaps the futility – of the IDF's containment strategy. Groundwater flow was no respecter of the blockade, any more than the tides obeyed King Canute. The coastal aquifer stretches under both sides of the border fence, and the fluid it contains cannot be controlled in practice. It is the same story along the edge of the West Bank, where the mountain aquifer stretches far beneath the political border with Israel.

Gazan pollution threatens Israel by sea as well, because the tides in the eastern Mediterranean naturally push the filth pumped into the sea northwards up the coast. In July 2017, a public swimming beach at Ashkelon, barely 15 kilometres from where I now stood, had to be closed due to contamination. A year earlier, much more seriously, the water around the intake pipe of Ashkelon's large desalination plant became so foul that the plant was twice forced to shut down. This event caused much alarm in Tel Aviv. The plant at Ashkelon, the first to be built in Israel, provides 15 per cent of all the country's domestic drinking water. Gaza's continuing sanitation crisis thus represents a direct threat to the water security of the state next door.[14]

Yet this threat is as nothing compared to the implications of a pandemic on Israel's doorstep, which were potentially existential long before the advent of the Covid virus. As the director of the Israeli organization Ecopeace, Gidon Bromberg, warned: 'When people are drinking unhealthy water, disease is a direct consequence. Should pandemic disease break out in Gaza, people will simply start moving to the fences. And they won't be moving with stones or rockets. They'll be moving with empty buckets, desperately calling out for clean water.'[15]

The Israeli public, according to Bromberg, are supportive of the IDF's harsh repression of the fence demonstrations because the policy is presented to them as 'national defence'. But he thought that turning away people in obvious need of medical assistance would be a much harder narrative to sell, and that public support for the IDF could quickly evaporate.

'At the moment, the IDF is facing a few tens of thousands of people on the fence. If there's a pandemic, they could be facing many hundreds of thousands – and what then?'[16]

The risk of a pandemic in Gaza is difficult to quantify, especially from a distance, whether in Israel or abroad, where the right sometimes dismiss it as fear-mongering by the activist left. But I had no doubt that dirty water was a genuine health concern for ordinary Gazans. I had heard it articulated by Sana'a Lubad in Jabaliya, and again in a different way by Mostafa Nahed, a twenty-nine-year-old architect who, being unemployed, had thrown himself into humanitarian work instead. His latest project, which he intended to pay for by crowd-sourcing US$25,000 internationally via social media, was to sink a new well, 50 metres deep and powered by a solar array of his own design, to supply a cluster of four large primary schools in central

Gaza City. 'I checked with the PWA, and they said the water in the aquifer under my site is good,' Mostafa told me enthusiastically. 'We have to do something. The kids' water at the moment is *yellow*.'

One quiet day, looking for detail rather than anecdote about the health risks of dirty water, I went with Mostafa to the Shifa hospital, Gaza's main medical complex. Inside, we had the luck to stumble upon an informal staff meeting of nine of the hospital's most senior doctors, all squeezed into a single small office. Not all of them were pleased to see me. The most senior among them, Zakaria al-Agha, was the former head of Fatah in Gaza, an old PLO stalwart also known as Abu Ammar. 'Don't tell the foreigner anything,' he growled. 'It will only get back to the Jews.'

Happily his younger colleagues ignored him. A cardiologist, Ashraf Sha'at, took the lead, and answered my question about pandemics. 'There has been no cholera outbreak here since 1995, but it remains a definite possibility,' he said. One reason that there had been no repeat of a waterborne epidemic, according to a colleague, was that Gazans were good hand washers. 'This is not Yemen,' he said reproachfully. 'We are an educated people, with a good understanding of the importance of personal hygiene.'

Even so, the doctors were in no doubt that Gaza's sub-standard water supply was bad for public health. Reliable data was in short supply, but cases of renal failure were rising by 13 per cent a year. Sewage on the beaches caused skin infections, shigellosis, spirillosis. Diarrhoea was common. They were seeing more cases of hepatitits and meningitis. Most worrying of all, perhaps, was an increase of natal disorders like methemoglobinemia, or 'blue baby syndrome', a condition linked to a surfeit of nitrates.[17] 'But the biggest problem for Gaza is the economy,' Dr Sha'at added, to nods all round.

For the previous two years, the doctors in this room had been on half pay. Some were working for a third of their former salary. 'People without jobs cannot afford to eat properly,' he went on. 'There is a lot of malnutrition, and poor water exacerbates the effects of that. Fifty per cent of our school-children are anaemic. These are the precursor conditions of a pandemic.'

One airless evening, Ahmad Yaqubi invited me to dinner with his family in the centre of town. It was interesting to see that it wasn't just the poor who were forced to cope with the lack of basic services. The stairwell of Ahmad's apartment block was so dark that I had to feel my way up, and the apartment itself was also in darkness. The municipal electricity supply was, evidently, off. 'This is our reality,' he shrugged, as I tripped through his front door.

The Yaqubis bought in privately produced well water like everybody else. Municipal water, when it functioned at all, was piped from a hydrant in the street to a rooftop water tank via a pump that Ahmad had rigged up himself, set to come on automatically whenever the power did.

Ahmad led me upstairs to the roof, where his seventeen-year-old son Wahid fired up a small, noisy generator, just enough to power a string of light bulbs hung above a table and chairs. A soft breeze blew here, making it mercifully cooler than the swelter of the streets below. The city stretched out before us, lit up here and there by private generators, edged to the west by the dimly glittering sea. Ahmad's kindly wife produced bread, hummus, olives. For the first time in days, I felt almost relaxed.

The neighbourhood still bore the scars of 2014, Operation Protective Edge, a seven-week conflict in which more than 2,000 Palestinians died, and nearly 11,000 were wounded, a third of them children, according to the UN. The Israelis also razed more than 7,000 buildings, including a youth centre across the road from the Yaqubis. We looked down on its shadowy remains from the parapet. The piles of twisted metal and broken slabs of concrete, Ahmad said, were slowly diminishing, thanks to scavengers. In Gaza, even rubble had a market value.

We were joined on the roof by Rehby al-Sheikh, an old friend and colleague of Ahmad's and the serving deputy head of the PWA. The talk quickly turned to their sons. Rehby's had the good fortune to be studying abroad; he had managed to leave via the Rafah crossing into Egypt, an exit route that had since been closed. The Yaqubis hoped their son might also study abroad, but had no idea how they would obtain the necessary permits.

'We are cut off from all the world here,' Mrs Yaqubi sighed. 'There are only thirty-nine countries where we are welcome without a visa, all of them in the Third World, and none of them Arab ones.'

It was a common Gazan complaint. When foreigners, and indeed Israelis, think of Gaza, they tend to think of crowded refugee camps blighted by poverty and radicalism, but I had already uncovered the inaccuracy of that stereotype. There are 140,000 graduates among the Strip's young population, almost all of them frustrated; people like Mostafa Nahed, the go-getting yet unemployed young architect I had met. His cohort carried the hopes of a sizeable middle class, with all the desires and ambitions recognizable from home. Their untapped potential was as awful a tragedy, in its way, as the conflict that had turned their forebears into refugees in the first place.

Rehby had just come from a water crisis meeting with UN officials. In the last three months, he had learned, daily municipal supply had dropped from 85 litres per capita to 53 litres: just 3 litres above the World Health Organization's recommended minimum of 20 to 50 litres per capita. 'People must burst,' he said. 'They cannot afford to live like this, however resilient they are.'

He said that Israel had played a double game in Gaza for many years, always giving with one hand while taking with the other. At Oslo, he explained, Israel had agreed to sell Gaza 5 million cubic metres of drinking water per year, to be piped in via a new branch line from Israel's national network. This was far below what Gaza's booming population needed, but it was at least something. The main collection point, however, was Al-Muntar reservoir, the construction and operation of which had been obstructed for years by the Israelis. Then, in 2014, the reservoir was 'completely destroyed' in an airstrike.

'Airstrikes caused US$34 million of damage to Gaza's water infrastructure,' Rehby noted bitterly. 'It is collective punishment. Israel just wants to harm Gaza.' In 2015, when the violence had subsided, Israel magnanimously agreed to double the amount of water they were prepared to sell to Gaza, to 10 million cubic metres. But the damage to Al-Muntar meant that Gaza had nowhere to store the extra water. 'Israel just wants to make life here as difficult as they can – but without making it impossible – while maintaining the ability to say to the international community that they are trying to help.'

Rehby reserved particular scorn for the IDF's restrictions on dual-use imports, which consistently hamstrung attempts to maintain or repair Gaza's creaking water network. 'They say we can't have new pumps because they could be used by tunnellers, but why would tunnellers need pumps when the water table is mostly 50 metres deep? We give them photographs of how and where we propose to use the pumps, but it's never enough.'

He acknowledged that some parts of the Israeli state machine, including in the upper echelons of the Defense Ministry, apparently did understand the dangers of letting Gaza's humanitarian situation worsen, and that Palestinian desperation could spark yet another war. Every so often, the IDF would permit the import of a container of material necessary for the repair of water infrastructure. Sometimes, outside players such as Qatar were allowed to make an emergency donation of fuel, and the chronic power shortage would briefly reduce. Overall though, it seemed to Rehby that nothing ever really changed, because progress was too often a case of 'one step forward and one step back'. The most charitable explanation, perhaps, was that Netanyahu was hamstrung by his coalition partners, some of whom were even more right-wing than his own Likud party, and so he could do no more than the minimum, to maintain the fragile status quo.

Halfway through the evening, municipal electricity was abruptly restored, to a faint cheer from the street below. Wahid had just been explaining his ambition to study engineering design, because, he said, he 'liked drawing'. With the lights back on, he took me downstairs to his bedroom, where he shyly showed me a pencil sketch of a pretty girl on the wall above his desk. This pin-up, with oversized eyes that glistened with repressed tears, was no ordinary schoolboy fantasy, however. Wahid had drawn her with one clenched fist raised, and she was wearing a military jacket. It was a portrait of Rouzan al-Najjar, a twenty-year-old volunteer nurse shot dead by snipers at a fence demonstration in June 2018: a new martyr and the perfect idol for Gaza's frustrated male youth.

Wahid said he had been to a fence demonstration once, but hadn't liked it. 'My dad was furious,' he confessed. His bedroom wall spoke nevertheless to the folly of Israel's Gaza policy. Even this gentle teenager was embittered by the isolation of his life. Israel's 'disengagement' strategy was framed as a security policy, but instead of making Israelis safer, it seemed to be doing the opposite, while storing up worse problems for the future. It seemed so obvious that the threat of violent reprisal could never be fully contained, any more than the Israel-bound flow of pollution in the ground and along the coast.

CHAPTER TWO

The Dying Dead Sea

My interest in Gaza's water crisis had long antecedents; they dated back, ultimately, to the day in 1987 when I first saw the empty River Jordan, and wondered where all the water had gone. So it was with some excitement that, thirty years after my first visit, I finally saw it again.

The circumstances, this time, were rather different: I was on a short, half-term holiday tour with my father, my wife, and our four young children. We visited all the usual tourist spots: Tel Aviv, Jerusalem, Bethlehem and, of course, the Jordan and its terminus, the famous Dead Sea. These latter places are in the occupied West Bank, but they are also such well-established waypoints on the Israeli-dominated tourist trail that the children barely noticed we had crossed a border to reach them.

We went to the Dead Sea first. The children were excited to visit the lowest point on the surface of the earth, and they were not disappointed. The Israeli-run beach resort we visited was surprisingly expensive to enter: a safe, cossetting cocoon, a world away from the poverty and violence of Gaza. Under a broiling sun we bobbed like corks in water ten times saltier than the ocean, so dense with salt that it is impossible to sink. Afterwards, we slathered ourselves in smelly black mud scooped from holes in the foreshore, and lumbered about like zombies as it dried and cracked on our limbs.

The hydrogeology of the Jordan Valley[1] is not an abstract matter to visitors to the Dead Sea. Parts of the coastline are spectacularly striated with crystallized salt deposits, forming weird caves and pillars like stalagmites. Elsewhere, the foreshore is a morass of dangerous sinkholes, formed by the retreat of the sea and the desaturation of the bed beneath. The foreshore everywhere is broadening with spectacular speed. The beach resort we visited was a new enterprise, yet the wooden jetty built for the convenience of bathers now stopped 100 metres short of the waterline. We had to climb off the end of the jetty with the help of a rope. The expanse of mud between made us all wonder what had happened here. The water level, we were told, is dropping by a metre a year: faster, clearly, than the beach resort's architects ever anticipated. It was hard to compute that this was no sea loch, but a tideless inland lake.

After the Dead Sea, we drove twenty minutes north to the spot on the River Jordan where Christ was baptised by John. The site, called Qasr al-Yahud – the 'Tower of the Jews', the Arabic name for the nearby monastery of St John the Baptist – proved to be just as big a draw for foreign tourists as the Dead Sea, although the crowd was different here, since the visitors were mostly Christian pilgrims. We found an enormous bus park, changing rooms with showers, and a gift shop selling fridge magnets and little bottles for the pilgrims to fill, the labels marked 'Holy Water' in all the languages of the world, although most of them were in Russian: Святая Вода.

Tiers of timber decking descended the slope to the water's edge. We stopped at the top and gazed down on a party of Americans, all wearing diaphanous white shrouds, who were undergoing a full baptismal immersion. Their accompanying pastor, stern and efficient, pushed their heads beneath the surface with such force that my children got the giggles. One after another of the group came up spouting, to cries of 'Hallelujah' from the small crowd, who fist-pumped the sky with trembling, fleshy arms. It was very reminiscent of the baptism scene in the Coen brothers movie, *O Brother, Where Art Thou?*, in which escaped convict Delmar O'Donnell announces: 'Well that's it boys! Ah've been redeemed! The preacher done washed away all my sins and transgressions. It's the straight and narrow from here on out, and heaven everlastin's mah reward!'

It was doubtful whether this actual Jordan water could wash away anything much. In 1848, when Lieutenant William Lynch of the United States Navy explored this stretch, he described a 'serpentine' and 'impetuous' river that in places was 180 yards wide. Between a 'desperate looking cascade' and a 'fearful cataract', he wrote, the Jordan 'flowed broad and deep, yet maintaining much of the character of a torrent'.[2] Now, however, the river flowed sluggishly, if at all, between banks choked by reeds. It was also absurdly narrow: Jordan, the country, was barely 30 metres away. The pastor was almost halfway across, and still only waist-deep. It was so easily fordable that there were signposts warning pilgrims not to wade in too far, on pain of arrest by border guards on the other side.

The Jordan, I had to remind myself, is 250 kilometres long: the only major river in this part of the Middle East, fed by tributaries that rise in Lebanon, Syria and Jordan as well as Israel-Palestine. Its name is thought by most historians to come from the Semitic word *Yarad*, 'the Descender';[3] others think the name derives from the ancient Egyptian *ye'or*, 'big river', compounded with the Akkadian *dannum*, 'powerful'.[4] Either way, it seems likely that the river as described by Lieutenant Lynch in the 1840s was as it had been for at least the previous three millennia. The shrinkage had to be entirely modern.

The ditch before us made a mockery not only of the river's etymology but also of the Bible stories about it. This was not just the site of Christ's baptism but, according to tradition, the place where the Israelites, after their escape from Egypt and years of wandering in the desert, forded the river and at last entered the Promised Land. The Book of Joshua, written in the thirteenth century BC, describes in detail how God erected an invisible dam upstream of the crossing point, so that

> ... the waters of Jordan shall be cut off from the waters that come down from above; and they shall stand upon an heap ... And the priests that bore the ark of the covenant of the Lord stood firm on dry ground in the

midst of [the] Jordan, and all the Israelites passed over on dry ground, until all the people were passed clean over.[5]

There would, we observed, be no need for any such miracle now.

And then there was the colour. The water was not the purifying kind, but an opaque greyish brown: dirtier, even, than I remembered it in the 1980s. This was despite the intervention of the tourist authorities, which had tried to sanitize the stretch that is open to the public by introducing clean water via a pipe hidden around the corner, just upstream. In some summers, I had read, the Jordan's natural flow is so reduced that the only fluid it contains is agricultural run-off and effluent from farms and settlements.[6] The pilgrims here seemed as likely to ingest E. coli as a dose of heavenly redemption. I didn't need to warn the children not to drink it.

The river might have been a disappointment, yet I knew that we were historically fortunate, as tourists, to get so close to it. When Israel drove the Jordanians from the West Bank in the Six Day War of 1967, they laid more than 300,000 mines to make sure they didn't come back. Israel made peace with Jordan in 1994, but the mines mostly remain. It was not until 2011 that Israel cleared a road between them, allowing pilgrims and tourists to reach Qasr al-Yahud for the first time in forty-four years.

It was hot and claustrophobic at the baptism site, and I longed to wander away from the crowds along the bank to look at the river in its unmanipulated state. Around the corner beyond the artificial inflow pipe, I suspected I would find the kind of dirty ditch I had once seen beneath the Allenby Bridge. We were hemmed in, however, by barriers as tall and strong as a deer fence on both sides of the access road, all the way back to the highway. The fence was also decorated with many signs warning of unexploded mines. I supposed that no sane person had strolled at leisure along the banks of the lower Jordan for more than fifty years. Not even the IDF venture in much, since the mines obviate the need for many border patrols.

For all its fame, the lower Jordan flows largely unseen by the world. Qasr al-Yahud is almost the only point along a strip of riverbank 70 kilometres long where public access is possible. The Palestinian West Bank, I reflected, is a place in name only, since its territory is utterly cut off from the riverside it describes. There were, revealingly, no Palestinians at Qasr al-Yahud, with the exception of one or two certified tour guides. Despite its West Bank location, the baptism site looks and feels like an exclusively Israeli tourist trap.

It is hard to make sense of the occupied West Bank without reference to the Oslo Accords, a pivotal moment in the modern Middle East The period when the Accords were signed, in 1993 and 1995, were years of unparalleled hope, signalling as they did the end of the First Intifada, and the best chance ever for a resolution to a conflict that has roiled the region for a century. A handshake on the Clinton White House lawn between the Israeli premier, Yitzhak Rabin, and the PLO chairman, Yasser Arafat, remains one of the world's best-known symbols of peace.

However, the longed-for new era got off to a disastrous start when the principal Israeli proponent, Prime Minister Yitzhak Rabin, was assassinated by an Israeli ultranationalist in November 1995. In elections the following year, Rabin's replacement, Shimon Peres, was narrowly defeated by Netanyahu, ushering in a period of harsher rhetoric and harder positions on both sides of the divide. Arafat and his support for the Oslo Accords was undermined by the machinations of Hamas and an increasingly violent Islamic Jihad.

The Oslo agreement ultimately contained the seeds of its own destruction, for it never led to the Final Status agreement that was supposed to have been reached within five years of signing the Accords. Instead, the supposedly interim arrangements for the occupied West Bank – which were, arguably, never compatible with the creation of an independent Palestinian state – remain in place three decades on.

To the West Bank's 3 million inhabitants, perhaps the most iniquitous of Oslo's many interim arrangements was the agreement to divide their territory into three 'areas of control', known as Areas A, B and C. Area A comprises the West Bank's major population centres, where the PA is theoretically autonomous; Area B comprises Palestinian suburbs and certain small towns and villages, where administrative authority is shared; while Area C means everywhere else – effectively 'the places in between' – and remains under full Israeli military control.

Ceding control of relatively sparsely populated lands did not look like such a bad deal to Arafat's negotiators at the time. Even today, Area C is home to an estimated 300,000 Palestinians,[7] compared to some 2.8 million in Areas A and B. However, Area C accounts for almost two-thirds of the West Bank's total land area, including almost all of the Jordan Valley, with the important exception of the city of Jericho and its environs. The Area ABC agreement was supposed to bring peace to the West Bank by ensuring that responsibility for security was shared. The reality was a deal that ended up extending and deepening the Israeli military occupation, while pushing territorial autonomy for Palestinians further out of reach. The PA has arguably never been an authority, because it has never held jurisdiction over more than a third of the West Bank's actual territory. Its claim to leadership was diminished even further in 2007, when Hamas ousted it from Gaza.

To make matters worse for Palestinians, Oslo Area C became the campaigning ground for Israel's West Bank settlement programme, which is still dramatically expanding. Since the day in 1980 when President Jimmy Carter first described the West Bank's settlements as 'illegal', settler numbers have risen fifty-fold, to some 650,000 people. The movement accelerated in 2009 when Netanyahu's Likud coalition government returned to power, and was boosted again following the 2016 election of Donald Trump, whose support for Netanyahu and disdain for the opinion of the UN were more pronounced than any past American president. In 2018 alone, settler numbers grew by 3.5 per cent, almost twice the rate of population growth in Israel proper. According to one projection, West Bank settlers could number more than a million by 2041.[8]

With the emergence of new, pro-settler parties after the intifadas, and the peculiar circumstances of Israel's fractured political landscape that brought them to power, support for the settlement movement entered Israel's political mainstream. The Orthodox Jewish and religious Zionist party, HaBayit HaYehudi – 'The Jewish Home' – which was founded in 2008, seeks Israeli sovereignty over the whole of Area C; its leader until 2018 was the prime minister, Naftali Bennett. Jewish Home's agenda sounds drastic, yet there are other Israelis for whom the annexation of even the entire West Bank would not go far enough, because according to some interpretations of the Bible, the land promised to Abraham by God, *Ha'aretz Hamuvtakhat*, is a territory that stretches east as far as Iraq.[9] Israel, the controversial British theologian Stephen Sizer once observed, 'must be the only country in the world that has not yet recognized its own borders'.[10]

The explosive growth of this 'creeping annexation', as critics sometimes dub the settlement programme, is no accident but part of a long-term security strategy, first enunciated in 1977 by Mati Drobles, a Likud politician and chairman of the World Zionist Organization's settlement department. In a document called the Master Plan for the Development of Settlements, Drobles wrote: 'The aim is to render it difficult for the minority Arab population to unite and create territorial continuity.'

Forty years on, the Drobles vision looks fulfilled. Even excluding Arab East Jerusalem, where some 250,000 Jews now live, there are 132 settlements in the West Bank that the Israeli government regards as 'legal'. There are also another 121 outposts that do not enjoy official recognition, although this does not necessarily signify government disapproval: since 1991, the authorities have removed only two outposts.[11] The Palestinians, for their part, are powerless to resist the spread because the settlements are all on land they no longer control, in Oslo Area C.

In 2009 a French cartographer, Julien Bousac, published a quirky but revealing map in *Le Monde Diplomatique* that reimagined the West Bank as a complex archipelago of tiny Palestinian islands afloat on an Israeli-controlled, Area C sea.[12] Thus, Ramallah occupies its own island, the 'Île Capitale', cut off from the 'mainland' to the north by the 'Canal d'Ariel', and from Hebron in the south by the 'Canal de Jerusalem', with a constellation of tiny rocks and islets in between. Jericho is represented as the distant Ile de l'Est, which floats alone in the widest and longest expanse of blue on the entire map; this is Bousac's rendering of the fertile Jordan Valley. The map is a devastating illustration of the challenge – or, some might say, the futility – of establishing a viable independent Palestinian state, the basis of the two-state solution that has underpinned the efforts of generations of Western peacemakers.

Bousac's aqueous analogy is clever because the settlement programme is fuelled by water. It is well known, almost a cliché among international aid workers, that the average per capita water consumption of Israelis versus Palestinians is four to one. Israeli *settlers*, however, are not average: they typically consume twenty times as much water, per capita, as their West Bank Arab neighbours. I was to learn and hear much more about this water-blessed segment of Israeli society, the advance guard of a government programme regarded as unconscionable even by many Israeli liberals, as well as illegal by the UN.

In 2019, an election year in Israel, the settlement programme received a significant boost when Netanyahu announced his formal intention to annex almost all of the Jordan Valley, should he be re-elected. At a televised press conference, he pointed enthusiastically at a coloured map with a stick. 'We haven't had such an opportunity since the [1967 war], and I doubt we will have such an opportunity in the next sixty years,' he said.[13]

Jordan Valley annexation has been proposed before in Israel – in fact, regularly, ever since the occupation began in 1967. The notion has been successfully resisted until now, whether by Palestinians, domestic political opponents, religious peace movements, or by a spectrum of foreign governments and institutions, on the grounds that annexation is illegal under international law; most likely it would also be fatal to the prospects of the two-state solution agreed in Oslo.

Netanyahu had to be taken seriously now, however, because this time the plan had the implicit support of the US. Earlier in 2019, Washington had surprised the world with an out-of-the-blue endorsement of Israel's claim to sovereignty over the long-occupied Golan Heights. Netanyahu, encouraged, now wanted to go further; indeed, he was soon to gain the explicit support he needed, with the publication of the Trump Peace Plan, which declared that Israeli sovereignty over the valley was necessary because it was 'critical for Israel's national security'.

Great trouble, therefore, was brewing in the Jordan Valley, where it looked as though 'creeping annexation' was about to become entrenched. Israel had already appropriated the water in the Jordan river. Now it was after its western littoral as well. The territory in Netanyahu's sights amounted to 22 per cent of the total land area of the occupied West Bank. Not only is it Palestine's best farming land; it is also Palestine's geographic link to Jordan, millions of whose citizens self-identify as Palestinian. Annexation therefore threatens to cut the de facto 'Palestinian nation' in two. Saeb Erekat, the lead Palestinian negotiator at Oslo,[14] warned that enactment of Netanyahu's proposal would amount to a 'war crime'.[15] To Palestinians like him, the threat was existential – because what kind of an entity would the West Bank become, or even be called, if it no longer possessed the territory after which it is named?

After my family holiday, I was keen to return to the source of so much contention. I wanted to see the occupation of the Jordan Valley from the Palestinian point of view, through local Arab eyes. However, the valley's centrepiece, the river, was physically closed off to local Arabs – and I needed to see this too. My best chance of reaching it at all would, I calculated, be in the company of Israelis.

My first thought was to try the military. Perhaps I could persuade the Defense Ministry to let me tag along on a border patrol? I posted some emails; but the IDF's bureaucracy quickly proved almost as impenetrable as the minefields along the riverbank. I thought about approaching from the Jordanian side, but the East Bank too turned out to be a military zone, where local farmers need special permission to enter.

Eventually I read about an Israeli campaign to turn the mine strip into a nature reserve. It seemed that the fifty-year absence of people here had proved excellent news for wildlife, rather as it has been in the exclusion zone around Chernobyl. According to the Society for the Protection of Nature in Israel (SPNI), a powerful lobby group, the river zone has become a haven for endangered gazelle, jackal, hyena and caracal. It is also an important corridor for birds migrating between Africa and Europe. Then I learned that the crumbling bunker posts abandoned by the IDF in 1994, which still overlook the river, have been colonized in many instances by a dozen species of rare bats. These colonies, I read, were closely moni-tored by Israeli ecologists working with the Israeli Nature and Parks Authority, in collaboration with the IDF. Could this be my way to the riverbank?

I contacted an ecologist, Shmulik Yedvab, who said he would be happy to show me the roosts. A fortnight later, I found myself deep inside the mine-field at last, but underground, in an eerie, pitch-dark labyrinth of concrete barrack rooms. Shmulik seemed quite at home in it. Shaven-headed and powerfully built, he was an officer in the army reserve when he wasn't study-ing bats. I stumbled after him, his head-torch flickering over the rusting frames of bunk beds, and on the wall of a cookhouse, the neat painted outlines of frying pans and cooking utensils, testament to the soldierly discipline of the long-departed occupiers. A thin layer of dust lay over the once gleaming kitchen surfaces, undisturbed for years. In the narrow space below one eave, some bored conscript had created a kind of frieze out of empty white ciga-rette packets. They were all the same brand, the most popular one in Israel, called TIME. The word was repeated around the eave until it became a subversive comment on the tedium of national service; unless it was just a way of marking it, as a prisoner chalks gates on the wall of his cell.

Shmulik had a phone app that both recorded and identified different species of bat by the frequency of their ultrasonic squeaks. We turned left, then right, and came at last to a hot and evil-smelling cul-de-sac, the far wall of which was dripping with guano beneath a black chandelier of inverted chiroptera. Disturbed by the sudden light, a pair of them broke from the roost and flitted for the exit, so close by our heads that we felt the swish of their wings.

'Hm. Nothing special, I'm afraid,' he said, consulting his phone. 'It's maybe a bit late in the season.' The creatures were trident leaf-nosed bats, *Asellia tridens*; he had been hoping to find a rarer variety called *Rhinolophus clivosus*, or Geoffroy's horseshoe bat.[16]

We returned to Route 90, the highway that parallels the river along the edge of the mine strip, and drove south to another roost, the location of which felt, if possible, even eerier than the abandoned bunker. These bats had colonized the underground pump room of the swimming pool of a ruined hotel, the Lido, very close to Kalya, an early potash-mining kibbutz near the mouth of the Jordan where it decants into the Dead Sea.

Built in the 1920s, the Dead Sea Lido was once a fashionable resort, popular with Europeans stopping off on the Imperial Airways seaplane route to Africa, India or the Far East. Its present-day dereliction was eloquent. In the 1920s, the Lido sat right on the shoreline. Now, thanks partly to natural processes and climate change – but mostly to Israel's diversion of the Jordan upstream – the water's edge was a good 2 kilometres away. From the cocktail terrace of the blue-painted, art deco-curved swimming pool – empty and scattered with rubble now, but still intact – we looked out across a wilderness of cracked, dun-coloured mud, with the Sea a mere glint in the distance, its shoreline demarcating the latest, deepest point on the surface of the Earth. In the foreground, on the spot where Short Empire flying boats once taxied, leaned the decaying remains of an old pleasure cruiser, surreally marooned.

The Lido's customers stopped coming as the Dead Sea receded, and the resort's fate was soon sealed. As the shore dried out, deep fissures and sinkholes appeared, and the hotel began to slump into its foundations. The structure eventually became so dangerous that IDF engineers felt obliged to blow it up. Shmulik and I climbed over rubble and twisted metal, crunching across smashed painted tiles and coloured glass. Buried among the detritus inside we found heaps of mould-spotted old books: the remains of the hotel library.

The titles evoked an age when Israel was young and full of hope. I found an English language primer for German-speakers, a *Selbststudium der Englischen Sprache*, printed in the 1940s in Gothic blackletter: the former property, I imagined, of a German Jewish émigré who had fled the Nazis. There was a 1950s survey of *Qi Min Yao Shu*, an agricultural encyclopaedia from sixth-century China: just the sort of book that might have inspired the farmer-pioneers of the new Israel. Most poignant of all was a study by a group of Oxford economists called *What Everybody Wants to Know About Money*, published in 1933. It contained some startlingly accurate predictions about the coming crisis in Europe, the collapse of the gold standard, and the international banking revolution that would follow. Here at the mouth of the Jordan, however, their cleverness read like hubris. Not one of them had foreseen that the planet would one day warm, and that rivers would dry and seas retreat, or that this grand hotel in consequence would soon crumble back into dust, as forlorn and forgotten as Shelley's broken statue to Ozymandias.

The bat roosts were interesting but, as a ploy for getting to grips with the river, my excursion with Shmulik was not a success. For sensible military reasons, the IDF bunkers were generally located on high ground, tantalisingly close to but never actually on the water's edge. I had hoped to get my feet wet. But Shmulik's permission to enter the closed zone with me, hard-won from the authorities, was tightly circumscribed; and nothing I said could persuade him to venture off-piste.

My frustration increased when I learned that he was in fact one of very few Israelis who did sometimes venture into the river itself. Earlier in the year, he revealed, he and two colleagues had mounted an expedition to monitor the lower Jordan's growing population of otters. They had tried to navigate a 30-kilometre stretch in a canoe, but found it so shallow that they were continually forced to pull the boat out and drag it along the bank. 'The mud was terrible,' he recalled. 'We came out of there stinking.'

He offered to take me on his next otter-hunting expedition, but I was already wondering if this was really the way to go in my research. It was not the fauna of the valley that most interested me, but its human occupants; and it was becoming ever clearer that Shmulik, as an Israeli, was probably not the right guide for me. For all his enthusiasm for the natural world, the West Bank to him was still occupied territory. His perception of it was necessarily circumscribed by security concerns, and skewed by the distrust between Israelis and the Arabs who called the area home; and tensions had recently been heightened by the renewed talk from Jerusalem of annexation. It would be difficult, if not impossible, to meet local Palestinians in his company.

SPNI's bid to turn the riverbank into a nature reserve – what Shmulik called 'an ecological corridor' between Europe and Africa – was much more controversial than it sounded on paper. With Palestine's population growing at 3 per cent a year (and Israel's at 2 per cent), pressure on land is mounting all the time. The closure of the border zone is theoretically temporary, pending the Final Status talks that are supposed to lead to a two-state solution. A new nature reserve, however, would likely render Palestinians' exclusion from the riverbank permanent; and most Palestinians feel that they have lost too much land to Israel already, whether through settlement, military requisition, or environmental schemes of this kind.

Shmulik's passion for bat conservation was genuine, but Palestinian suspicion of Israeli motives was understandable. There are, already, more than two dozen designated nature reserves in the Jordan Valley, accounting for 20 per cent of the total land area.[17] To Palestinians, therefore, SPNI looks like just another tool of the occupation; and even Shmulik conceded that Ramallah was unlikely to smile upon a proposal for yet another nature reserve.

CHAPTER THREE

The Jordan Valley

Tales from the Riverbank

I T WAS OBVIOUS that I would need a Palestinian's help to get beneath the skin of this complex place, so eventually I enlisted the help of Bassam, a professional guide based in Ramallah. He was, among other things, a keen motorcyclist, the leader of a club of fellow enthusiasts who sometimes toured the West Bank together at weekends. It sounded an excellent mode of transport for another foray into the Valley – and Bassam had a friend, a successful shawarma foodshop owner, who was willing to lend me his machine.

This turned out to be a Korean knock-off of a Harley Davidson called a Hyosung Aquila. The bike was long and low, a mean-looking street cruiser with chopper-style handlebars and tassled saddle bags, but with an engine of just 250cc. It seemed a dubious prospect. The electrics were temperamental, and we had to bump-start it. But I gave it a quick test drive, a wobbly figure-of-eight in a car park beneath a block of flats, and then we were off, weaving through the chaos of Ramallah's rush hour.

On the north edge of town, we came to an IDF checkpoint: a permanent one, marking the limit of Area A Ramallah, and the beginning of Israeli-controlled Area C. I was struck by how close it was: the city centre was barely a ten-minute drive away. Although the sense of enclosure in Ramallah is not nearly as intense as in Gaza, the checkpoint, part of a ring around the city, was a reminder that it is still a kind of cage. Bassam said the checkpoint was usually unmanned – but today turned out to be an exception. Bassam, leading, cheerfully ignored the waiting cars, and we scooted to the front of the queue. We were immediately stopped by two incensed-looking soldiers with M16 rifles clipped to the fronts of their immense bulletproof vests. Then Bassam, to my consternation, indicated that I should do the talking.

'Whydja skip the line?' growled the corporal in charge, in a flawless Brooklyn accent. He seemed ridiculously young, with a wisp of blond on his chin. I decided to play the clueless tourist – and luckily, he softened when I showed him my passport.

'What are you doing here? Don't you know how dangerous this town is?'

'Dangerous?' I replied, all astonished.

'Sure! There was a shoot-out here last night. Right over there.'

I thanked him for the warning, and he asked where I was from.

'Scotland,' I said.

'Cool,' he replied, 'I'm from Liverpool.'

His accent had no trace of Scouse, but this was not the moment to ask about his family's no doubt rich migratory backstory. I smiled, and he waved us both through.

We rode south around the eastern edge of Ramallah on Route 60, between desert hilltops dotted with red-roofed houses, the standard design of Israeli settlements. There were other tell-tale signs of the occupation: a remote bus stop, for instance, guarded by a lone IDF soldier for the protection of commuting settlers; or a road junction overlooked by a cluster of CCTV cameras mounted on poles. Bassam said the cameras logged every passing number plate, so that it was impossible to drive anywhere in the West Bank without being watched and recorded. The entire landscape was under surveillance, and it did not feel comfortable to travel through, even for a non-Palestinian.

Yet the road slowly opened up, and with the city behind us, I at last began to relax. We joined Route 1, which leads east from Jerusalem, winding down the escarpment that forms the western side of the Jordan rift. We passed a rock marked 'Sea Level', and wadis to either side that offered fleeting glimpses of Bedouin encampments: rickety shacks, ragged children playing, a hobbled camel. I had taken this road before with Shmulek, in search of bats, but it felt and looked marvellously different now, travelling in the company of this maverick Palestinian. Motorcycling was important to Bassam because, he said, it helped him shake off, however temporarily, the feeling of oppression that the occupation gave him. He had written about it online – 'You can't ride very far if you live in the West Bank, unfortunately, but at least freedom is imaginable when you're out on the road' – and on my Korean Easy Rider machine, buffeted by the desert air, I sensed what he meant.

Our ears popped as we descended. The valley rose into view, a carpet of dark green laid out between buff-coloured hills. At the valley bottom I followed Bassam north into what, for me, was uncharted territory. It was many degrees warmer here than in the highlands around Ramallah, making me sweat inside my borrowed leather jacket, even when we were on the move.

The Jordan Valley, especially in its northern reaches, contains the most fertile farmland in Palestine. Millennia of run-off from wadis, as well as the flow of the Jordan itself, have filled the cleft between with many metres of nutrient-rich, clay-based soil. Farmers have always coveted it; the Book of Genesis calls the valley's plain 'well-watered everywhere . . . like the garden of the Lord'.[1]

We passed between long acres of medjool date palm plantations. Some of them, on Area A land around Jericho, were Palestinian-owned, but the majority belonged to Israelis; several were flying the Star of David. Thanks to plantations like these – all of which belong to settlements deemed 'illegal' by the UN – Israel has dominated the medjool date market for years, and not just regionally, but globally.

Yet, as Bassam later explained, the kibbutzim and moshavim that run them[2] did not exist merely for the production of dates. In line with a plan devised after the 1967 war by Minister of Labour Yigal Allon – perhaps Israel's most successful military leader during the Arab-Israeli war of 1948 – the oldest of these agricultural settlements were also designed as a second line of defence in the event of another Arab invasion. Strategically located and semi-fortified, they were just as militarily important as the minefields and bunkers just to their east. The 'Allon Plan' was frank in its ambition to annex most of the Jordan Valley to Israel, in the interests of self-defence; Allon suggested that the Arab population centres to the west should be returned to Jordanian control, if they did not become autonomous. The plan, however, was rejected outright by the Jordanian King Hussein.

Israel's continued military presence in the valley has still other indicators. Swathes of land are off limits to the public because they are marked out as 'firing zones' for army training purposes – far more land, it is widely suspected by Palestinians, than the IDF really needs. The valley's 65,000 Arab residents outnumber Israeli settlers by a factor of about six, yet are barred from using 85 per cent of the available land, including of course the edge of their most obvious water source, the river.[3]

After 1977 – when Menachem Begin's Likud party came to power, forming the first right-wing government in Israel's history – Yigal Allon's original half-dozen 'security settlements' along the main north-south highway were joined by many new 'ideological' ones. Today there are twenty-seven of them in the valley, becoming yet more 'facts on the ground': outposts of an occupation that Netanyahu, in 2019, announced he wanted to make official and permanent. Allon's annexation agenda was back on the table for Israel – if, indeed, it had ever really left it.

We stopped at Al-Auja, a farming town just north of Jericho. There was a self-sustaining eco-hotel here that Bassam wanted to show me, but we found it shut up as we turned through the gates. The front of the building was painted with palm trees, though not in a way that quite camouflaged the air-conditioning units poking through the walls. The paint was faded and peeling, and the garden at the front, which contained a children's play area made of tyres, along with the gravel-filled basins of a wastewater filtration system, looked so down at heel that Bassam whistled, and wondered if the place had gone bust since his last visit. But just as we were about to leave again, a man of 60 or so appeared on a moped, carefully balancing a bucket of minnows on the back.

His name was Ali, doing a favour for his good friend, the absent caretaker of the hotel. He explained that the eco-hotel was not bust at all, but merely closed for the winter season. It might look scruffy but, he insisted, all the equipment here – the gravel filters, the solar oven – was working as it should. The minnows were to help clean the water in another filtration system, in a greenhouse around the back.

We followed him there to watch him tip in the fish. The hotel, he told us, had opened in 2009 with generous grants from foreign aid donors. USAID had contributed US$500,000 to the project, hailing it as an exciting new model of community sustainability, a harbinger of a brighter, eco-friendly future for the whole valley. But the foreigners' attention, along with their dollars, had since turned elsewhere. Ali admitted that the eco-hotel was now struggling to make ends meet. His friend the caretaker was the only hotel worker left, on a fraction of his former salary, and he stayed on more out of loyalty to the concept of the hotel than from strict economic need. Bassam grumbled that it was typical of foreign donors, who were always splurging dollars on tick-box development projects like this one, but who seldom stuck around once the headlines had faded. As usual the NGO cavalcade had moved on, whimsical, fickle, forever applying sticking plasters, never tackling the underlying causes of the problem.

The spring to which Ali's town owed its existence was once one of the best in the valley, capable of producing 1,800 cubic metres of water an hour. Al-Auja means 'the meandering one', after the wadi from the spring along which the town was built. Farmers had always made use of its waters, but business boomed in the 1960s and 1970s, when the bananas and oranges they grew were sold all over Palestine. From a hamlet of 250 in the 1930s, Al-Auja became a thriving market town, with as many as 20,000 people making their living on its land.

Little water meandered in the wadi now, however. The spring, Ali said, all but dried up in 2000, when nearby Israeli settlers sank six wells for themselves. These days, Al-Auja is forced to buy even its drinking water from Israel. For the farmers, boom had inevitably turned to bust. Al-Auja today is home to no more than 5,000 people.

The town's decline was an object lesson in the mechanics of the occupation. Ali explained that Al-Auja was a part of the Jericho governorate, which was designated as Area A at Oslo, but that four-fifths of its land lay beyond the boundary, and so was designated as Area C, denoting full Israeli military jurisdiction. This meant that anyone wishing to sink a new well there, or even to repair an old one, had first to apply for permission from the Civil Administration, the branch of the Israeli military that handles civil matters in Area C. But the Civil Administration, he said, almost never granted such permission to Palestinians, while Israeli settlers appeared to have an entirely free hand.

Life here now, Ali said, was tougher even than it appeared. Hardly anyone farmed for themselves anymore. The only employment available was labouring work on Israeli-owned farms. But the Israelis, he said, didn't pay the local labourers enough to support their families. For this reason, the labourers tended to take their sons out of school early – sometimes at a very young age – in order to put them to work so that they too could contribute to household income. This in turn meant that educational standards were slipping, condemning Al-Auja's youth to a servile future with no prospect of betterment.

'Go down Route 90 any early morning in the harvest season, and you'll see what I mean. There are children touting for work all along the roadsides. It's like a slave economy. The settlers say, "If it wasn't for us, you'd have no work at all." But we only work for them because they stole all our water! It would be funny if it wasn't so sad.'

Ali was in no doubt: Al-Auja had been both impoverished and subjugated by the requisition of its water supply. His town, he said, was the victim of a deliberate policy of 'hydrocolonialism', a term that I had not often heard Palestinians use before. Most of its inhabitants these days, he said, were refugees from elsewhere, with no traditional connection to the local land. The core of the community he had once known had gone, and the pride they had once taken in their farming prowess was all but destroyed.

It wasn't just Al-Auja's spring water that Ali accused Israel of stealing. Ali's father had once owned farmland that ran down to the river, but was forced to give it up after the '67 war when the military sowed it with mines. And he was not the only one: as many as 30,000 dunams[4] of the town's land, a third of the pre-1967 total, was lost in the same way.

To add insult to injury, Ali's family's land had eventually been cleared of mines, but it was then handed over to Israeli date farmers. Armed with title deeds, the family went to court to try to get their land back. If the land could be farmed, they argued, then why should it not be returned to its rightful owners? The court agreed, but said it was a matter for the military. The military, however, said it was a matter for the civil courts. And no land was ever returned to the family.

'The settlers leave the minefield warning signs up in order to scare us off. Around here, we joke that they must be smart mines – because they only blow up Palestinians, never Israelis.' The river was barely a couple of kilometres from where we stood, beyond a dense green canopy of date palms on the other side of Route 90, yet it had been years since Ali had been anywhere near it.

'The river is holier to my family than it is even to Christians,' Ali said. 'We used to go there often before 1967. We swam in it, and caught fish in it. It was clean enough to see the gravel bottom in those days, and 200 metres wide. I took my old father to see it again once, up at the baptism site when they opened it. When he saw what has happened to our river, he cried.'

Ali blamed the etiolated state of the Jordan squarely on Israel. The river's natural flow, he said, was obstructed by a dam built at Degania, at the head of the Jordan Valley where it glides from the south end of the Sea of Galilee. All the water in the river these days, he claimed, was raw sewage from settlements, or else antibiotic run-off from the many fish-farms around the Israeli town of Beit She'an. In 2013, he recalled, he had attended a USAID-sponsored conference on the River Jordan in Amman, as a representative of his town. 'I said, "Thanks very much, USAID, for the half a million dollars for our eco-hotel. But if you give me just US$500 more, I can restore the river permanently for you – by renting a bulldozer for a day, and destroying the dam at Degania."'

It wasn't fair of Ali to put all the blame on Israel. For many years, Jordan, Syria and Lebanon had dammed the Jordan's tributaries, diminishing the upper river's natural flow before its waters even reached Israel. Years of drought and climate change had also taken their toll, as they have on every hydrologic system in the Middle East. Nevertheless, it was true that Israel had always taken the lion's share from the Jordan system, extracting more than 500 million cubic metres from the Galilee in some years,[5] with inevitable consequences for the river that the lake feeds. But whoever or whatever was responsible, there was no doubting Ali's passion and sorrow at what the beautiful river of his youth had become.

Our next stop was a farm on the edge of a village called Zubeidat, for a rendezvous with two farmer brothers, Hani and Mohammed. We had trouble finding their farm at first, and stopped for directions in a grubby roadside hamlet. A crowd of schoolboys materialized, competing to touch our parked motorbikes, glamorous visitations from another world. We were only there for five minutes, but that was long enough for a formal celebration. A dozen boys lined up in order of age and launched into a cheery Bedouin wedding song, a monotone solo couplet from each of them with everyone clapping along.

After a welcome push-start, Bassam and I arrived at last in a concrete yard where labourers were loading crates of okra, zucchini and cucumber onto a trailer. Work immediately stopped, a table and chairs were produced, and we all sat down to drink tea in the shade of a shed. The air was hot and filled with flies, and we had to shout to be heard above the roar of trucks passing along Route 90.

Hani and Mohammed were Bedouin of the Jahalin clan, traditional shepherd nomads who had become settled farmers. Their family had lived at Zubeidat for at least half a century. They said that some 20,000 Jahalin lived in the valley, a third of all the Bedouin here, and that the great majority were now settled, as they were.

There was, I heard, another serious water shortage here, despite the crates of vegetables all around us. The village relied on three wells, all of which were yielding less with every passing year. The wells were all shallow ones, which meant that the water they produced was brackish, good only for irrigation. And they no longer produced enough: some fifty dunams of their land were irrigable only using water borrowed from neighbours. The village's drinking water, meanwhile, all had to be tankered in.

'We'd like to drill a deeper well to reach the fresh water, but we're not allowed to go below 90 metres,' Mohammed explained. As at Al-Auja, such drilling restrictions did not apply to the local Israelis. 'When they slaughter a camel, we only get the ear,' said Mohammed drily.

The best well, a deep old one that his father had once used, was now off-limits in the precinct of Argaman, an Israeli moshav established on land confiscated, in part, from Zubeidat. Argaman's inhabitants, all 128 of them, grew thirsty crops like grapes and herbs as well as dates, and had all the domestic water they needed; more, at any rate, than Zubeidat, which was a much bigger community of 2,000, organized into 240 families. Numerically, at least, the community appeared to be flourishing. 'Bedouins have lots of children,' Mohammed winked. Because of this, in fact, their most immediate problem was not water but a shortage of housing.

'We need to build, but the Israelis won't allow us to extend our footprint because we are in Area C here. If we put up a house without permission, they come and demolish it. So now we're going vertical,' he said, pointing at the treeline over his shoulder where the top of a half-finished five-storey building was visible.

The new building looked solid enough, but its permanence was illusory. Again because of Area C regulations, the land it stood on could only be rented, not bought, which meant that the Civil Administration had the power to evict its occupants at any time. The tenuousness of Zubeidat's existence became clearer when Mohammed examined a roadmap I had tossed on the table.

'Look, everyone. Zubeidat is on it! Is your map French? No, it's Israeli – really? Praise the Lord: Alhamdulillah!' he cried, his fingers and thumbs pressed together as he looked up to the sky, 'Al-ham-du-lil-lah!'

Bassam had warned me to expect a narrative of oppression in the valley, and indeed we heard variants of this theme wherever we went. At Jiftlik, another farming community of Jahalin Bedouin, the head of the local council, Ahmad Ghawanmeh, described how the IDF regularly conducted training exercises through the middle of his village, just to show that they could. The exercises sometimes took place at night, often without warning. His children, he said, were terrified by the noise, the smoke, the soldiers manoeu-vring between the houses with their rifles on their shoulders.

Area C building restrictions were so rigorously enforced at Jiftlik that the electricity pylons were mounted in cubes of cement. Anything smacking of permanence, he said, even a simple pole buried in the ground, was auto-matically nixed. From the terrace of his house, Ghawanmeh pointed to a scrap of weedy ground at the bottom of his garden, the former site of a small house that he had built for his brother without Israeli permission; the house had been summarily demolished. Ghawanmeh was in no doubt about what Israel ultimately wanted in the valley. 'There are twenty-seven Israeli settle-ments along Route 90, and they are all expanding. They want all the land, and eventually they will drive us off it.'

Ghawanmeh, another courgette farmer, added that he had not given up the nomad's life by choice, but because the shortage of grazing had made it unviable, a shortage that he blamed on Israeli settlers and their land-grabbing ways. 'I still keep sheep, just thirty of them, to remind me of my heritage,' he said wistfully. He worried that if the Jiftlik community was dislocated again, the next stopping place would likely be Jericho or Nablus or Ramallah; and with citification, he feared that the Bedouin's ancient connection to the land would finally be broken.

His fears were not unjustified: rural Palestinians, I knew, were already migrating to the cities at the fastest rate in the Arab world.[6] Nothing good, Ghawanmeh thought, could come of the renewed Israeli talk of annexation. The Jahalin Bedouin had, after all, been 'moved on' before. In Ottoman times, perhaps for centuries, they had grazed lands in the northern Negev desert in an area known as Tel Arad, a tradition that came to an abrupt end when Israel expelled them after the war of 1948. They initially hoped their expulsion would be temporary, but it soon became clear that they would not be returning to their ancestral lands. In the 1960s, Arad became Israel's first 'planned city', which has since grown into a town with a population of 25,000, the majority of whom are Jewish; its industries include textiles, electronics, and the manu-facture of phosphoric acid using brine collected from the Dead Sea.

We were joined on the terrace by Ghawanmeh's quiet and deferential son, Osman, who had a university degree in financial management, yet had failed to find any kind of appropriate job. Instead, he worked as a labourer on an Israeli farm. 'The work is poorly paid, seventy or eighty shekels [US$20–23] a day only,' said his father, 'but there is no other work here. So 90 per cent of us who can, work for Israelis. We are their slaves.'

It was a familiar lament. Yet I wondered if the Arab-Israeli relationship in the valley was really as binary as Ghawanmeh suggested. What he seemed to be describing was a kind of uneasy symbiosis. His people were not quite slaves. The labour Jiftlik provided was cheap, but it was not free – and it also appeared to be indispensible to the Israeli farmers.

'If they could find good substitutes, we'd be out tomorrow,' Ghawanmeh acknowledged. 'They do bring foreign labourers – Chinese, Thai, Turkish, Ethiopians, Sudanese, Jewish volunteers from Europe. But they all need accommodation, insurance. We are much less of a burden to the Israelis, and we know the land. So, in a manner of speaking, the Israeli farmers here protect us – for now.'

The Palestinians are useful to the settlers in other ways, for instance by providing Israeli date farmers with a means of circumventing the growing power of the international campaign to boycott, divest and sanction (BDS) Israeli produce from the West Bank, which poses a threat to the lucrative medjool export market. Palestinians also grow dates in the valley, in the Area A land around Jericho; and BDS, alongside organizations such as the Islamic Human Rights Commission, have long accused Israeli date farmers of deliberately deceiving customers around the world by labelling their boxes 'Produce of Palestine'.[7]

The Israelis are useful to Palestinians, too. Throughout the valley, Israel proper provides the most important market for the crops they grow – including the zucchini grown by Ghawanmeh – and many Arab farmers, perhaps most of them, see no contradiction in selling their produce over the border. As another farmer later explained to me, the politics of the occupation were 'different' in the Jordan Valley because 'here, it's all about business'.

The imperative of economic survival, it seemed, has created strange distortions in the standard narrative of suppression and exploitation. The occupation has gone on for so long that in the Jordan Valley – and perhaps elsewhere in the Occupied Territories – the two sides have in significant ways become co-dependent. It was striking that not all of Ghawanmeh's bitterness was directed towards the occupiers. He referred constantly to 'the fat cats in Ramallah', the PA, who he said had enriched themselves with foreign aid money, but who did nothing to create the local jobs that might help communities like Jiftlik escape the Israeli yoke.

Even Ghawanmeh averred that some Israeli farmers were kind to their Arab neighbours. Some were even on friendly enough terms to turn up at Arab weddings or funerals, a state of affairs unheard of in most other parts of the West Bank. This did not mean that their coexistence was happy, necessarily. Ghawanmeh described a sort of social schizophrenia, whereby an Israeli farmer could behave like an old friend in private one day, but might refuse eye contact the next if, for instance, he was in the company of other Israelis. Every social exchange, even the simplest ones, contained an unspoken subtext of fear and suspicion.

Jiftlik had water supply troubles similar to those at Zubeidat and Al-Auja. Water used to flow freely from a local spring, Ein Shible, until the local moshav sank a well 500 metres deep nearby. These days, Ghawanmeh said, water from Ein Shible had to be coaxed out with pumps, while the village's own new wells were, of course, restricted to the regulation 90 metres. They had ways of evading such restrictions in Jiftlik, however.

'The Israelis laid a 60-centimetre water pipe right through the village,' Ghawanmeh said. 'They allowed us two taps. But there are 12,000 people in this village. So sometimes we make our own taps. We Bedouin have a saying: "Water does not flow past the thirsty."'

Did the local Israelis turn a blind eye to such pilfering? If so, it was another pointer to the unspoken truth that they did not, necessarily, want to see Palestinians driven from the land, whatever local leaders like Ghawanmeh said.

Bassam confirmed that the settlers here were not all as ideologically driven as those one usually heard about, the zealous new generation in the hills to the west; many of them had been in the valley for decades – the kibbutz at Beit HaArava, for instance, was established by Jews fleeing Nazi Europe in 1939 – and they had since developed their own distinct ethos. They generally belonged to a secular, leftist tradition, as descendants of the first pioneers of old Israel, when the land was less crowded and times were somehow kinder, and Arabs and Jews could be fellow sons of the soil. Neighbourly cooperation, I could easily guess, must once have been vital to survival in this unforgiving part of the world.

Later, at a service station south of Yafit, Bassam and I met an Israeli date farmer who had stopped in to buy cigarettes. 'You came here by bike from Ramallah? Fantastic!' he grinned. 'Such a nice town. I used to go there for the restaurants before the intifada. Not any more, of course.'

He was friendly and easy-going and didn't at all seem the merciless colonial exploiter type. Nor, from the ramshackle state of his car, did he appear rich. He wore his hair in a ponytail with sunglasses propped on his head, framing a grizzled face burnished dark by a lifetime in the desert sun. If he had an ideology, it seemed to be the hippyish, peace-and-love ethos of the 1970s, in which decade he had in fact first moved to the valley. Did he make a good living out of dates? 'You can survive,' he shrugged. Foreign competition, he explained, meant that the date business was not as lucrative as it had once been, and now everyone was struggling. Many Israeli farmers had diversified into other businesses, although not always successfully. 'Just look over there,' he said, nodding towards a stout chain-link fence abutting the service station. 'That's a sad story.'

Beyond an array of 'Keep Out' signs in English, Hebrew and Arabic, a ruined visitor's centre mouldered. The entrance path led through the open jaws of an outsized crocodile's head rendered in plastic. The date farmer explained that an Israeli entrepreneur had tried to farm the reptiles for their meat and skin, but was thwarted in 2012 when the Israeli government ruled that crocodiles were an endangered species. An attempt to turn the farm into a visitor attraction then also failed, for lack of visitors. 'I think maybe some tourists got eaten,' he said, crossing his eyes and chomping the air with outstretched arms.

The crocodiles, hundreds of them, were still lurking in their pools beyond the faded signs. It was like the plotline of *Jurassic Park*. 'No one knows what to do with them,' he said. 'They escape, sometimes. Seventy of them got out a few years ago, and it took three days to recapture them all. God knows what will happen if they ever make it to the river.'

The crocodile farm was kooky, but it did not feel out of keeping with this beguiling place. To Arabs, the fertile Jordan Valley represents a vital economic opportunity, mostly: a breadbasket-in-waiting for future Palestine. To many Israelis, though, it means something quite different, especially the valley's southern stretch and the western edge of the Dead Sea. The weird lunar landscapes, silent desert wadis, and extremes of heat and geological depth of that region make it a magnet for hikers and nature lovers. It also attracts wannabe frontiersmen, dreamers and trailblazers, or simply eccentric social misfits seeking a life off the grid. I had read, for instance, about a thriving nudist hippie colony at Metzukei Dragot, 64 kilometres south on the shore of the Dead Sea, that was full of drop-outs from Israeli cities – 'a haven,' as one visiting journalist put it, 'for people who have been broken by the world, who don't have a cent, whose possessions consist of a tent and sleeping bag. The option they get here is the sea in the morning and the stars at night, the possibility of sex and freedom, and the ability to create and to talk.'[8]

The valley, though, is an imperfect locale for the live-and-let-live philosophy. In early 2020, a group of Israelis proposed to hold a festival for 15,000 people on IDF-controlled land near Jericho called the 'Dead Sea Burn', a version of the famous Burning Man festival that has been held in the Black Rock Desert in Nevada annually since 1986. The patch of Area C chosen for the festival even resembled Nevada. In accordance with the 'radical inclusion' principle of the American original, Palestinians were invited to join in the fun. The plan, however, immediately ran into local opposition. Saeb Erekat, the veteran politician and one-time resident of Jericho, called the invitation 'an insult that unveils the colonialist mentality of the organizers'.

'So they come to occupied territory, to an area … where our natural resources are stolen and our rights in general are negated, and then they tell us "you can attend" in a closed military area,' he said.[9] Erekat's remarks were telling: the theft of water and land remains at the heart of all Palestinian grievance. In this harsh and water-stressed land, the festival's traditional centrepiece – the ceremonial burning of a human effigy, 12 metres tall – was perhaps more apt than the festival organizers realised. They were crestfallen, but their well-meaning idealism was defeated; and the Dead Sea Burn seems unlikely ever to take place.

Bassam and I rode on towards Bardala, a village in the far north-east corner of the West Bank, as far up the valley as it is possible for a Palestinian to go. Along the way we passed a small side road, where a brown tourist sign indicated that it led to a beauty spot: a spring, Ein Asakout, that our satnav map showed was located unusually close to the river. We broke our itinerary, and doubled back for a look. The spring turned out to be surrounded by land once farmed by Arabs, now cleared of mines and expropriated by Israelis: precisely what had happened to Ali's family at Al-Auja. Barbed wire and minefield warning signs had been left up to deter trespassers, just as Ali described.

Jolting along a farm track, we came to a fork where an old 'Keep Out' sign had been allowed to hang from one nail so that it pointed straight down at the ground, making it impossible to know which way we were supposed not to go. Off to one side, a settler in a shiny new tractor was ploughing neat furrows in a field; mine-cleared land, Bassam was sure. We were about to ask him for directions, but our bikes had Ramallah licence plates, and the settler gave us such a glare from his cab as he rumbled past that Bassam thought better of it. Instead, we rode off to the right, Bassam laughing grimly that it would be fine, probably, so long as we kept our wheels within the old tire tracks just visible in the dust.

The spring was a waterhole filled with reeds and birds, with the river no more than 400 metres to the east, its course demarcated by a line of willows. The water looked as clean and clear as the kind you get in supermarkets: a marvellous natural bathing spot, although the dilapidation of the parking area suggested that few tourists ever ventured here. No doubt they were discouraged, as we were, by the mine warning signs and rusty barbed wire that topped the near horizon. It didn't feel like a place to linger, and we did not.

At Bardala, we pulled up at the village shop, and chatted to the elderly owner, Haji Sultan Rajid Sawafta. He produced a flask of tea, our conversation over the counter interrupted from time to time by small boys pestering him for sweets, or on errands for their mothers to buy eggs, biscuits, or a tin of *ful medames*.

By some vagary of the Oslo Accords, Bardala and its surrounds, an area of 20 square kilometres, is designated Area A, making it the only piece of land under full Palestinian control in the whole north-eastern corner of the West Bank, a status that made it important to believers in the independent state promised at Oslo. Sawafta was a Bardalan born and bred – this was a traditional clan village of perhaps 2,000 people, 90 per cent of whom belonged to the same family – and he described himself as another *murabit*, a defender of the land. 'We live in the Empty Quarter here,' he said proudly. 'If I leave this place, the Israelis will take it over tomorrow – and then we will lose it forever.'

Bardala is ancient, and was once blessed with an abundant water supply, enough to service a bathhouse in the early Islamic period; when archaeologists excavated the bathhouse's ruins, they discovered it to have been built atop a Byzantine church erected in AD 400. Like every village I had visited in the valley, however, Bardala was now short of natural local water. Following a pattern becoming all too familiar, Sawafta described how the local springs began drying up when Israelis from the nearby settlement of Mehola sank their first well in the area, and used it to grow thirsty crops, such as bananas. Since 1967, Bardala had relied for its supply on the Israeli water grid. Sawafta added that he himself had helped to drill Mehola's first well, a revelation that sat oddly with his claim to be a *murabit*. 'It was the only work available at the time,' he shrugged when I asked why.

It sounded rather as though he had colluded with the occupation, but Bassam found this unremarkable when I asked him about it later. Poor villagers like Sawafta, he explained, often had no choice about whom they worked for, and added that this was accepted throughout Palestine. He drew the line, though, at high officials who exploited the occupation to enrich themselves – something he said happened depressingly often. The example he gave was a widely reported scandal from the early 2000s known as 'Cementgate', in which several businessmen, with the alleged collusion of senior Fatah politicians, were found by a Palestinian parliamentary inquiry to have sold cut-price cement to Israeli firms who used it to build illegal settlements – even as those same politicians publicly fought against the occupation.[10]

Bardala's Area A status, I learned, meant that it traditionally received special treatment from the PA in Ramallah, who paid the Israeli water utility, Mekorot, to supply the village with water. Bardala was supposed to pay the PA back each year, but for nearly twenty years the Bardalans had routinely ignored their rates bills, calculating that the PA would continue to pay Mekorot come what may, out of macro-political expediency. 'It's our land, and our water that the Israelis are selling back to us,' said Haji Sawafta stoutly. 'Why should we pay for it?'

The independent-minded villagers had for some time been demanding the right to drill their own new wells, although so far without success, despite their campaign having gained attention and support from as far afield as Boston, the headquarters of a pressure group called the Alliance for Water Justice in Palestine. 'There's enough water in the ground to go around,' Sawafta insisted. 'Bardala is sitting on top of a lake.'

In Bardala, as in Jiftlik, the Mekorot mains pipe ran right through the village. As in Jiftlik, the villagers helped themselves to extra water when necessary. Sometimes, despite Bardala's Area A status that theoretically precluded it, the IDF took firm action. In April 2017, a squad of forty soldiers raided the village and confiscated hundreds of metres of illicit hosepipe. The following month, 500 villagers staged a water rights march that the IDF broke up with tear gas, injuring 5 youths.[11] It sounded heavy-handed; although according to Sawafta, the IDF usually left the village alone, calculating perhaps that it was easier to keep Bardala pacified by turning a blind eye to water theft.

The status quo was fragile, however. The villagers had recently learned that Mekorot was planning to re-route their pipeline away from the village. The new pipe was to be buried much deeper than the old one, and would be equipped with high-tech sensors to warn Central Control of any unexpected loss of pressure along the line. Sawafta added that the source of this devastating news – a Mekorot contractor – was an Israeli Arab.

It was clear, from the almost casual way Sawafta threw in this detail, that it added only a little insult to the injury; he did not seem to regard this

Mekorot contractor as a traitor to the Palestinian cause. Perhaps in honesty he could not, when he, too, had once worked for the occupiers. It was another reminder that the rights and wrongs of the occupation are far more complex than they first appeared to me. The rival occupants of the land of Palestine live in each other's pockets, as intertwined as they have always been, a modus vivendi that throws up constant practical as well as moral conundrums for its citizens.

It is sometimes forgotten by outsiders – although never by Israelis – that fully 21 per cent of Israeli citizens are Arabs.[12] Not all Arab villagers on the Israeli side of the border were driven out, or chose to flee, during the Nakba. Hundreds of thousands stayed put, too, during the war of 1967. Their descendants now number 1.9 million people who live in communities all over Israel, although there are some significant concentrations, notably in East Jerusalem; in an area along the north-western border of the West Bank known as 'The Triangle', centred on the city of Umm al-Fahm; and in Israel's northern district, where Arabs constitute a slim majority, particularly in Nazareth, the so-called 'capital' of Arab Israel. Eighty-four per cent of Israeli Arabs are Muslim, with the remainder made up by Christians as well as Druze.[13]

Although there are important variations in their treatment, Israeli Arabs collectively remain much discriminated against, despite the size of their minority. They do enjoy some political representation – at the beginning of 2022 there were 14 Arab and Druze MPs out of a total 120 in the Knesset – but neither their representation nor their influence across Jerusalem's fractured political landscape is as great as it democratically should or could be. Opinion polls consistently find that a majority of Jews feel threatened by the domestic Arab presence, and suspect them of disloyalty to the state. This was especially the case during Israel's 2006 Lebanon War, which Israeli Arabs strongly opposed.

It is apparent to them that many Israelis do not want them in their country at all. In 2018, the Knesset passed the instantly infamous 'Nation State Law', which among other measures formally relegated Arabic, the first language of a fifth of Israel's citizens, to a language of mere 'special status'. Netanyahu later clarified that Israel was 'not a state of all its citizens [but] the nation state of the Jewish people – and only it.'[14] This chilling assertion prompted dismay among Israeli Arabs, who accused Netanyahu of 'planting the seeds of an apartheid state'. It sparked outrage abroad, too, with the EU leading the criticism.[15]

In May 2021, following clashes between Palestinians and security forces in Sheikh Jarrah, a neighbourhood of East Jerusalem where four Arab families faced eviction by a Supreme Court ruling, dismay turned to anger. In towns up and down the country, Israeli Arab youths formed stone-throwing lynch mobs, and burned shops, schools, restaurants and synagogues. Gangs of Jewish youths responded in kind. There were clashes around Temple Mount in Jerusalem, prompting a volley of rockets from Gaza, and Israeli airstrikes in response.

The epicentre of Israeli Arab violence was in the small mixed city of Lod, south of Tel Aviv, where emergency powers were invoked to restore order: reportedly the first time this had been necessary, in an Israeli Arab community, since the 1960s. Netanyahu promised to deploy 'an iron fist if needed' to 'stop the anarchy'; the Israeli president, Reuven Rivlin, warned publicly that the country could slide into civil war. The anarchy may have been sparked by events in Jerusalem and Gaza, but the tinder was already there: years of perceived discrimination against Israeli Arabs.

'The way we are treated is as though we shouldn't be here,' observed Diana Buttu, a Palestinian lawyer and political analyst based in Haifa.[16]

Despite that, it is not always clear what Israeli Arabs want for themselves. For all the resentment they justifiably feel at their status as second-class citizens, a great many of them also acknowledge, with varying degrees of reluctance, that residency in Israel has distinct advantages over life in the West Bank or Gaza: more economic opportunity, better security, a higher standard of living, as well as freedom from the frequently dysfunctional and corrupt administration of the PA.

If Arab attitudes towards Israel are sometimes ambivalent even in the Occupied Territories, as I had found, then they are naturally more so among Israeli Arabs, who exist in a state of permanent identity crisis. Are they Israeli Arabs, or Arab Israelis? This is no dry semantic question, but the subject of hot and constant media debate in the Arab-Jewish world. Israeli Arabs do not necessarily identify as 'Palestinians', as a casual foreign observer might assume. From the point of view of Israel's security establishment, of course, the fewer Israeli Arabs who do, the better. Following one recent survey, the *Jersualem Post* – a news organization routinely accused of right-wing partisanship – reported that the proportion of Israeli Arabs defining themselves as 'Palestinian' had dropped to just 7 per cent.[17]

The implications for any future peace settlement, depending as this does on where the border between Israel and Palestine is ultimately drawn, are significant. During the Al-Aqsa Intifada, a 'Populated-Area Exchange Plan' was proposed, according to which the territory of the Triangle around Umm al-Fahm, along with its 300,000 Palestinian residents, would be transferred to PA control in return for formal annexation of a number of Israeli settlements in the West Bank. This territorial exchange, later championed by the influential right-winger Avigdor Lieberman, is still touted as a potential pathway to peace; it also featured in Jared Kushner's peace plan of 2020.[18] Yet a poll conducted in Umm al-Fahm when the plan was first mooted found that 83 per cent of residents opposed the transfer of their town to Palestinian rule. Perhaps this was unsurprising, for who but the most ardent Palestinian nationalist would choose to live under Israeli military occupation if they didn't have to?[19]

The loyalties or otherwise of Umm al-Fahm were not of much consequence to Haji Sawafta in Bardala, however. The old man knew what he was: a proud Palestinian defender of this isolated patch of Area A. His troubles were closer at hand, for he was in no doubt that the plan to re-route the water pipe away from his village would have serious consequences. His community's farming future – perhaps its very existence – was in jeopardy as never before.

I could only guess at Mekorot's motive for moving the pipe. Were they simply fed up with the plundering ways of the locals, and acting as any utility might, in the interests of operating efficiency, or profit? Or were they, as many activist organizations have argued in the past, acting in collusion with the Civil Administration, or following orders from even higher up, in pursuit of some deeper strategy of Jordan Valley annexation? In a report in 2013, the research centre Mi Marviha? (Who Profits?) called Mekorot 'the Israeli government's executive arm in the OPT for water issues'.

Mekorot, which has run all water infrastructure in the West Bank since 1982, when it took over that role from the military,[20] was certainly capable of that. Founded in 1937, it is one of a handful of Yishuv institutions surviving from those heroic pre-state days.[21] Israelis tend to associate Mekorot with Zionism itself, which makes it a water utility with a very special status; one that, in the view of many Israelis, is literally engaged on a holy mission.[22]

The occupiers could be cruel and machine-like in their efficiency, but their policies were not always consistent or joined up. The different agencies of authority – the Civil Administration, the IDF, Mekorot, local settlers – could and often did contradict one another. Unpredictability was perhaps not a conscious Israeli strategy, but I could see that it might suit the occupiers to keep the Bardalans guessing. It meant that the villagers lived in a perpetual state of anxiety, which only added to the sense of oppression that all the Arabs of the Jordan Valley shared. By refusing to pay its water bills, furthermore, Bardala had almost certainly alienated the PA in Ramallah, the one authority that was supposed to support them. What, if any, role had Ramallah played in the decision to re-route the pipe?

The politics of the occupation made even Palestinian heads spin. I needed to learn more about how they worked, and gain a better understanding of the fall-out from the Oslo Accords, above all in the matter of water allocation and management. The clarity I needed would evidently not be found in the villages of the occupied Jordan Valley, but back in the de facto capital of the West Bank: Ramallah.

CHAPTER FOUR

Ramallah

Wet City

M Y FIRST VISIT to the administrative capital of the West Bank surprised me. I arrived soon after my visit to Gaza, on a bus caught from the Damascus Gate in Arab East Jerusalem, an old and grubby vehicle packed with tired labourers returning home after their day's work. At Qalandiya, the heavily fortified border crossing, an IDF conscript climbed aboard for a cursory inspection of our papers, which the passengers all produced expressionlessly, and in silence, so used to the routine that they hardly seemed to notice the humiliation it implied.

I remembered Ramallah from news programmes in the early 2000s during the Second Intifada. It was a battleground then, as the IDF attempted to dislodge Yasser Arafat from his bunker in the city centre. I expected therefore to find ruined buildings, broken infrastructure, and more of the social disorder, tension and poverty to which I had grown accustomed in Gaza. Instead, a mere sixteen kilomtres north of Jerusalem, so close that there was barely a break in the suburban sprawl in between, I found a prosperous and attractive small city of khaki-coloured tower blocks that marched purposefully across the Samarian hills. The contrast with Gaza could hardly have been greater.

A village in Ottoman times, Ramallah only emerged as Palestine's administrative centre in 1995, when the Israelis withdrew and handed control to the newly created PA. The 'Oslo years' that followed led to a boom that seemed not to have abated. Every other street corner revealed dramatic vistas of recent development. The planners had kept the architects in check as Ramallah expanded, leading to a certain uniformity of design unusual in the urban Middle East; to the emergence, even, of a bold new Palestinian vernacular.

Money was much in evidence, along with a certain brassy confidence among its citizens that I had also not anticipated. I saw fashionably dressed young men impatiently revving the engines of souped-up sports cars with exhaust pipes deliberately left unbaffled. There were trendy coffee shops, fast-food restaurants, even shops selling alcohol, an unthinkable thing in puritanical Gaza. The hotel I stayed in on my first night, the newly refurbished *Caesar*, boasted a glass-walled martini bar on its top floor. Ramallah, I had forgotten, is historically an Arab Christian town, and it retains a sizeable Christian minority. But such overt lack of religiosity still came as a surprise, at odds as it is with the city's doleful international reputation.

At first sight, water supply in Ramallah did not seem to be much of a problem. I noticed immediately how every tower block was topped by a battery of water tanks, squat cylinders in regulation black or white that seemed to cluster with intent, like armies poised to invade in the board game *Risk*. Situated nearly 900 metres above sea level, Ramallah is a naturally wet city. Indeed, it was spotting with rain when I arrived there, a blessed relief after the swelter of the coast. I later learned that Ramallah receives more annual rainfall even than London – 715mm per year, compared to London's 584mm – another surprise, at the centre of one of the most water-stressed regions of the world.

Ramallah's wet climate is not why Arafat chose the city as his seat of power, but it is a useful attribute. The ability to supply water is the key to political control throughout the Middle East, where leaders are often fond of demonstrating their mastery over the resource. It is no coincidence, for instance, that the 800-metre-high Burj Khalifa tower, the greatest vanity project of the Maktoum sheikhs of Dubai, is fronted by a thirty-acre man-made lake studded with swivelling jets that shoot water 150 metres into the air, all choreographed to music. Geysers of oil are all very well, but in a desert, it is fountains of water that really impress the locals.

The West Bank's leaders could never compete with the showmanship or wealth of the Maktoums, but I nevertheless detected an echo of Dubai in the centrepiece of the Palestinian Authority regime, the mausoleum of the late hero-of-the-revolution, Yasser Arafat. His tomb occupies a modernist, glass and marble cube in front of the *Mukata'a*, his former headquarters where he was besieged by Israeli forces for more than two years, until his death in November 2004. The cube, guarded around the clock by a pair of ceremonial guards with bayonets fixed, is perched above an improbably lush and close-cropped lawn set around a placid blue pool, which sends refracted sunbeams dappling across the ceiling of the mausoleum's cool white interior.

The mausoleum is not the only architectural attempt to demonstrate control over water. In the contiguous city of Al-Bireh I found a saltwater aquarium large enough to support 250 species of marine life: an extraordinary public amenity in a territory cut off from the coast. The water that sustains it comes not from the Mediterranean – because it cannot – but from a nearby factory where fresh water is artificially salinated. 'People here can't visit our sea, so we bring it to Palestine so everyone can see it,' the aquarium's owner-manager, Sofian Qawasmeh, told a magazine interviewer.[1] To drive home the point, the aquarium is housed in a building shaped like an ocean liner, the surreal silhouette of which soars like a mirage above the city skyline.

The aquarium-ship proved that Jews have no monopoly on *chutzpah*, but as a symbol of defiance it still rang a little hollow. The regimented water tanks visible on every rooftop were evidence of good municipal organization, no doubt, but they also pointed to the need to store and hoard the resource. They were thus a symbol not of plenty but of shortage – and no aquarium or ceremonial water feature could change that reality.

The truth, I was to discover, is that Ramallah depends on Israel for its networked supply – and that not even this city receives as much as it needs. Summer shortfalls are common, forcing the Palestinian Water Authority to supply the city's neighbourhoods in rotation. The shortfalls are most severe in outlying areas, especially those on higher ground, where communities regularly go for weeks or even months without any network supply at all. Ramallah is better off than most other parts of the West Bank, and of course far better off than Gaza. Nevertheless, and in spite of its natural wetness, the city's water supply – and by extension, the capital's notional political autonomy – is entirely in hock to the PA's close client relationship with the Israeli state.

This baleful situation is another legacy of the Oslo Accords, which curtailed Palestinian ability to construct the new dams and reservoirs needed to trap rainfall. Worse still, Oslo effectively prevented the excavation of new wells, the West Bank's means of accessing a source of water far more important than the River Jordan ever was: the groundwater in the mountain aquifers. Water officials on both sides of the divide knew, long before Oslo, that the rate of extraction from the region's aquifers, increasing every year to meet demand from fast-growing populations, could not be sustained. The condition of the largest aquifer, 'the western mountain aquifer' which extends beneath the western border of the West Bank, and so is of vital interest to Israel too, looked particularly perilous by the early 1990s. Restraint on both sides was needed. This required a cooperative approach, which found its expression in the creation, in 1995, of a Joint Water Committee: the JWC.

The committee was intended to manage all water and sewage infrastructure in the West Bank and, crucially, to reach joint decisions on the approval of all new water projects, as well as the maintenance of old ones. An equal number of Israelis and Arabs sat on the committee, requiring all decisions to be reached by consensus; this also meant that both sides theoretically enjoyed an equal power of veto.

Like everything negotiated at Oslo, it was only ever intended as an interim arrangement, pending a final settlement that, it was envisioned, would allocate precisely how much water each side could withdraw from the aquifer in the future. But the final settlement never materialised, which meant that the interim arrangement, just like the Area ABC designations, stuck.

To begin with, the JWC functioned as it was supposed to. As time went by, however, it became apparent that the system was desperately unfair. As the occupiers, the Israelis were able to apply their veto – and repeatedly did so – to any water-related project anywhere in Area C: in two-thirds of the West Bank, in other words. Their veto was particularly rigorously enforced when it came to projects involving extraction from the trans-boundary western mountain aquifer. Projects in Areas A and B were affected as well, including in the district of Ramallah, which straddles the watershed between the western mountain aquifer and the eastern one that drains towards the Jordan Valley.[2]

The PA, by contrast, had no means of preventing the Israelis from sinking new wells in the western mountain aquifer on their side of the border, nor any way of monitoring how much was being extracted if they did. And they very much did: Israel today operates hundreds of deep wells in the western mountain aquifer's discharge zone; while the Palestinians, although permitted to draw water from existing wells, remain unable to sink any new wells at all. Israeli settlers in Area C of the western West Bank, on the other hand, *are* permitted to sink new wells. The upshot of Oslo is that the water in the western mountain aquifer has never been fairly shared. Even in the Oslo years, between 1995 and 2000, Israel consumed an estimated 87 per cent of its yield.[3]

As negotiators at Oslo, the Palestinians had proved no match for the well-oiled and US-backed machinery of the Israeli government. Time and again, the Palestinians were bounced, via the JWC, into approving decisions that they might otherwise have chosen to reject – such as new pipelines for illegal Israeli settlements – in return for Israeli approval of their projects. Yet this quid pro quo almost never came.

Jan Selby, in a study of the JWC's operations between 1995 and 2008, found that the Palestinian Water Authority had approved every application to connect Israeli settlements to the mains – as many as a hundred of them – while Israel had vetoed every single Palestinian application to sink a new well in the western mountain aquifer. The JWC, he concluded, was used as a tool of the occupation; it was an example of what he called 'domination dressed up as cooperation'.[4]

Palestinian projects were routinely obstructed by bureaucracy, which sometimes took years to overcome. The Israeli JWC members had to take into account the views of no fewer than twenty-two different government departments and partisan interest groups, which included the Yesha Council, an umbrella organization for the settler movement. Even with JWC approval, a water project in Area C still needed permission to proceed from the military, who very often refused it, citing nebulous 'security reasons'.

As an Amnesty International report in 2009, quoting the World Bank, drily noted: 'The JWC does not function as a "joint" water resource governance institution because of fundamental asymmetries – of power, of capacity, of information, of interests – that prevent the development of a consensual approach.' In practice, decision-making on the JWC was entirely in the hands of the Israelis. One international observer, who attended several JWC meetings, described the interaction between the two sides more bluntly as 'an exercise in subjugation and humiliation'.[5]

The JWC staggered on for a decade longer than originally intended, seldom meeting, and agreeing little if anything to Palestinian advantage when it did. Formal Arab-Israeli cooperation in the water sector finally died in 2010, when the PA ran out of patience with the one-sidedness of the arrangement, and formally withdrew from the JWC. Its creation had led not to enhanced cooperation in the water sector, but to a disastrous worsening of Palestine's overall supply. At Oslo, Israel gained, and retains, control of some 80 per cent of all the groundwater in the West Bank.[6] There has never been enough water for Palestinians: per capita water use in Palestine has declined by 20 per cent since 1995.[7] As the West Bank's population grew, and demand increased, the PA faced a shortfall that it has only ever been able to meet by buying in water from Mekorot, who deliver it via a network that was mostly laid in the 1950s, and is creaking and leaking with age.

The bureaucracy imposed at Oslo – according to which any new pipe over 5 centimentres in diameter, let alone any new well, requires prior approval from Israel – has proved a particular disaster for the West Bank's poorest. As I heard throughout the Jordan Valley, rural communities who take matters into their own hands, and who build pipes or cisterns or even simple field toilets without waiting for Civil Administration approval, have for years had their construction efforts demolished by the IDF, almost as a matter of routine. Indeed, the demolition of 'WASH-related infrastructure'

– the acronym stands for water, sanitation and hygiene – has accelerated, according to the UN, who recorded ten instances of it in the first three months of 2019 alone.[8] In the most serious incident, in February 2019, the IDF destroyed a 750-metre pipe intended to connect the villages of Beit Fourik and Beit Dajan to the mains in Nablus, to the detriment of their 18,000 residents.

'The two villages are like islands, surrounded by settlements to the north and south, a military training area to the east, and a bypass road to the west that we are not allowed to use,' said Awad Hanani, the head of the Beit Fourik village council. 'We only have one source of water, a well that the villages share. But in recent years, [output] has more than halved . . . To fill this gap, people are forced to rely on tankered water, with a higher price than tap water . . . Especially in summer, when the demand is intense, we have to wait more than a month to receive the tankered water, due to delays and other difficulties.'

The UN says that overall, some 270,000 residents of Area C are directly affected by Israeli WASH restrictions, 95,000 of whom receive less than 50 litres of water per day – the World Health Organization's recommended minimum – while more than 83,000 receive bad quality water, or are forced to resort to buying expensive and unregulated water from private suppliers.[9] As the American philosopher Noam Chomsky put it, 'The outcome of cooperation between an elephant and a fly is not hard to predict.'[10]

I spent several days interviewing water officials in Ramallah, and found that the failure of the Oslo Accords was their constant theme. Every conversation circled back to it; it was the source of all their woes. Indeed, other Palestinian troubles seemed conspicuously absent from their thoughts; most strikingly, Gaza. The sewage and supply problems of the Strip did not come up in my conversations unless I raised them. The plight of their countrymen there, including even the bloodshed at the weekly fence demonstrations, appeared to be a matter they mostly knew about at one remove, from the news.

The West Bank of course has its own, different water troubles, stemming from the occupation and, especially, from the remorseless march of Israel's settler movement. Gaza's problems, it could further be argued, were now for

Hamas to deal with, since the PA had been pushed from power there in 2007. But I still found this state of affairs remarkable. Gaza City, by far the largest urban concentration in Palestine, is a scant 80 kilometres from Ramallah, yet most of my interviewees had not been there for years; some had never been there at all. The contrast in lifestyle, prosperity, and political outlook reminded me of East and West Germany during the Cold War. Ramallah felt like a city in an entirely different country. What prospect was there now for a two-state solution, when the region was effectively evolving into a three-state one?

I went to meet Abdulrahman Tamimi, a former adviser to the Palestinian Water Authority, who for many years has headed a lobby organization called the Palestine Hydrology Group. He sat me down in his office and drew the word Oslo for me on a piece of paper, with the Os enlarged and a double-headed arrow linking the two: 'For twenty-five years now, we've been running between two fat zeros, one big and one small – you see?'

Oslo, he meant, had promised a better future for Palestine, but it was all snake oil. The JWC, supposedly one of the 1995 Accord's greatest achievements, had turned out to be merely 'window-dressing,' and 'joint' only in name. 'How can there be real cooperation when 8,000 of our people are in Israeli prisons?' Tamimi said.

Groundwater in the West Bank, he continued, had never been fairly shared, even during the years of hope that followed Oslo. Israel, in his view, had betrayed the spirit of the peace accord with their JWC machinations. 'Water is a basic human resource – a human right,' he insisted, 'yet in Fasayil [in the mid-Jordan Valley], it took the JWC two years to grant permission to lay a connecting pipe that was 4 metres long.'

Tamimi was right: water is a basic human resource, and a person's right to it has been recognized, in varying ways by different societies and cultures, for millennia. In the twenty-first century, we tend to take this for granted. But I also remembered, from my days as a hydrogeology student, that the notion of any specifically 'human' right, with all the international legal implications that such a fundamental concept implies, is not as simple or obvious as it first appears. Ascribing 'human right' status to water is especially problematic. The Universal Declaration of Human Rights of 1948, one of the foundations of the global peace settlement that followed the Second World War, focused on the basics – the human rights to life, liberty, and freedom of expression, among many others – but it made no mention of a human right to water. It took the UN decades of international wrangling, and much abstruse jurisprudence, to come up with a formula on water rights that all its members could agree to. In fact, the UN did not recognize access to water – and its closely related cousin, sanitation – as a full-blown 'human right' until 2010.[11]

In the view of the UN, the implications of that recognition ought to have been clear to Israel: as the military occupier of the West Bank, the country now bore legal responsibility for the safe and adequate water supply of the citizens under its control. The difficulty for the UN – and for Palestinians – is that Israel does not refer to the West Bank as 'occupied' but as 'disputed' territory, pending a resolution based on the Oslo Accord. It therefore argues that no such responsibility exists.[12] The UN naturally disagrees. But, armed with its own legal advice, the political leadership in Jerusalem has consistently ignored the 'human right to water' argument. The hurt and passion behind protestations like Tamimi's appear to have cut no ice at all.

Tamimi had an intriguing theory about the infamous separation barrier that Israel began to build between themselves and Palestine after the Second Intifada, and that now snakes for over 700 kilometres around the West Bank. Ordinary Israelis tend to defend it as a security measure to keep out suicide bombers, something to be regretted perhaps, but also unfortunately necessary; they echo the rhetoric of Donald Trump on Mexico that when it comes to keeping out undesirables, nothing works better than a wall. Tamimi, however, reckoned there was more to it than that.

He produced a map, and traced the barrier with his finger, solid where it was completed, dotted where it was still under construction. The route, he showed me, does not follow the so-called 'green line', the political border set by the armistice following the Arab-Israeli war of 1948, as might be expected. In fact, as I saw, it mostly follows a path well to the east of the green line, the route of which it only approximately shadows; for there are many places on the map where it extends deep into the West Bank.

The total area of the land trapped between the green line and the barrier, the so-called 'seam zone', is substantial: once completed, the barrier will surround more than 8 per cent of the West Bank's territory. The seam zone is densely populated with Israeli settlements; it is also home to hundreds of thousands of unfortunate Palestinians. Palestinian non-residents cannot enter the seam zone without a special permit. Israelis, on the other hand, are free to come and go as they please. Most Palestinians understandably regard the seam zone as a naked piece of expansionism: an attempt by the Israelis to grab as much land for themselves as possible.

The Israelis counter that the armistice line is not easily defensible. The barrier, they say, had to be built within the West Bank in order to create an effective security buffer zone, and that the longer, finger-like incursions into Palestinian territory – some of which extend as far as 18 kilometres beyond the old green line – are simply a matter of topographical necessity; that is, the barrier follows the high ground in order to make it easier for the IDF to patrol or defend. It was also argued that the high ground had to be secured to prevent militants from using it to launch missiles at incoming civilian airliners.

Tamimi, however, did not believe that it was mere military advantage that the barrier-builders were after, nor even the extra territory. The barrier's route, he noted, almost exactly follows the recharge-discharge line of the western mountain aquifer. He was convinced that the real prize for Israel had always been the water in the ground beneath the seam zone, where, he claimed, the Israelis now operate as many as 350 deep groundwater wells.

This hidden, hydrogeological agenda, he believed, was in play long before the Second Intifada. He recalled how in 1991, the year of the Madrid Conference when Israel was negotiating peace with Jordan, the minister of agriculture, the ex-general and war hero Raful Eitan, placed a full-page advertisement in the *Jerusalem Post* arguing that Israel could not cede control of the 'mountains' of the West Bank because of their importance to his country's water supply. For that reason, Eitan brazenly suggested, Israel and Jordan should agree on a 'new green line', to be placed between 5 and 6 kilometres east of the original one. Then, at Oslo in 1995, the defence minister (and another ex-general, Itzik Mordechai), proposed the line be pushed back even further, to 8–10 kilometres beyond the 1949 ceasefire point – and it was along this line that the separation barrier was eventually constructed. So the barrier, to Tamimi, was simply another tool of hydro-colonialism; its route proved it.

The two-state solution has long been predicated on the old green line, but Tamimi feared that the fertile seam zone land beyond the barrier had gone for good. He pointed out that before 1967, some 14 per cent of Palestine's agricultural land was irrigated, a proportion that has since dropped to 1.8 per cent. The cornucopia of fruit and vegetables that Palestinians used to grow had been replaced by a meagre basket of rain-fed produce, principally olives.

'If Final Status negotiations ever come, Israel will present the destruction of our agriculture as another fact on the ground. They will say, "Why do you need this water from the discharge zone when you have no agriculture?"' The stranglehold on Palestine's water supply, he added, did not just suppress agriculture, but also held back industrial development, and tourism. 'Bethlehem gets water once a week. How can we build modern hotels in such circumstances? Who will come to stay there?' It pained him that the PA was obliged to pay Mekorot to provide municipal water. I asked what would happen if Israel were to supply it for free instead of selling it, a proposal often heard on the Israeli left. 'But this is our land, our water we are talking about!' he said, almost thumping his desk. 'It is not for Israel to either sell or to give.'

Tamimi was the former mayor of Nabi Saleh, a West Bank village famed for its campaign of resistance to the occupation. His cousin Ahed Tamimi, who was arrested, aged sixteen, in 2017 for slapping an Israeli soldier, became a global icon known as 'the Palestinian Rosa Parks', a Joan of Arc figure in the male-dominated world of the resistance.

With her leonine blonde curls and fearless round blue eyes – a trait that Tamimi shared – Ahed's looks upended lazy European (and Ashkenazi Jewish) assumptions about the Israel–Palestine dispute. Weren't resisters supposed to be dark-skinned young men? And weren't the white, blond ones the good guys? Ahed's looks didn't fit the stereotype, and that made her a potent symbol of resistance; particularly, perhaps, because of the awkward reality of the IDF, the ranks of which are filled – disproportionately so, according to some critics – with darker-skinned Mizrahim, Sephardim and Druze. Her arrest in 2017 was an ongoing public relations disaster for Israel. In the week I arrived in Ramallah, she was in Spain being fêted by the entire team of Real Madrid.

Water rights were at the heart of Nabi Saleh's campaign, which began in 2009 when Jews from the nearby settlement of Halamish appropriated a local spring. The spring was on privately owned Palestinian land, but that did not prevent the settlers from fencing it off, changing its name from Ein al-Qaws to 'Meir Spring' after Halamish's founder, Meir Segal, and creating a pretty bathing area at the spot, complete with a pergola and picnic tables. For seven years the villagers staged a protest every Friday, symbolically marching towards their stolen spring.

They never once reached it. Instead, they were routinely dispersed by the IDF, using the full panoply of weapons at their disposal, including rubber bullets and, sometimes, live ammunition.[13] Some 350 villagers had been injured over the course of the campaign. Tamimi's kinsman Mustafa was killed when a tear-gas canister was fired into his face at close range. His cousin Bassem, Ahed's father, had been arrested twelve times, and had spent years in administrative detention without trial. The price, in the end, was too high, so in 2016 the Tamimi clan called a halt to their village's weekly marches.

'The social fabric is broken in my village,' Tamimi said. 'Two-thirds of the children have spent time in an Israeli prison – even twelve-year-olds. There is a lot of psychological trauma. I worry even for Ahed. I tell her father not to put too much on her shoulders.' As a lobbyist for water rights, Tamimi's gloom sounded justified. Violent resistance had achieved nothing. The occupation continues, and the spring remains off-limits to the villagers of Nabi Saleh.[14]

The man held responsible for Palestine's formal withdrawal from the JWC in 2010 was Shaddad Attili, the water minister of the day, who argued bluntly that the committee had become 'a forum for blackmail … no different to asking us to approve our own occupation and colonization'.[15]

I went to meet Attili in a ritzy coffee shop. He was a controversial figure in Ramallah, an ambitious man with an imposing physique who had risen high from humble beginnings as a junior adviser to Arafat in the days of the PLO's exile in Tunis. Although he had resigned from government in 2014, he still had influence with the present regime, his status perhaps paraded by the shiny upmarket 4x4 vehicle he arrived in. It was clear from the way he ordered his cappuccino that the coffee shop was a regular haunt of his.

'Yes, I'm the man who ended coordination with the Israelis,' he sighed, rolling his eyes. He made it sound like a faux pas in an HM Bateman cartoon. Palestine's withdrawal had been condemned by Israel, of course, but also internationally; some foreign commentators still lament the demise of the JWC, citing it as a rare example of cross-border cooperation, and thus a lost stepping-stone to peace.

Initially, Attili said, he had done all he could to work with the Israelis. Access to water, he explained, was a 'fundamental human right', and he took his politician's duty to provide it very seriously. 'Even during [the Gaza war of] 2014, when buses were blowing up on television and F16s were killing us, Israelis and Palestinians kept talking within the water sector,' he insisted. Such informal contacts, however, were of limited use. The JWC's approval was still required for all major water infrastructure projects, but by 2013, Attili had long since concluded that formal cooperation with the JWC was not in Palestine's interests, and had already pulled the plug.

'I called myself the Virtual Minister,' he recalled, 'because the reality was that Israel decided everything. As they still do.' I asked him if there was any past precedent for true cooperation in the water sector. Oslo, including the will to establish the JWC, had to have built on something. 'The Johnston Plan?' he replied after some thought.

It was revealing, and depressing, how far back in time he had to go: Eric Johnston was a special US ambassador dispatched to the region by Eisenhower in 1955, with orders to work out a water-sharing agreement between all the squabbling neighbours of the Jordan Basin. It was an unlikely appointment – Johnston was the head of the Motion Picture Association of America, not a water engineer – yet the formula he arrived at was perhaps the closest the region had ever come to a sustainable water settlement. Unfortunately, the supranational Arab League was unwilling in those days to agree to anything that implied formal recognition of Israel, and rejected it. Arab attitudes hardened further following the Suez Crisis in 1956, ensuring that the Johnston Plan was never ratified.

Peace talks with Israel, Attili believed, urgently needed reopening, and the Oslo Accord renegotiating – although he was gloomy about the prospects of that happening. There were no peace talks to speak of at present, he said. America, in the view of Palestine's ageing president, Mahmoud Abbas, had 'withdrawn' from its traditional role as peace mediator in December 2017, when Donald Trump decided to recognize Jerusalem as Israel's capital, and then moved the US embassy there from Tel Aviv (a move that Trump's successor, Joe Biden, announced in 2021 would not be reversed). Attili, however, reckoned that the standstill in peace talks long pre-dated the machinations of Trump. He was also surprisingly frank in pinning some of the blame for the lack of progress on Abbas.

'Abu Mazen is the most peaceful man, but he has no plan. I tell him: we must review Oslo. But his approach is, "if negotiations fail … we must negotiate some more." That is not a plan.'

Abbas had recently returned from the UN General Assembly in New York, where he had delivered a speech that even I noticed failed to land any sort of blow on Trump, or to say anything new; or indeed to say anything much at all.[16] Abbas, Attili strongly hinted, did not really 'get' the water issue, or understand how critical it was to Palestine's development. This was in frustrating contrast to other PLO stalwarts of Abbas's generation, for whom Israel's denial of Palestine's water rights was an important *casus belli*: Sakher Habash, for instance, a founding father of Fatah known as Abu Nizar, who was an Egyptian- and American-trained hydrogeologist.

Attili recalled going to meet Abbas one winter morning in his office where he found him in cheerful mood, gazing through his garden window at the rain cascading outside.

'Yanni,' he remembered Abbas asking him, 'what is the average rainfall these days?'

'Mr President,' Attili replied patiently. 'It's good that it is raining. But the rain sinks into the ground – and what use is it if our farmers can't get permission to trap it, or dig wells to get it out again?'

Like Abdulrahman Tamimi, Attili regarded the West Bank's natural water, whether it flowed in rivers or underground, as Palestine's by right. Israel's historic diversion of the River Jordan remained a particular and continuing cause of resentment, even after so many years. The Israelis, he explained, tended to defend their control of the Jordan by arguing the right of 'prior use'; that is, the resource 'belongs' to them simply because they got to it first, in an era when – according to their version of history – no one else was using it. One of the most popular Zionist slogans of the 1890s, which served both to recruit new nation-builders and to justify what happened next, was 'A land without a people, for a people without a land': a slogan that still resonates in Israel today. Israelis also argue that the present-day Palestinian claim to sovereignty over the river is legally null and void, because the West Bank in the 1930s, when Israel first dammed the river, was under Jordanian or Mandate British rule, when 'Palestine', as a separate entity, did not exist.

To Attili, however, all this was sophistry.

'This is visceral for us,' he said fiercely. 'We are a riparian country. It is not acceptable that the settlements benefit more from our river than we do.'

His choice of words revealed much about the tangled geopolitics of Israel-Palestine. What, I wondered, did he mean by the phrase 'riparian country'? The independent Palestine envisioned under the two-state solution comprises Gaza as well as the West Bank; yet Gaza can hardly be described as 'riparian'. It made no sense, unless Attili had a three-state solution in mind – which I was sure he did not. He was jumping the gun in any case, because Palestine is not, yet, a 'country' in the normal international sense. It is recognized as a state by many UN members, but not by the ones that matter most, Israel and the United States (or, indeed, by the United Kingdom). In 2012, a major diplomatic row ensued when the UN upgraded Palestine to the status of, merely, a 'non-Member Observer State'.

Attili's description was, perhaps, another product of the inward-looking nature of the discourse on the peace process in Ramallah, and the tendency to ignore or forget about Palestine's other, Hamas-dominated half. However, his remark did also underline the importance of the River Jordan to the

West Bank's specific identity. I knew that he was not talking about something so ephemeral as his homeland's nomenclature: the issue was 'visceral' to him, I understood, because the old Israeli narrative – that no one else was really using the river, or indeed its West Bank littoral, until the first Zionists turned up – is untrue.

The Jordan is the centrepiece of a hydrologic system that has been tapped for irrigation purposes for millennia, underpinning an Arab economy and society that flourished in the centuries of Ottoman rule that preceded the Zionists. Following the Roman expulsion of the Jews in AD 70, Palestine was occupied by, among others, Ummayads, Abbasids, Seljuks, Crusaders, Ayyubids, Mongols and Mamluks. In other words, the land the Zionists colonised – or re-occupied, depending on one's point of view – was never 'without a people'.

The Ottomans, who arrived in 1516, were fond of a census, and kept good records. Even in 1550, Palestine's total population was calculated at around 300,000. Around a quarter of these lived in the six main towns, which included Nablus, Hebron and Gaza, as well as Jerusalem; their food was produced by peasant farmers in the surrounding villages, who grew everything from grapes to wheat.[17] Their success as farmers may be seen in the growth of Palestine's population, which reached 600,000 by 1900, an estimated 94 per cent of whom were Arab; Jews, even at that date, accounted for no more than 5 per cent of the total.[18]

Ancient history is a live battleground in Israel-Palestine. Zionists argue now, as they did a century ago, that the Ottomans grossly mismanaged Palestine's natural resources: its soil, its forests, and its water. They then use this argument to justify Israeli intervention as a tool of essential environmental repair. Some of this argument is justified. It is true, for instance, that by the tail end of the Ottoman Empire in the late nineteenth century, Palestine was a depressed and neglected province, where civic infrastructure was in dire need of updating. Its water infrastructure was especially rickety in the expanding cities. 'The suffering of the inhabitants of Jerusalem, the main cause of which is the lack of water, has made public opinion rank water supply highest among all the issues which involve the Holy City for more than ten years,' wrote the Ottoman engineer Franghia Bey in the late 1880s. 'As the days go by, the need becomes more pressing, more urgent.'[19]

Nevertheless, the charge of mismanagement needs to be treated with as much caution as the claim that the land was 'empty'. The Ottomans had a talent for central organization, which sustained an empire that spanned 3.2 million square kilometres, at its height, and that lasted for 700 years. The coda to Franghia Bey's complaint is that in 1891, Jerusalemites were granted the new municipal water system they craved: Palestine's first in modern times.

Out in the countryside, meanwhile, it was also true that centuries of overgrazing and logging had denuded the soil. Yet the land was far from 'barren' and 'desolate', as the Zionist narrative claims. Palestine's agrarian society was intact, and still paying taxes to Istanbul. The region's irrigation system was ancient, but the Ottomans understood that it was key to their province's productivity, as well as its political stability, and so they maintained it as best they could. In 1985, a geographer at Tel Aviv University, Zvi Ron, mapped the remains of some 250 subterranean irrigation channels around Israel, and found many of them to be pre-Roman; other examples of these so-called *qanats* – an ancient Assyrian word for a reed, and the root of the English words *channel* and *canal* – are found all over the Middle East.[20]

Palestine's Arabs continued to operate their qanats long after the Ottomans had gone. Following the Nakba, however, when up to 600 Arab villages were abandoned or destroyed, the system that once served them was allowed to collapse – a development that Zvi Ron called 'a human, ecological and cultural tragedy'. From the Palestinian Arab point of view, it is not they who were guilty of mismanaging Palestine's water infrastructure, but Israel.

Water use in Ottoman Palestine, finally, was never an unregulated, environmentally disastrous free-for-all as Zionists claim, but closely controlled by the authorities. The Quran views water as a gift from God, and the sharing of it as a holy duty – and Ottoman water law integrated traditional Muslim practice. From the sixteenth century, although 'artificial' water drawn from wells or qanats could be privately owned, any surplus water belonged to the community, and had to be made available for public use;

and in no case could a private well owner deny water to the thirsty. In the 1870s, this deceptively enlightened approach was adapted and secularized into the Mecelle, the Ottoman civil code, which stipulated that all water resources, even water on private property and from wells, were subject to government regulation and control.[21]

Modern Israeli water management, ironically, owes much to the Ottoman system. The Mecelle continued to apply in Mandate Palestine after 1920, and was eventually integrated into the Israeli Water Law of 1959, which enshrined the principle of public ownership of all water. Seth Siegel, the best-selling author of a study of Israel's water revolution, calls this 1959 law 'transformational'; it remains the legislative keystone of water management in Israel. The Mecelle was not fully superseded in the Israeli statute book until 1984.[22]

This debt to the Ottomans has largely been forgotten in modern Israel. But to Palestinians who know their history – and Shaddad Attili is certainly among these – the narrative that so blithely ignores the region's common heritage is the worst kind of insult; 'visceral', indeed.

I was no longer staying at the Caesar hotel, thanks to Bassam, my motorcycling guide in the Jordan Valley, who kindly lent me a spare bedroom in the back of his office, a spacious basement flat in a scruffy suburb of Al-Bireh. It was interesting to observe the local community here, and to feel the rhythm of day-to-day life in the neighbourhood. It was a gentle, unthreatening place, and as I grew more familiar with it, the anxiety I felt as a newcomer fell away.

I was soon on nodding terms with the old men who sat all day outside a garage, playing dominoes as they shooed away stray cats. I made friends with the teenage boys who manned the till in the local mini-mart, swapping English words for Arabic ones as I shopped for baklava, olives, fresh pitta bread, and hummus, of which there were at least a dozen brands. I took to walking into the centre of Ramallah for my meetings, and went for other long trudges up and down the city's tarmacked hills. One day I was caught in an immense rainstorm, and returned to Al-Bireh with feet so wet that my shoes fell apart. The rain made roofs leak, and flooded the road junctions at the bottoms of the hills. Ramallah's wetness was a constant and instructive surprise.

Yet, after some days of this, I found myself itching to get out of the city again. For all Al-Bireh's charms, I knew that Ramallah was atypical of the West Bank, a bubble of ease far removed from the experience of most Palestinians. I had much to learn about the wider role that water played in West Bank society, and the cultural and socioeconomic significance of its scarcity. The views outside the rarefied world of the capital were bound to be very different.

Bassam was a thoroughly urbanized Ramallah-ite, but one day he revealed that he had been born and brought up on an orange farm at Al-Hafireh in the upper Jezreel Valley, where his brother still tilled the land. It sounded like a good opportunity for an expedition. Bassam, though, was reluctant to take me. As a teenager, he said, he had been desperately bored by life in the country, and had left the homestead as soon as he was old enough, thirty years ago. He said he seldom revisited his birthplace, and apparently felt none of the homeland nostalgia that traditionally afflicts so many of his displaced countrymen. He and his brother, he added, did not get on so well following the death of their father three years ago, and they didn't much keep in touch.

The more I heard about his old family home, however, the more I wanted to see it. Bassam described how his father's orange groves were irrigated by a series of wells and cisterns that had dotted the landscape for millennia. The farm, he said, lay in the shadow of a great ruin, the ancient Canaanite city-fortress of Dothan, which derived its name from the ancient Chaldean word *doth*, a well or fountain. The well nearest the farm, he added, almost in passing, was called Jubb Yussef, or Joseph's Well.

It took me a moment to realise that Bassam was describing the centre-piece of one of the most famous stories in the Old Testament: the actual pit into which Jacob's son Joseph was thrown by his jealous brothers before they sold him into slavery in Egypt, as per 'Poor, poor Joseph', the song in *Joseph and the Amazing Technicolor Dreamcoat*, the 1970s musical by Tim Rice and Andrew Lloyd Webber that was forever being staged by schools when I was child.

I simply had to see this key piece of Old Testament hydro-mythology. And so, with a little more nagging, Bassam finally agreed to drive me there, on the understanding that we wouldn't go anywhere near his estranged brother.

It was a three-hour drive from Ramallah, and late afternoon before we reached Al-Hafireh, a scattered hamlet not far from Jenin, the West Bank's most northerly city. Bassam was evidently not the only resident to have abandoned the place. Many of its old stone buildings were in ruins. We made way for a tractor pulling a trailer with three old women aboard, but apart from them there was no one about.

The primary reason for Al-Hafireh's decline was, once again, a shortage of water. The village had suffered much the same fate as Al-Auja, the orange-growing town north of Jericho: drought, over-extraction of ground water, and Israeli interference had all played their role. 'The wells started drying in the 1980s,' Bassam recalled. 'The farmers tried to sink new ones, but the Israelis came and destroyed them if they drilled too deep. That happened to my brother twice.'

The desolation felt significant. As Shaddad Attili told me, the upper Jezreel is the only region of the West Bank with enough groundwater for Arab farmers to practise irrigation for themselves on any significant commercial scale. Jenin governorate, on the edge of which Al-Hafireh is located, is also the only governorate out of eleven in the West Bank where a majority of the land is designated as Area A, denoting full PA control. This was the consequence, in part, of Israel's 'disengagement' policy in 2005, when the IDF, seeking to rationalise its security arrangements in the outlying Occupied Territories, moved four settlements out of the Jenin area, at the same time that they withdrew altogether from Gaza. Yet it was clear that this had not translated into autonomy over the governorate's ground-water, least of all in its outlying areas.

For all his earlier indifference, Bassam grew nostalgic as we approached the village centre. 'All this area would have been packed with people in the old days. Workers. Young people. It's completely changed.' He pointed at a big empty field, its rich brown earth speckled with chunks of white limestone. 'All that used to be orange grove. And that field over there – and that one. But you can't grow oranges without a lot of water. They were marvellous, the orange groves. We used to play in them as kids, and chased girls through them as teenagers.'

The district had always been fought over. It was, for instance, the scene of the opening tank battle between Israel and Jordan in the Six Day War of 1967. From where we stood, the landscape's most conspicuous feature was the ruin of Dothan. For millennia, the city-fortress's buildings had been cyclically razed and rebuilt from the rubble, the foundations rising in layers above the valley floor until they formed their own hillock, a tell-tale trapezoid shape known as a *tel*. Archaeologists in the 1950s dated its lowest layer to the early Bronze Age, 3,000 BC, which made it as old as Troy. And yet Tel Dothan barely makes it onto the tourist maps of the Holy Land, where ruins of such antiquity are commonplace.

The story of how Bassam's family ended up there was a Palestinian classic. His late father, Salah, was a tent-dwelling Bedouin born in Sheikh Munis, a village just north of Tel Aviv. As a young man he kept cows and grew vegetables that he sold in the city from a handcart. But then came the Nakba, and Zionist militiamen who forced the villagers from their homes. Salah fled eastwards, pitching his tent and subsisting on the war-ravaged land wherever he could, wandering for a decade before settling down here by Tel Dothan.

Like hundreds of other pre-Nakba Arab villages, Sheikh Munis no longer exists: not even in name. Its streets were subsumed by Tel Aviv as the city expanded along the coast, becoming a suburb called Ramat Aviv; part of its former land is now occupied by the city's university. Bassam later forwarded me a remarkable article, published in 2009 by the liberal daily *Haaretz*.[23] It was by the author and journalist Gideon Levy, a prominent critic of the occupation who lives in Ramat Aviv, and who in an earlier column had mused wistfully about the unknown Arabs who once called his suburb their home.

On reading that column, Bassam had emailed Levy to inform him that his father had once lived where he now did, and sarcastically thanked him for his implicit offer to return the family's land. Levy, to his credit, went to Al-Hafireh to meet Salah, then eighty years old, and wrote about the encounter, recording Salah's many memories of life in Sheikh Munis. It was a deeply moving article, a snapshot of a lost, pre-war paradise when Jews and Arabs could and often did coexist in peace. What caught my eye was how lovingly both Levy and Salah dwelt on the vanished village's primary water source, a hilltop irrigation pool 45 metres square that Salah had once splashed about in as a boy, and which was subsequently replaced by a municipal swimming pool used by Levy.

Jubb Yussef lay at an intersection of farm tracks. Bassam turned off the engine, and we got out in a cloud of settling dust. The well's location was barely indicated: just the skeleton of a signpost, an empty rectangle that framed a plot of tobacco plants – a crop, Bassam said, that didn't need much irrigating – and a sloped edge of Tel Dothan beyond.

'Tourists used to come here a lot when I was growing up in the '70s,' Bassam said. 'They came to see the well, and the tel. I used to guide them up there. It's how I first learned English.' The well itself was a storage cistern rather than a true well. Its mouth was open to the sky, an empty cylinder of polished ashlar over 2 metres across and 10 deep in perfect condition, despite its purported age. If Joseph was thrown in here, I thought, he was lucky not to break his neck. We peered in, and looked down at the canopy of a spindly fig tree, stretching up towards the light from the bottom where it had seeded itself. Bassam said there had been no significant water in the well for thirty years.

'Do you really think this is the *actual* Joseph's Well?' I asked.

'Who knows?' he shrugged. 'It's the story we were brought up on as kids. But there are lots of wells around here, and some people say it happened at one of them. It's like that with all the old Bible stories.'

The Holy Land is indeed splendidly awash with competing claims to biblical 'authenticity'. It sometimes seemed as though every rock and stone had been ascribed some special religious significance in the past. As Mark Twain acidly notes in *The Innocents Abroad*, his classic account of an early package tour of the region undertaken in 1867, pilgrim-tourists are willing to believe almost anything, and have in consequence been misled by local

Arab guides for centuries. The importance of water features, Twain found, was particularly prone to misrepresentation and exaggeration:

> Every rivulet that gurgles out of the rocks and sands of this part of the world is dubbed the title 'fountain', and people familiar with the Hudson, the Great Lakes and the Mississippi fall into transports of admiration over them ... If all the poetry and nonsense that have been discharged upon the fountains and bland scenery of this region were collected in a book, it would make a most valuable volume to burn.[24]

This Joseph's Well, perhaps, was like a piece of the True Cross, one of those splinters of wood venerated in churches around the globe, so numerous that, as Erasmus put it in the 1500s, 'If all the fragments were collected together, they would appear to form a fair cargo for a merchant ship.'[25]

Bassam and I took photographs in the mellow light of the fading afternoon. Crickets chirped in the still air. All was bucolic calm. Bassam pointed to the ruined farmhouse where he was born, just up the hill. I suggested we take a closer look, but he demurred. 'Not all my memories of this place are good ones,' he muttered.

He began to talk, then, about growing up here with his brothers and sisters. There had been ten of them, but five of them had died before their time. One brother, a three-year-old, was killed by a scorpion bite: 'one of the hazards of the farmer's life,' Bassam shrugged. Another died in a motorcycle crash. There was a sister who died of cancer, and another 'of grief'.

The death of the third sister, though, was the worst. This sister, eighteen years old, disappeared one day. Her worried family and then the rest of the village sent search parties into the thick-leaved orange groves, but there was no sign of her. Eventually, after three days, her father thought to look in the cisterns around the farm.

History had not quite repeated itself: Joseph had been luckier by far than Bassam's sister. In one of the cisterns, Salah found his daughter drowned. Her broken fingers suggested she had somehow toppled in and then scrabbled to get out for quite some time, her desperate cries for help unheard. At last I understood Bassam's reluctance to bring me to Al-Hafireh, and felt not a little guilty for having persuaded him. Water had played a deeper and darker role in his life than perhaps even he had realised.

'I saw her body being pulled from the water,' he said quietly. 'A very funny colour, after three days. I was four at the time. It's why I still don't swim.'

CHAPTER FIVE

Samaria

Where the Hills Have Eyes

A
L-HAFIREH WAS in decline because Israel restricted its ability to
sink irrigation wells, and as I continued my exploration of the
northern West Bank, I came to see that there was nothing remotely
unusual about that. To put things at their simplest, groundwater was reserved
wherever possible for the use of Israeli settlers.

With its densely populated spine of desert hills that runs south, via
Nablus and Salfit to Jerusalem, Samaria – or Shomron, in Hebrew – was
once an independent Israelite kingdom, which flourished in the ninth
century BC over its rival, the kingdom of Judea, to the south. As so often
in Israel-Palestine, the old names are contentious. 'Judea and Samaria' is
the formal Israeli term for the West Bank, a phrase that implies that
the land is Israel's by historical right, while conveniently ignoring the
awkward modern narrative of an occupation that most of the world regards
as illegal. Palestinians understandably loathe the Israeli descriptor, and
prefer their own names. Samaria is still sometimes referred to as 'Jabal
Nablus', the 'Nablus Mountains', its name in Ottoman times. For 400 years
before Israel reclaimed the name 'Samaria', 'Jabal Nablus' was one of six
administrative *sanjaks* in Palestine, all of which were sub-districts of the
vilayet of Damascus.

But whatever it is or should be called, Samaria's ancient Israelite legacy made it an attractive proposition for modern settlers bent on reclaiming the land of Zion. Its most famous leader in Israelite times was Omri, a warrior king who dominated the ground from his hilltop capital, Shomron, after which the northern kingdom was eventually named. Shomron means 'Watch Mountain', and remains an apt name; because as I soon discovered, Omri's martial legacy is flourishing in modern Samaria, where hostile eyes still stare down on strangers entering its remoter areas. The uneasy truce between occupiers and occupied that I had detected in the Jordan Valley did not pertain here. The local IDF appeared to me to be much less even-handed, and the settlers I encountered belonged to a very different breed of Zionist.

In 1998 Ariel Sharon, a former general who later became prime minister, and a noted champion of the settler movement, urged young Israelis in a radio broadcast to 'grab the hilltops'. Three millennia after Omri, the key to domination had not changed. The idea now was to drive parallel wedges of control eastwards, advancing like a giant game of 'join the dots', with the goal, transparently, of linking up with the already colonised Jordan Valley. Once established, these west-east fingers of highland could be thickened, squeezing out the Arabs who lived in the valleys below, until they conjoined to subsume their land.

'Everyone that's there should move, should run, should grab more hills, expand the territory,' said Sharon. 'Everything that's grabbed will be in our hands. Everything we don't grab will be in their hands.'[1]

Bassam and I went to meet a family of Bedouin tent-dwellers on the edge of a nature reserve called Umm Zuka, in an encampment nestled in a small U-shaped bowl of dusty rock-strewn hills. We zig-zagged up a track on our ridiculous townie motorbikes. The camp was 800 metres from the main road, and our wheels slithered sideways in ruts full of sheep muck. A car was parked facing us on the crest of the hill, along which a smart new tarmac road marked out by flags led to an equally new hilltop army base. The car's position suggested that its owner wanted us to know that our progress was being watched – an impression that was strengthened when I caught a flash of sunlight reflected from a pair of binoculars.

We were met as we reached the camp by a pack of snarling sheepdogs, course-haired and crop-eared; I recognized them as examples of an ancient Middle Eastern breed, known as the Canaan Dog. An old man with a small moustache, dressed in proper Bedouin rig – *thobe*, *kufiya* and *igal* – emerged from a shack of corrugated iron to call them off.[2] 'Sorry about that,' he said, as we killed our engines. 'The dogs mistake you for settlers.'

His name was Haji Abed, the family patriarch. He explained that local settlers sometimes raided the camp, tearing around the shacks and tents on quadbikes, frightening the sheep in their pens and showing the Bedouin who was in charge. From the dogs' response to our arrival, I inferred that such incursions were routine.

He led us past empty sheep pens to to the 'majlis', an open-sided structure at the centre of the camp, and the only one with a concrete floor, where a grandson produced tea. It was late morning, so the middle generation of the family were away tending their flocks somewhere on the hills above. Haji Abed had a septic finger and asked Bassam if he had any plasters. Bassam fetched a first aid kit, and was dressing the old man's wound when a clanking of bells announced that the shepherds had come back unexpectedly early. The wadi was suddenly filled with returning sheep, 600 of them streaming over the lip of the hill. There were dogs and children with sticks everywhere, hustling the flock into their pens.

Haji Abed's son, another Abed, was a wiry man in a grubby grey sun hat, who soon joined us in the majlis looking hot, tired and troubled. 'No day is good,' he began. 'We have just one hill left to us – just one. There's no grazing left on it. And today we ran into the settler's cows. We had to turn around.'

His nemesis, he gave me to believe, was a settler he referred to as Uri who, two years previously, had taken up residence with his 200 cows in a hilltop outpost nearby. From here, his cows ranged wherever they pleased. If Abed or the other shepherds came too close to them, he said, then the army was called in, leading to encounters that seldom ended well for the Bedouin. Sometimes the shepherds were detained for the whole day, while their untended sheep scattered to the hills.

'They even blindfolded us once,' Abed went on. He produced a photograph by way of proof: three gnarled shepherds surrounded by a group of

IDF soldiers. 'Two of them are just girls. Do you see?' Two of them did indeed look like very young women, which for Abed was evidently an extra humiliation, an emasculation. No explanation for the blindfolding was ever offered.

It was clear that Haji Abed's family was barely clinging on here. It turned out that the occupant of the car who had watched us entering the valley was an Israeli activist, a member of Ta'ayush, 'Coexistence', a left-wing group who campaign for an end to the occupation, and for civil equality between Arabs and Jews. Its volunteers were regulars at Umm Zuka, turning up in rotation to act, in effect, as the shepherds' shepherds.

'The activists can't do anything but they can document abuses, which does act as a deterrent,' Abed said. 'We have to wait for them to arrive before we can go out. And sometimes they don't come. Still: if it wasn't for the activists, this way of life would already be finished.'

The watcher on the hill was the first evidence of such activism that I had yet encountered in the West Bank, and I felt heartened by it. Until now, the conspicuous absence of such people tended to uphold a complaint I had often heard, that the voice of Israeli liberals is strangely absent from the domestic moral debate over the occupation. The Palestinian writer Raja Shehadeh, whom I met at the Edinburgh Literary Festival in 2017, shook his head when I asked who spoke up for Arab rights on the Israeli side. 'They are very few,' he said glumly.

Raja regretted that the mainstream Israeli left, once the natural political home for peaceniks and dissenters, had become such a weak and divided force since the heady days of the early 1990s, when Yitzhak Rabin's Labor coalition paved the way for the Oslo Accords. The fissiparous nature of Israeli party politics has served the right wing much better than the left: there has been no left-wing government in Israel since Ehud Barak's shaky 'One Israel' coalition fell in 2001. In opposition, meanwhile, progressive liberal parties like Meretz – meaning 'Vigour' – have demonstrated anything but that.[3]

There are, however, organizations like Ta'ayush for Israelis who find the occupation unconscionable, and who are prepared to do something about it. B'Tselem, a Jerusalem-based NGO founded in 1989, is on a similar mission to document human rights violations in the Occupied Territories. Another organization called 'Breaking the Silence' is even more explicit in its goal to prick the consciences of what it sees as a supine citizenry in the Israeli heartlands. Breaking the Silence was established in 2004 by a group of IDF veterans, who were appalled by the treatment of Palestinian civilians they had witnessed during their tour of duty in Hebron. The organization has since attracted funding from a number of European governments, including Britain's;[4] it remains a thorn in the side of those in the Israeli government who would prefer the grim reality of the occupation not to be so exposed.

In the Umm Zuka majlis, in the traditional Bedouin way, an oversized lunch was suddenly produced, aubergines stuffed with lamb, flatbread, and Sprite to wash it down. I doubted they could afford it, but there was no declining their hospitality. Haji Abed ignored our protests and loaded extra food onto our plates. His father, he said, had been born in this area. In the days before 1948, he remembered, the shepherds had ranged with their flocks as far as Haifa on the coast. Sixty Bedouin herding families had once lived in the area. There were now just four left. 'My cousin left last year,' said the younger Abed. 'He sold all his sheep. Finding pasture is just too tough.' His early return from the hill today meant that his flock would have to be fed with barley bought in for the purpose.

Uri the Settler was never far from these Bedouins' thoughts. He seemed to hover over the camp like a malign spirit, in counterpoint to that other shadowy body, the guardian angel parked on the shoulder of the hill. Because of the camp's location, the Abed clan lived with the permanent sense of being watched. It was creepy; I could feel it even as I ate my lunch.

'The army supports him,' Abed went on. 'The IDF have designated this land as another "firing zone" for military training – but it is obviously nothing of the sort . . . We've tried reporting him to the police, but they can do nothing here because this is all Area C.' I asked why the family did not simply move on, in the traditional nomadic way, but Abed said it was too risky. If the hunt for new grazing land failed, he explained, they wouldn't even be able to return to this valley, thanks to a Civil Administration ruling specifically outlawing the reoccupation of abandoned camps. They were, in practice, stuck.

The Civil Administration, he said, barely tolerated their presence here even now. The military bureaucrats naturally hated the Bedouins' untidy encampments, which the herdsmen set up wherever they could in the shrinking empty spaces of the desert. At the side of the entrance track from the road, Bassam and I had passed a tall slab of pre-fabricated concrete that the IDF had erected there, instantly recognizable as a single section of the West Bank separation barrier. Stencilled across it, like an epitaph on a giant tombstone, were the words: 'Danger. Firing Area. Entrance Forbidden'. Earlier on our journey, we had passed the entrances to other Bedouin camps in other roadside wadis, all of which were marked out by the same forbidding sign. The message was unequivocal, the official discouragement systematic. As Bassam pointed out, these wadi entrances were the *only* places on the road where the signs had been put up.[5]

Uri's farm was an unauthorized outpost, illegal under Israeli law. Yet neither feeding nor watering his cows was a problem for him. When he had moved into the area two years previously, according to Abed, the army secretly supplied him with water via a spur of pipe especially laid for him from their nearby military base. That arrangement was stopped when local activists challenged it in the courts, he said, but it made little difference. According to Abed, the residents of the farm were now connected to the mains by a pipe 10 kilometres long – the first step, he explained, towards 'regularization' of the outpost, and the eventual transformation of Uri's farm into a legally recognized settlement.[6]

There was, of course, no mains connection for these Bedouin. Their water all had to be tankered in from Tubas, the nearest large Palestinian town. They needed 3,500 litres of it every week, which cost them almost 900 shekels (US$260). The only way Abed could afford this, he said, was to sell off his flock, little by little. 'We settle our bills in the lambing season. Until then, we are always hundreds of thousands of shekels in debt.'

The choking off of their water supply, it seemed to me, had the potential to drive Haji Abed's clan from this land faster even than the dispossession of their pastures.

From the Bedouins' description I initially took Uri for a hick on a quad bike whom the military were unable, not just unwilling, to control. He sounded half-crazed – and perhaps he was. The further I travelled in Samaria, however, the more I realised that men like Uri were commonplace pawns in a much bigger, state-sponsored game.

Israel's takeover tactics became clearest to me in the remote hamlet of Yanoun, a few kilometres south-east of Nablus. Outwardly this was a beautiful spot, a picturesque cluster of ancient mud and stone cottages between neat terraces of fruit and olive trees on a hillside that looked as though it had never changed. A single column of cooking smoke rose into the still air. Sheep baaed in the meadow below. But, as at Umm Zuka, the village huddled in a horseshoe of hills that again seemed full of unwelcoming eyes. I felt watched even on the approach road, which was the only one in or out, snaking almost 5 kilometres up the wadi bottom from the town of Aqraba to the south.

The village well was the cause of much-documented trouble at Yanoun. The settlers who lived on the heights reportedly favoured a passive-aggressive technique. Brash young men would turn up on summer days to wash in the cistern as if they owned it. They would bring their dogs and wash them too, calculating, no doubt, that this would offend conservative Muslims who regard dogs as unclean. Sometimes, if there were women around, they would strip naked, and jeer if anyone dared to object. The invaders were said by the villagers to be members of *No'ar HaGva'ot*, the notorious 'Hilltop Youth', whose founder and inspiration was Avri Ran, an organic chicken farmer with four convictions for assault. His outpost, barely 2 kilometres from Yanoun, was called Giv'ot Olam, 'The Hills of Eternity'.

I found the well just below the village, protected by a heavy chain-link fence and an imposing pair of metal gates paid for, according to a sign, by the European Commission in Brussels.[7] The well itself was dwarfed by its defences, a tiny pump housed in a rusting white box that filled a short watering trough smelling strongly of sheep. It seemed quite undeserving of all the international fuss it had caused – something I was rapidly getting used to in the West Bank.

Yasser Fahmi, the head of one of the Yanoun families, was perched on a rock in front of his house, watching his sheep grazing beyond the well. Broken bits of machinery lay scattered around his yard, at the centre of which sat a battered truck on blocks with its wheels off. With his magnificent white walrus moustache and sun-leathered face, Fahmi looked like an Old Testament prophet. I was shocked to discover that he was 53, almost the same age as me.

It didn't take him long to get into his stride. The Israelis, he explained, pressed in on his village from three sides, and did so more closely than could in any way be called reasonable. The village limit to the north, a low bluff beyond his house, was about 100 metres away. Fahmi said he owned the line of olive trees along it, but that he wasn't able to pick their fruit without first coordinating with the IDF. Even then there was a risk of hassle from the settlers. Harvest time, he said, almost always led to trouble between the two sides. 'When the settlers attack us, we are supposed to contact the Liaison Office, who send the army to investigate. But the settlers have always gone by the time the army gets here. The soldiers will pick up a thrown stone and say, "What stone?"'

The IDF, he complained, had declared all the land above the village a closed firing zone, yet allowed the settlers to plough it. They and the settlers, he insisted, were literally a single enterprise. Not for nothing was Avri Ran, the founder of the Hilltop Youth, once nicknamed 'The Sheriff'.[8] 'My neighbour had an argument with a settler recently, about access to his orchard. He said, "Let's get the IDF to sort this out." The argument ended when the settler went to his car, fetched a gun and put on a uniform, and came back and said "OK, I'm the army now." They are all reservists. Even the Haredim have to serve these days.'[9]

The village of Beit Fourik – a much larger community, with dire, settler-related water troubles of its own – was once a ten-minute walk away over the hill through his olive grove. Generations of Yanoun villagers had gone there for work or to sell their produce; their respective sons and daughters were much intermarried. It was, however, no longer possible to walk to Beit Fourik, the path to which passed near Avri Ran's chicken farm. The only way to reach it was by car, a circuitous journey via Aqraba that took an hour and half. For all its open skies and glorious views, Fahmi's pretty village was a gilded cage.

Fahmi described himself as another *murabit*, a defender of the land. His family, he said, had lived in Yanoun for eight generations. 'We will never leave this place,' he said doughtily. But the arithmetic of the village suggested otherwise. Yanoun had once been home to thirty shepherd families – now there were only six. His children, tellingly, were not preparing to take over from him. One son was studying IT in Saudi Arabia; another was a trainee air-conditioning engineer in Nablus. Fahmi himself had once owned a hundred sheep, but had reduced his flock to thirty, for lack of grazing. Fahmi conceded that in a couple of years he would likely have no sheep at all.

As a working shepherding community, Yanoun was on life support, its existence sustained by foreign aid money and the attentions of human rights activists, just as at Umm Zuka. Yanoun's connection to the electric grid, I learned, had been funded by Belgium. Its domestic water supply, by pipeline from Aqraba, was paid for by Germany. The well, Fahmi explained, was vital for the watering of livestock, but had never been clean or reliable enough to provide domestic water. Until 2016, Yanoun had depended like so many other villages in Palestine on tanker delivery. The new pipeline was a boon, although it could hardly be described as secure. The Civil Administration had never approved its construction, and had placed a demolition order on it almost as soon as it was completed. Germany's diplomatic clout in Jerusalem protected it, for now. 'If it wasn't for the foreigners, Yanoun would already be finished,' Fahmi acknowledged.

As he spoke, a group of women, instantly recognizable as European, appeared on the terrace of a house nearby. They were middle-aged ladies who wore a uniform of sorts: sensible walking boots and dun-coloured safari waistcoats that bore the logo of EAPPI, the Ecumenical Accompaniment Programme in Palestine and Israel. We were all startled to see each other – Yanoun is as remote a village as you can find in Palestine – and they laughed when I called out a greeting. One of them turned out to be from the south side of Edinburgh, my home city.

Her name was Margot, a housewife with grown-up children, who had volunteered for a three-month mission here through her local church. Yanoun, she explained, became a cause célèbre for human rights organizations like hers in 2002, when settlers first invaded the village and forced the residents to evacuate. The invasion prompted an international outcry and, with a small army of foreign volunteers in attendance, the villagers were eventually able to move back in. Rotating teams of foreigners had stood in over-watch ever since.

Using a village house as their base, the ladies from EAPPI set out each morning on a long hike around the area, seeing and being seen, sending a message that this village had not been forgotten, maintaining the fragile status quo. Every incident was monitored and reported upwards, eventually, to the UN.

Margot described a children's playground, recently constructed in a nearby village by the NGO World Vision, which no one had been into following an incident six weeks previously when two small boys had been shot at. She and her colleagues sometimes accompanied Arab children on their walk to school, their presence helping to deter stone-throwing settlers, perhaps shaming the IDF into keeping the peace. 'The IDF are careful how they respond to us. They don't give us trouble. I'm sure it helps that we are mostly western women of a certain age. They generally just pretend we're not here.'

Hers was a quiet sort of activism, different to the kind practised by younger campaigners. She was no Rachel Corrie.[10] But her opposition to the occupation was no less effective for that, and no less brave, and I admired her determination to act on her principles. She was in no doubt that Yanoun would be finished without EAPPI's presence. The settlers were still circling, watching, waiting for any opportunity to provoke and harass. Two months previously, she said, a car full of them had driven into the village in the middle of the night, and gone for a noisy walk around the village, rattling bins, making the dogs bark. 'We just ignored them until they went away. We heard later that they told a flying IDF checkpoint that they'd found a bomb-making factory here.'

She waved a hand at the little houses around her: the chickens scratching in the dust, a child on a bicycle, a dog sleeping in the shade of an orange tree. 'Can you think of anything more ridiculous?'

Neither Umm Zuka nor Yanoun were my closest brush with the settlers in the hills. In 2017, while planning the same half-term holiday during which I took my family to Qasr al-Yahud on the Jordan, I spotted a listing on a holiday rental website for a 'family house' in an illegal West Bank settlement, one of several dotted along the Shiloh Valley 48 kilometres north of Jerusalem.

From the listing's photographs it was apparent that the house was another small, red-roofed cabin, no different to hundreds of other settler dwellings that I had seen around the West Bank. The owners had been renting it out for over a year, although perhaps not very successfully: there was just one previous customer review online, which stated blandly that the place was 'nice'. The asking price, around £150 a night, seemed steep. Still, the photos showed a table prettily laid for breakfast on a sunny terrace overlooking the Samarian hills. The listing's notes promised an LCD television, and a hot tub: water supply was evidently not much of an issue for its owners. Guests, I noted, were also invited to hire bicycles on which they could follow a trail of 'antique water holes': to whom, I wondered, did those belong? The calendar said the cabin was available. I quickly booked us in.

We set off from our boutique hotel in beachside Tel Aviv. The receptionist who organized our minivan and driver was saucer-eyed when I told her where we were going. 'Why?' she wanted to know. 'Won't it be dangerous?' But we were all reassured by Leon the driver, a huge man from California, who waved away such concerns and kept us all laughing on the road with a series of novel Jewish jokes.

'Why did the Jews end up in Canaan? Because Moses had a stutter. He was trying to lead us to Canada, but . . . Can – Canaa – Canaan.'

Our destination turned out to be one of several satellite outposts of Shiloh, a larger settlement established in 1978. The road signs to this place made my older children laugh: the name Shiloh Pitt, the daughter of Brad and Angelina Jolie, was their favourite spoonerism.

According to biblical legend, Shiloh was once the site of the tabernacle, the resting place of the Ark of the Covenant when it first arrived on the shoulders of Israelite priests returning from their Egyptian exile; the Ark stayed put for nearly four centuries before its transfer to the temple in Jerusalem. Shiloh is also said to be the spot where Joshua divided the Promised Land among the tribes of Israel. Archaeological evidence of this is scanty, although that has proved no obstacle to settlers, who still use the legend to validate their claim to the area. The settlements of south Samaria are all part of the Mateh Binyamin Regional Council, named after the tribe of Benjamin who once settled here. However, the outposts around Shiloh, including ours, go by a more informal but no less provocative name, the 'Daughters of Shiloh'.[11]

The outpost was approached – of course – by its own, newly asphalted access road. Big Leon grew quieter as we turned off the highway and wound up the hill. Just before the first houses, he stopped to ask directions from three youths carrying mattocks. Their faces were streaked with mud and sweat, and they wore their sidelocks long and thick: great shanks of hair that were crusted with filth like the tails of mountain sheep, or the matted dreadlocks of a tramp. They were entirely different to the delicate spiralled *payot* worn by the Jerusalem Haredim. These boys did not at first answer Leon. They peered nosily past into the depths of the van with dark suspicious eyes, feral and unwelcoming, filling the window frame: the faces of the Hilltop Youth.

We all flinched: even Leon. 'I don't know what they've been smoking, but I want some. *Not,*' he grumbled, once we had moved on.

Our hosts, happily, were more pleasant. Noah was a second-generation immigrant whose parents had made 'aliyah' to the Shiloh Valley from central Europe.[12] His wife, Naomi, wore a full-length country skirt and a scarf around her head. She was young and heavily pregnant, and counted on her fingers to show that the child she was expecting would be her seventh. There was a zealous quality to her, a certain simple religiosity that reminded me of the Mennonites, a community of Anabaptists who also embrace the mores of the past, as though the clock can be turned back to more devout times.

Naomi kissed the *mezuzah* by the door and showed us around with glowing pride. The cabin's interior was tiled and scrubbed to a state of sterile godliness. A French window gave on to a small terrace with long views over a valley strewn with jagged white boulders and thorns. The land at the bottom of the hill, though, was cleared of rocks to reveal soil of a rich ochre colour, which was planted with a flourishing green vineyard. It was as lovely as Tuscany. But then we noticed the IDF watchtower perched on the horizon, a concrete stub of gun slits and bulletproof glass, as incongruous as a spaceship. Not far down the valley, we could make out the minaret of an Arab village, Jalud, whose residents, I knew, had no love for the people here.

Later, as the day cooled, we ambled up the hill towards the centre of the settlement, which was organized into three rows of shack-like houses along the contours of the top of the hill. The homes we passed were mostly pre-fabricated units, rectangular and white, the type that can be delivered on the back of a lorry. Others, though, were built like our rental property, in the classic settler style with pitched red roofs. There was a lot of building work going on: plots marked out for new houses, or half-finished extensions being added to existing ones. The homes were small and basic and, to judge from the washing drying on lines in their scruffy back yards, crowded with young children. It all looked and felt a bit hillbilly, a bit backwoods: a harder, poorer way of life than I had expected to find. This isolated hilltop was certainly no place for the sick, or the elderly. The oldest resident here, I later learned, was less than forty-five years old.

Here and there we caught the unmistakeable whiff of marijuana, which sat oddly with the professed religiosity of the settlement. This was a community that refrained from driving on Shabbat. Our rented kitchen contained only disposable paper plates and plastic cutlery, in strict adherence to *kashrut* dietary laws, according to which a plate or fork used by a non-Jewish goy is rendered permanently unclean.

At the top of the hill, in the shadow of a synagogue and a tall steel watchtower, we found a playground covered in Astroturf. Naomi was there, cross-legged on the ground in a circle of five other mothers all dressed as she was, their many offspring swarming on a climbing frame. Young, pregnant Naomi was evidently not unusual here. Like their Benjamite forebears, these settlers seemed to be on a messianic mission to repopulate their Promised Land.

The mothers looked across at us, not hostile, but not exactly welcoming either. We smiled awkwardly and took up position on a bench opposite, from where my children shyly refused to budge, until Naomi gamely marched over to break the ice. Her gesture spoke volumes. I suddenly felt certain that her rental operation was a portal to the outside world that not everyone here approved of.

I admired Naomi's entrepreneurialism, and warmed to her friendliness and implied conviction that her community had nothing to hide. Yet it was absurd to present life here as being in any way normal. When a father turned up with an assault rifle dangling from his shoulder, the illusion popped. My children stared as he called a cheery greeting to the mothers before disappearing up the ladder of the watchtower to relieve another sentry-Dad. Many settlers, I had read, voluntarily underwent 'security training' from an organization called *Mishmeret Yesha*, the Guardians of Yesha, a collective Hebrew term for Judea, Samaria and Gaza. I recalled a jokey tourist T-shirt I had seen for sale in Tel Aviv bearing the phrase 'Guns N' Moses', which made more sense to me now, for that was exactly the ethos of this singular place.

It was a relief when Noah appeared, a toddler on his hip, and offered to show us the synagogue on the crown of the hill. This building was small with a white-tiled floor and pine-clad walls that reminded me of an alpine ski lodge. At the far end, pointing towards Jerusalem, red-cushioned benches were arranged around an ark for Torah scrolls. Noah explained that the synagogue was the first building constructed when the settlement was founded. The community had since outgrown it – there was, he said, a long waiting list of families wanting to join the settlement – so now they were planning to build a bigger one.

The draw for all the families, he confirmed, was largely ideological. He was unambiguous about this: he said that they were 'reclaiming' the Land of Israel for the Jews, and that he, like them, was 'of course' proud to be a part of that holy mission. I asked about the local Arabs who had once farmed the land they now occupied: didn't this settlement amount to theft? But Noah said that there was nothing here before their arrival: just rocks on an empty hill. He added that because the land was unused, their occupation of it could not be defined as theft, according to the law. I asked if local Arabs objected to this legal interpretation. He admitted, with a vague wave over his shoulder, that there been some trouble in the past. But all that was a long time ago; everything now, he insisted, was 'fine'.

I wondered about this. The road entrance to the settlement was unprotected by any kind of security barrier, which was unusual. Perhaps this was an indication that the two sides had reached an agreement of sorts, a non-aggression pact, maybe even the beginning of peaceful coexistence? But, no: the absence of a barrier, he explained, was a security strategy. Building a wall implied permission for those on the other side to come right up to it. Without a wall, they naturally stayed much further away; and the settlers maintained a clear field of fire right down the valley.

I doubted very much that the land these settlers occupied had been unused when Noah first came here. I suspected that the hilltop was previously empty only in the sense that it had never been built on, probably for the sound hydrological reason that groundwater collects at the bottom of hills, never at the top. No one ever chooses to dig a well on a summit, which is why farming villages are generally found in valleys. But 'empty' land is seldom valueless, especially in crowded Israel-Palestine, and does not imply that it is not owned. Hilltops can be grazed, or cultivated with rainfall captured in cisterns or terraces. How could Noah be so sure that local farmers never had a use for this hill? In any case, the settlement's footprint had expanded over the years, spreading downhill until it incorporated flat and fertile land that must surely once have been farmed by Jalud.

Like many settlers or their supporters, Noah argued that his community had not stolen any ground because the Land of Israel was a gift to the Jews from God, and thus was rightfully theirs in the first place; they were merely reclaiming it after an absence of two millennia, following their eviction by the Romans. Yet, to my mind, this kind of language gave him away. 'Empty land' was the sort of phrase once favoured by European colonialists to justify their appropriations around the world. The 'outback', to Australian aborigines, was a sacred homeland before that word was coined; the 'Wild West' never appeared 'wild' to Native Americans in the sense that cowboys meant it.

Noah led us to a lookout point from where we could see the vineyards that helped to sustain his community's economy. There were, I now saw, two abutting vineyards on the valley bottom. The nearer one, belonging to the settlement, was lush and green; the other, belonging to farmers from Jalud, was sparse and dry. Noah drew my attention to the contrast: evidence, he said, that the settlers knew how to make 'proper' use of the land. He seemed to speak as though Jews were intrinsically better farmers than their Arab neighbours: not just savvier but more industrious, with greener fingers; perhaps even naturally so, by dint of some divine communion with the land.

It soon became apparent, however, that irrigation had as much to do with the settlers' success. The Civil Administration, I learned, only permitted the farmers from Jalud to visit their vines once or twice a year. Noah seemed to make no connection between the scragginess of the Arab vineyard and the practical impossibility of watering it. The truth was that his community, like every hilltop settlement in the West Bank, could not survive for long without government-subsidized pumps, pipes and water. Yet he did not appear to consider this a privilege. His water supply was so cheap and plentiful that there was no need to worry about it – and so, to my mind, he didn't. Indeed, just beyond our cabin was the stone block outline of another unfinished building, larger than the other houses. Later, when I peeked through an empty window frame, I discovered a half-built indoor swimming pool.

Back at the cabin as night fell, we sat on our terrace and watched the settlement's powerful floodlights come on, illuminating a moonscape that now felt menacing. A distant dog's bark echoed in the silence. A white light winked in the IDF watchtower on the horizon, and the streetlights of Jalud twinkled a low-wattage yellow. It was no comfort to know that Israeli guns were trained on the darkness in between. The valley was a no-man's-land waiting for something to happen.

At dawn the following day I scrambled down the hill with two of my children, Gus and Mary, for a closer look at the vineyards. Noah had told us that we would find a work-gang harvesting early grapes at that time, and it seemed that we might be able to join them if we liked. The grape-pickers ignored us, however, more coldly even than the mothers in the playground.

I showed the children the hosepipes that snaked up and down the neat rows of vines, and followed the pipes back to an industrial-grade hydrant dug into the edge of the field. The hydrant's wheel valve was leaking so much that we sank into mud. Then we made our way to the vineyard next door where the earth was not red but grey, and the few stunted vines that clung on were mostly withered to kindling.

'I don't understand,' said Mary, her nine-year-old voice full of innocent wonder and anguish. 'Why can't these people just share?'

'Good question,' I said, 'and one the UN have been asking themselves for more than half a century.'

'Hm,' said Mary, pleased. And then, quietly, after a pause: 'What does UN stand for?'

The settlement made us all curious about the mysterious Arab village down the hill. Even the children understood that there are two sides to every story, and that we were unlikely to hear the Palestinian version from any settler. Noah's assertion that the land he occupied was empty before his arrival was something I was particularly keen to test, but it was another year before I was able to do so, with the help of the resourceful Bassam.

Jalud turned out to be a town of a thousand people, much bigger than it looked from up the hill. The head of the town council, Abdullah Haj Mohamed, was well organized: there was no airy wave of the hand from *him* about past 'trouble' with the neighbours. In his office in the town hall, one wall was covered with photographs documenting years of violent dispute with the Daughters of Shiloh. As recently as April, settler youths had crept into Jalud one night, slashing the tyres of parked cars and scrawling propaganda on walls. Some of their graffiti was still visible: 'Jews wake up!' it said in Hebrew. 'Our rights are in our own hands.'[13]

Councillor Abdullah found nothing unusual in my interest in Jalud. Foreign journalists, politicians and activists came here all the time, and all were shown this wall. He said that settlers from all the hilltops around had brought trouble for Jalud. Some of the settlements, he said, were linked to an extremist settler organization, Kahane Hai (Kahane Lives) that was named after the ultranationalist politician and rabbi, Meir Kahane, who was assassinated in New York in 1990. During the recent wheat harvest, he asserted, settler women and children from roundabout had obstructed a Jalud farmer by lying down in front of his tractor. When he and others tried to remonstrate, they were driven off by IDF tear gas. I looked closely at a photograph of this incident, half-fearing that I would recognize one of the settlers I had encountered among the protestors – and was relieved when I did not.

115

I was introduced to four Jalud farmers who trooped one after another into Council Abdullah's office. One of them, Mahmoud Mutabasi, was a big, gnarled, middle-aged man in a thick sheepskin waistcoat and a flat black cap, like the archetype of a Palestinian fellah.

'Empty? That land?' he said, pointing up the hill towards the settlement where I'd stayed. 'I remember when my father bought that land from a neighbour. The price was one bull. There is a sheep trough on the hilltop, 2 metres square, that my father dug out of the rock with his own hands.'

Mutabasi had fought hard for his birthright. He pulled up a trouser leg to reveal an old bullet wound that had left him with a permanent limp. Then he doffed his cap to show me another scar on his head. Both injuries came from clashes with settlers. 'I've still got olives up there. The last time I tried to visit them was in 2011. We came back with nineteen injured.'

I met the owner of the withered vineyard I had shown to my children. I didn't mention that I had actually been there, as a guest of settlers. The hurt and anger these men felt was raw, and I wasn't sure that they would appreciate the ethical niceties of balanced reporting.

'I have to get permission from the IDF to tend my vines,' he confirmed. 'They give us a couple of days, twice a year. It's not nearly enough. And the permission came two months late this year. By then the crop was worthless, but we went anyway. We get so excited when they say we can go! The settlers harass us, but it's worth it. If we don't go, they will just take it. We have to defend our land where we can.'

I asked about water supply. The settlers, they said, extracted 'huge amounts' of groundwater from a deep well near Huwara, 16 kilometres to the north-west, and brought it here through a pipe laid across Jalud ground. Water, I understood, was a worry for these farmers, although they did not dwell on it. It was of secondary importance to a more immediate and emotive grievance, the denial of access to their land.

Councillor Abdullah led us all up a staircase to a roof. It was apparent from here how crowded this district was, and how much pressure there is on the land. It was shocking to discover that the desert emptiness I had seen and felt on the terrace of my rental cabin was just another illusion. Abdullah turned and pointed in a 270-degree arc, ticking off the names of ten illegal outposts and two army bases that encircled his town. To the west we could see the tower blocks of Ariel, a settler city of 20,000, and beyond it in the haze, a suggestion of the Mediterranean coast.

'Their grip is tightening,' he said glumly. 'All the settlements are getting bigger. And the new houses aren't pre-fabs. They are built of wood and old stone. It's a sure sign that the outposts are becoming permanent settlements with legal status.'

The arc of newly settled land included the building site of Amihai, the first new West Bank settlement to be authorized for twenty-five years. Amihai was the consolation prize for the residents of yet another settlement in the region, Amona, who were evicted in 2017 following a ruling by the Israeli Supreme Court that the land it was built on was stolen. Jalud was now paying the price of this rare Palestinian legal victory: Amihai was expanding so fast that it would soon subsume Adei Ad, an unauthorized outpost built on land that once belonged to Jalud. Once Amihai was finished, Abdullah said, Adei Ad would gain de facto legal status, becoming yet another irreversible 'fact on the ground'. Jalud's jurisdiction was shrinking all the time: of the 17,000 dunams once under its control, just 4,500 remained.

The farmers fought the settlers in the fields, and they fought them through the courts, but neither tactic worked. When the settlers planted their first olive trees in 2000, the farmer whose patch of land they had requisitioned, Mahmoud Haj Mohamed, went to court to get it back. He was armed with all the necessary deeds, yet it was not until 2013 that an Israeli judge finally acknowledged his ownership, and ordered the new olive trees be uprooted. 'Everything that has happened here since has been to avenge that,' Mahmoud said.

He led us later to a promontory at the edge of the village, and pointed up the hill to the land he had fought for. 'The olive trees the Jews planted were uprooted five years ago, but I still can't get there. We'd be shot for sure if we tried.'

Even keeping within the confines of the town was no guarantee of safety. Almost every window was protected by a sturdy grille. In the nearby village of Duma in July 2015, the Dawabsheh family were firebombed as they slept: three died, including an eighteen-month-old baby. The killer, Amiram Ben-Uliel, 21, was traced to the outpost of Adei Ad, and eventually imprisoned in 2020; in September 2022 he lost a High Court appeal.[14] 'I remember the Duma attack well because it was the day of my wedding,' Mahmoud said. 'It's just kids who do it. Hillboys, we call them. They are pigs. Even the IDF hate them, because they make things harder for the army.'

Mahmoud worried that the Duma attack could be repeated in Jalud. Settler attacks had tripled since the previous year, and the Shiloh Valley was a particular hotspot.[15] He invited us to his house, a grand old stone mansion in the centre of town. In Ottoman times, he explained, Jalud was an important administrative centre, ruled over by his ancestor, a local *mutesellim* who collected taxes for the Turks, and who had built this very house. It was a remarkable building from up close, with massive carved corbels and a flying buttress staircase that seemed to rebuke with its elegance the cheap pop-up architecture of the settlements. Mahmoud was no precious conservationist, however. He knew little about his home's history: not even the century of its construction. The majlis where he served us coffee, a tall, tiled chamber with a deeply domed ceiling, was furnished with an incongruously modern suite of ugly brown sofas.

'What matters is that the house is older than anything the Jews have built,' he said. 'It proves that we were here first, and that this is our land.'

CHAPTER SIX

Bethlehem, Qalqilya, Battir

Bursting at the Seam

As conscientious tourists on a family holiday, we had to visit Bethlehem. We paid a guide to help us jump the astonishing queues in the Church of the Nativity – Christendom's second-biggest tourist trap, after the Holy Sepulchre in Jerusalem – and photographed each other at the supposed site of Jesus's manger, a marble slab behind a curtain in a sweaty subterranean grotto. There was no sign of the humble stable of the children's imagination. The church over our heads was huge, a compound of three monasteries covering 12,000 square metres.

We moved on to the Chapel of Shepherd's Field, the spot where a herald angel announced the birth of Christ. The children sang the requisite carol – the profane British schoolchild version, naturally:

While shepherds watched the box at night, all tuned to ITV
The Angel of the Lord came down and switched to BBC.

There were, however, no flocks of sheep here, no dark pastureland over which an angel might visitate – only half-finished tower blocks sprouting on hilltops in every direction. The 'little town' the children sang about at Christmas had turned into a teeming metropolitan area of 220,000,[1] far removed from the 'deep and dreamless sleep' celebrated in that carol. The chapel itself was a modern Italian affair, in the middle of a small, parched municipal park. By the entrance, a long line of empty tourist buses waited for their passengers to return, their engines throbbing, and aircon units dripping. Parked nose to tail with their antennae-like mirrors, they resembled a column of giant killer ants, and seemed just as out of place.

Bethlehem beyond the tourist spots seemed a sad, tense place, and it was clear that the twenty-year-old separation barrier that runs through the city's northern edge, sealing off its Arab residents from the world beyond, had much to do with that. Jerusalem, with which Bethlehem has effectively been twinned for centuries, is barely 9 kilometres away. Our young guide, Mohammed, paused at the top of a hill and pointed out the Al-Aqsa mosque and the Dome of the Rock, its golden roof shimmering in the urban haze. Jerusalem's Old City, he reminded us, is a part of East Jerusalem, occupied by Israeli forces in 1967, then unilaterally annexed to Israel – illegally, according to the UN – by the Knesset's 'Jerusalem Law' of 1980.

'I have never even been to Jerusalem,' Mohammed told us with practised bitterness. 'Al-Aqsa is the third holiest Muslim site in the world after Mecca and Medina, yet I cannot pray there.'

As a young single Muslim man, he explained, he matched the profile of a terrorist, and so was automatically suspect in Israeli eyes. Until he married and had children, or until he became old, he said it wasn't even worth applying for permission to cross the border. All Palestinians complain, with good reason, that the separation barrier has divided families and whole communities, while strangling trade, investment, development and economic opportunity of all kinds. But Bethlehem was where the gravity of the barrier's social consequences was first really brought home to me.

Cut off from Jerusalem, young men like Mohammed are forced to find work locally. But work is in short supply: the local chamber of commerce claims the city has the highest unemployment rate in Palestine, at 29 per cent.[2] Pickings from tourism, the one industry thriving in Bethlehem, are also often thin, because the visitors mostly arrive, as I did with my family, on tours booked and paid for in Israel. So, although some 2.3 million tourists come to Bethlehem each year, the benefit to the local economy is marginal.

Meanwhile, for any Palestinian lucky enough to have a job in Israel, along with the permit required to commute to it, the dystopian chaos of the traffic jams at every one of the crossing points into Jerusalem is a humiliating daily reminder of their status as second-class citizens, tolerated for the cheapness of their labour, seldom welcome, always under suspicion. 'The wall is like a cold,' a friend of Bassam's once observed. 'Every sickness begins with one.'

In his Declaration of 1917, Arthur Balfour made British support for a Jewish homeland conditional on the understanding that 'nothing shall be done which may prejudice the civil and religious rights of existing non-Jewish communities in Palestine.' Instead, in the view of the activist historian Ilan Pappé, Israel has turned Palestine into 'the Biggest Prison on Earth', with a barrier that flies in the face of the values of liberal democracy, above all, the freedom of movement of goods and people, the cherished principle that underpinned the rebuilding of western Europe after the Second World War.[3]

The tourist attraction in Bethlehem that surprised us most was a hotel set up by the Bristol graffiti artist, Banksy. The 'Walled Off', as this satirical monument to the occupation is archly named, opened in 2017 to mark the centenary of the Balfour Declaration. Its location, a corner plot hard up against the barrier, was carefully chosen. The front-facing rooms open directly onto graffiti-covered concrete that blots out the sky – 'the worst view in the world', as the hotel literature proudly states. Guests come and go under the gaze of an Israeli watchtower across the street.

We found the entrance guarded by a life-size model of a chimpanzee dressed as a bellhop – an incompetent one, since the suitcase he was carrying had fallen open, its contents tumbling on the ground. The lobby was a gaudy pastiche of an English country hotel, all flowery chintz wallpaper and silk-shaded standard lamps. CCTV cameras of various sizes were mounted on one wall like a collection of big game trophies. A trio of surveillance drones, small, medium and large, flew above a fireplace like china ducks. There was a painting in the style of Constable of a classic English thatched cottage in an apple orchard, whose picturesque inhabitants were fleeing a vast armoured bulldozer.

There was also, fantastically, a life-size wax model of my great-great-great-uncle, Arthur Balfour. The man known to my great-grandmother as 'Nunky' was now a parody of an Edwardian grandee complete with wing collar, tweeds and a handlebar moustache. Seated at a desk beneath a chandelier, he was captured – of course – in the act of signing his famous Declaration. His arm was motorised, so that at the press of a button the pen in his hand jerked across the paper before him, back and forth like a barograph on the blink.

The tableau was all frightfully British. Big Ben loomed above Westminster Bridge through the fake window over Balfour's shoulder. Before him on his desk, which was gilded with the royal coat of arms, sat a dainty teacup and saucer. There was also an Empire-era map of Palestine on the wall behind him, embellished with a quote from a memorandum he wrote in 1919:

> We do not propose even to go through the form of consulting the wishes
> of the present inhabitants of the country.

I knew I was not responsible for my ancestor's actions, and so felt no familial guilt, but these words of Balfour still made me wince. The cynical disregard for Palestinian rights that they implied was the precise opposite of his public insistence on protecting those rights in his Declaration of 1917. Could he really have been so callous?

It is easy to condemn the injustices of Britain's imperial past with the benefit of hindsight – and perhaps unfair. Yet the Declaration had terrible consequences, and Balfour did bear some responsibility for those, even if they were unintended. Past injustice is still injustice. Furthermore, if the consequences of the Declaration *were* unintended by Balfour, as I wanted to believe, then that only increased the moral obligation on Britain, on whose behalf and in whose interests Balfour signed, to now try to put the wrongs right. My country, in other words, was still inculpated. I looked at Balfour's ridiculous mannequin and felt, if not exactly ashamed, a distinct and uncomfortable sense of remorse. I thought ruefully of that useful word coined in post-war Germany, *Vergangenheitsbewältigung*, 'the societal struggle to over-come the negatives of the past'. Perhaps, I thought, I was more British than I realised. The teacup on the table, after all, was one of my cultural identi-fiers, too.

It was clear that in Palestine, unlike in Britain, Balfour is more than a half-forgotten figure from history. He is regarded instead as a key architect of Arab misfortune, and thus a bogeyman of the present. This was especially so in 2017, the centenary of the Declaration when Banksy's hotel opened. The actual anniversary, 2 November, was marked by street demonstrations not just in Palestine but also in London, Dublin, New York. In Bethlehem, the demonstrators marched behind an effigy of Balfour very like the one at the Walled Off. The footage of their march is still viewable on YouTube: chanting furiously, they stop before a line of grim-faced Israeli soldiers, where one of them removes a shoe and beats Nunky's face with it. In Ramallah, 3,000 people marched on the British Council office, where another effigy was burned, side by side with one of then Prime Minister Theresa May.[4] I had not previously appreciated that I was descended from the Arab-Palestinian version of Guy Fawkes.

The real business of the Walled Off was in the back: a small and angry exhibition that documented without satirical spin the injustices of the occupation. It included many revealing details about Israeli attitudes to Palestinian water supply. My eye was drawn to a photograph of a rooftop water tank that was riddled with bullet holes. 'Palestinian water tanks are often plastic, not metal,' observed the caption, because 'plastic tanks are easier to repair when bored Israeli soldiers shoot holes in them.'

The exhibition focused, naturally, on the separation barrier, with quotes from UN Resolution ES-10/15 of 2004 – the one that most unequivocally asserts its illegality under international law[5] – although its overall target was broader than that. 'The UN calls any system of racial segregation Apartheid, and regards it as a crime against humanity,' I read, next to a set of aerial photo-graphs revealing the Escheresque craziness of Israel's segregated road system.

A section on the hardware of state suppression was especially attention-grabbing. The IDF arsenal, much of it operable by remote control, boasts 'skunk trucks' that blast rebellious neighbourhoods with almost indelible chemical filth; 'venom launchers' that can drown whole villages in tear gas; and a Humvee-mounted weapon called The Scream (also known as the 'Shofar', after the ram's horn blown during Jewish religious ceremonies) that emits a sound loud enough to make ears bleed. There was also a model of a mini-cannon stone thrower, manufactured by the Israeli firm R.D. Peled, which described it as 'an innovative solution' to the problem of rock-slinging teenagers during the First Intifada. It seemed a long way indeed from the approach to retribution advocated in the Old Testament: the machine, capable of firing 600 stones a minute, threatened to take a hundred eyes for an eye. But perhaps the company could not be blamed. According to an interview that I looked up later, Peled – a clever inventor, and a patriot of the old school – had only developed the machine because he was asked to do so by the IDF, which bought sixty of them.

Responding to threat with disproportionate force, the so-called 'Dahiya doctrine', has long been the IDF way. The tactic is named after a Hezbollah-dominated neighbourhood of Beirut in which it was applied during the Lebanon War of 2006; it was formally adopted by the army in 2008. Peled, according to his interviewer, was a 'bit of a naif', a Professor Branestawm character who regarded his invention not as an instrument of dispropor-tionate force but as 'something that is humane, because the stone-throwers would be acquired in place of weapons' and was a 'machine . . . to prevent people being killed'.[6]

Worse than any of this, perhaps, was the exhibition's assertion that Palestine has become a vital testing ground for Israel's lucrative arms export industry, and that as a consequence Israel deliberately perpetuates the occu-pation out of economic self-interest. There was a damning quote from a government minister, Binyamin Ben-Eliezer, who observed in 2013: 'People like to buy things that have been tested. If Israel sells weapons, they have been tested, tried out . . . it brings Israel billions of dollars.'

Is the Jewish state really as cynical as Banksy believes? The IDF, I was relieved to read, had discontinued their use of R.D. Peled's fearsome mini-cannon – but I knew that was not the case with others of the weapons described in the exhibition. It seemed a wonder that Israel's authorities had put up with Banksy's hotel for as long as they already had.

If the separation barrier made Bethlehem feel claustrophobic, the effect at Qalqilya, the most westerly town in the West Bank, was akin to asphyxia. Once a bustling market town of 55,000, Qalqilya's own residents now describe it, Ilan Pappé-style, as 'the biggest prison in the world'. The border has been pushed eastwards to the town's north and south, so that today Qalqilya is hemmed in on three sides with only two ways in or out, one via a road leading due east, the other via a tunnel to the south. Both entrances are fortified, with military checkpoints at either end that can and often do close without warning. The territory within is bottle-shaped, with Israel in total control of the cork.

Bassam and I went to look at the barrier in the company of an official from the Mayor's office, another Mohammed, who led us down Qalqilya's high street to a point where it simply peters out. There were no cars, no people. Weeds pushed up through the disintegrating concrete. There were coils of rusting barbed wire along the roadsides, raggedy palm trees, and mounds of fly-tipped rubbish rotting in a thin, warm rain.

The desolation was eloquent. This was once a major trunk road to Tel Aviv, the natural market for Qalqilya's traditional workshop industry. But nothing had passed this way since 2004, prompting a disastrous 90 per cent drop in trade. Productivity halved, driving up unemployment, poverty and desperation, even as the population grew. The town has a reputation for terrorism, and it wasn't hard to see why that might be.[7]

We were so far west here that the air smelled salty. The coast is barely 20 kilometres away, so close that we had to shout above the noise of jets descending on Herzliya Airport. It was much hotter and lower than Ramallah, a semi-tropical region dotted with plantations of guava and banana. We were in the mountain aquifer's discharge zone, where irrigation should not have been a problem. The governorate, encompassing more than thirty farming villages spread over 176,000 dunums, is blessed with 76 working wells. Qalqilya, in one interpretation of the Arabic, means 'gurgling of water'.[8] But as I was to hear, the occupation, and above all the separation barrier, has cancelled out the hydrous plenty of this town.

There was a short bend in the road, and the barrier loomed into view. Its height was astonishing from up close, a sheer curtain of serrated grey, 8 metres tall. Along its top, for good measure, ran an inward-leaning pelmet of chicken wire connected to a motion-activated alarm system. A mushroom-shaped observation post poked up beyond, radiating menace and intent, the roof above its dark glass window slits crowded with floodlights, aerials and a remote-control CCTV camera, just like on the T-shirts sold at the Banksy hotel.

'We are in a miserable situation here,' observed Mohammed. Israeli propagandists tend to play down the size and permanence of their boundary construction, which they prefer to call a security fence, a barrier, or a 'line': anything but a wall. The Palestinians have other ideas: to them it is simply *jidar al-fasl al-'unsuri*, the 'wall of apartheid'. This war of words is fought all along the border, all the time. Israel, for example, generally refers to its heavily fortified border crossings as 'terminals' rather than 'checkpoints', as the Arabs do.

In most rural areas, which is to say, along 95 per cent of its 700-kilometre length, the barrier is indeed more like a fence than a wall. What the IDF calls a 'multi-layered fence system' relies heavily on barbed wire: two rows of it, 60 metres apart, with a third fence in the middle mounted with motion sensors; the barrier also features an anti-vehicle ditch, a strip of smooth sand to betray footprints, and patrol roads to either side. In certain hotspots, or in urban areas like Bethlehem and here in Qalqilya, the barrier comprises interlocking sections of concrete up to 8 metres high: not a fence but, unequivocally, a wall.

Foreign graffiti artists had been as busy here as in Bethlehem. At least one of them had had the same initial response as mine: *This definitely is not a fence*, I read. Some scrawls compared Zionism to Nazism, in reference to that popular troublesome trope, the mystery of how the victimized become victimizers. There were mentions of Belsen and Auschwitz, and the phrase *Palestine pays for Shoah*, the Hebrew word for the Holocaust. The wall itself reminded me, powerfully, of the Iron Curtain in Berlin, and again I was not alone: *This wall is sooo 1989*, I read, and *This wall will definitely fall*.

As a schoolboy in the early 1980s, I had chosen the Berlin Wall as my subject for an O-Level history project, and concluded, even then, that it could not last. History, I argued, showed that people eventually find ways around them, through them, under them. The redundancy of Hadrian's Wall, the Antonine Wall and the Great Wall of China all proved it. Bassam laughed as I explained how I vindicated my teenaged thesis in November 1989, when I flew out to Berlin with a rucksack, hammer and chisel, and joined the jubilant crowds as they reduced their wall to rubble; everyone in my family got a chunk of graffiti-splashed German concrete as a Christmas present that year.

Mohammed wanted to talk about drainage. Qalqilya is built on land that slopes gently towards the ocean. The rains of winter that don't sink into the ground are naturally carried westwards on the surface. The Israelis, Mohammed explained, had anticipated the wall's effect on surface water when they built it, and inserted a series of small square sluices to let the floodwater through. The sluices, however, contained metal grilles to prevent human traffic, and quickly became blocked with flotsam; and no Palestinian was willing to risk getting shot by crawling in to clear it. The IDF, for their part, couldn't care less, and weren't prepared to do the work themselves. Periodic floods were therefore the norm. Mohammed led us a short distance along the wall to one of the sluice gates, which was clogged with evil-smelling slime and rubbish. The ground for 50 metres about was water-logged and dotted with plastic detritus where floodwater had slowly receded. In bad winters, Mohammed said, the flow backed up so far that it flooded the town. A nearby girls' secondary school had on occasion been forced to close.

'Palestinians are like water,' Bassam mused, thinking still about the Berlin Wall. 'We can find a way around any obstacle, any barrier. We have a word, *leffe*: an alternative route. If there is no leffe available, we know how to wait. Then the water builds up, and the barrier is breached.'

We went to meet Qalqilya's governor, Rafa' Rawajbeh. He was a dapper middle-aged man with the luxuriously furnished office of a powerful appa-ratchik, one of only sixteen governors in the PA machine. His staff seemed to treat him with striking deference, treading lightly and speaking in hushed tones. As we sat down in matching leather armchairs beneath portraits of Abbas and Arafat, with a flag on a pole between us, an official photographer stepped forward to record the occasion for posterity.

I soon learned that securing the town's water supply was one of the mayor's biggest headaches, a major part of his job. The complaints poured out of him, faster than I could write them down. He had to deal with winter floods caused by the wall, and with wadis polluted by sewage from illegal settlements uphill to the east. Above all, his governorate didn't have enough water, either of the domestic or the agricultural kind, despite the region's natural, 'gurgling' wetness. The dryer, eastern half of his governorate was dependent on water pumped in by Mekorot, which was preposterous, in his view. As governor, he said, he wrestled with the injustice of the Oslo Accords every single day. 'If we could build our own network, we'd be fine. We are sitting on top of a lake in Qalqilya. But Israel blocks all new water infrastructure on principle, and monitors all the wells that we do have, and restricts how deep we can drill, and how much we can extract.'

His greatest challenge, perhaps, was the administration of his section of the seam zone, where several thousand Qalqilyans still live or farm. The southern Israeli salient, he said, was solidifying all the time, with 54 kilometres of wall already built, and new sections of it still going up. Before 2014, some outlying villages were no more than a ten-minute drive from Qalqilya. Now, in some cases, getting to market required an Israeli permit and a journey of two hours. The town's isolation was deepening with every passing year. The governorate already contained 25 Israeli settlements; some 36,000 dunams of Qalqilya's land, a fifth of the total area, equating to 70 per cent of all the land cultivable, had been 'lost'. As I had heard elsewhere in the West Bank, Governor Rawajbeh was convinced that Israel's strategy was simply to grab as much land as it could. 'Their goal is to make it so hard for farmers in the seam zone that they leave. Then, once the land is unused, they are entitled to take it, according to old Ottoman law'.

One of the principal methods the Israelis deployed to discourage farmers, he went on, was to restrict access to groundwater in the seam zone wherever they could. He said he had just come from a meeting with colleagues from the Palestinian ministries of agriculture and energy, where they had discussed the upgrade of six wells in the seam zone. 'The pumps run on diesel, which is expensive,' he explained. 'We've been trying for years to convert them to electricity, which is half the price, but the Israelis won't give us permission.' Combatting obstruction like this, he said, was a major part of his daily routine: the tedious reality of the Oslo-derived 'hydro-colonialism' that Abdulrahman Tamimi described in Ramallah.

The interview came to an end with an absurd formal handshake for the camera, before we were dispatched on a longer tour of the area with his employee, Mohammed. From a viewing platform on Qalqilya's outskirts, Bassam and I looked down into the seam zone, where three Israeli tractors were at work ploughing a field: the expropriation process in action. The wall through the town centre had given way here to a metal mesh fence, with a gate set into it guarded by three Israeli conscripts. A stooped old man in a yellow baseball cap was waiting by the gate, an impassive queue of one. Mohammed explained that he was the owner of a tiny orchard on the other side. With special permission from the Israelis, he was allowed in to water his trees at set times of the day, at eight, one and five o'clock. It was now five minutes to one. 'Don't talk to him while the Israelis are watching,' Mohammed warned. 'They will only detain him for questioning and cause him trouble.'

The orchard owner and I carefully looked away from each other; although, in truth, I hardly needed to ask what he thought of his situation. The humiliation of the occupation, the petty cruelties of its bureaucracy, the hundreds of hours wasted, the careful suppression of indignation learned over half a lifetime of this daily rigmarole – all were etched into the lines of his cracked and sunburned face. This gate, Mohammed said, was one of seventy-seven such gates up and down the border that led to Palestinian farmland in the seam zone. This one was unusual only in that it was opened up to the landowners on a daily basis: the great majority of seam zone gates were opened far less often than that.[9]

I looked over at the conscripts, two men and a fresh-faced woman whose glossy pigtails made her look too young to be carrying a gun. She laughed and smiled, preening in the attention of her comrades, who exuded combat chic in their mirror shades. The old man seemed completely invisible to them.

I understood that these conscripts were reprising a role that was not of their devising. They were bit players in a piece of theatre, a tired old show called *The Occupation* that had been running since long before they were born. So, were they guilty of inhumanity or cruelty towards the farmer at the gate? Watching them made me think of Hannah Arendt's famous phrase, 'the banality of evil', which she coined to describe the Nazi bureaucrat Adolf Eichmann at his trial in 1961. Eichmann, she controversially argued, was not the anti-Semitic monster of popular imagination but something even more sinister, a new type of killer, a 'desk murderer' motivated not by ideology but by careerism. As a small cog in the machine of the Nazi state, he 'neither considered the significance of his deeds nor accepted responsibility for them'. His crime, she argued, was 'thoughtlessness', an inability to think from the other's point of view.[10]

What did these young Israelis even see when they looked at the border they were guarding? Its appearance literally depended on which side one examined it from. In many of those places where it is an actual wall, the Israel-facing sides are painted with pretty patterns to make them less of an eyesore, in striking contrast to the abrupt concrete cliffs that typically mar the views from the Palestine side. In some other places – where it passes very close to new Israeli settlements, for instance – the barrier becomes a giant ha-ha, specifically designed to vanish into the landscape when viewed from the western side. In such cases, it can only be seen at all from Palestine.

'The wall doesn't just lock Palestinians in,' wrote Mariam Barghouti, an astute young Palestinian former student of international relations at Edinburgh University. 'It locks Israeli citizens out of the truth of what their government is doing. It shields Israelis not just from Palestinians, but from the visuals of what the occupation looks like – even from its very existence. It's a wall, but it's also a mask. The Israeli side of the apartheid wall is neatly tucked behind trees and colourful murals, serving as a cloak for Israel, a mental siege that ensures that Israelis as a population are not confronted with the product of their oppression. In other words, this curtain is strategically arranged to not only impede Palestinians, but to conceal from the Israeli populace what is happening to us Palestinians.'[11]

It isn't only Israelis who are invited not to see the barrier. Its impact is minimized as much as possible for foreign tourists and officials, too, almost as a part of some international marketing exercise – because of course it is harder to criticize something one has not felt or seen. Bassam related how Nicolas Sarkozy was once asked what he thought of the barrier at a press conference in Ramallah. The then French President, who had just been wafted there via Qalandiya in an armoured motorcade, along roads entirely cleared of the usual traffic, confessed that he had been so busy on his phone that he hadn't even noticed the border as he passed through.

Bassam and I said goodbye to our guide and drove on to Azzun Atma, one of Qalqilya's outlying villages. The community here had suffered greatly from the barrier, which effectively cut it in two when construction began in 2002. Israel's security regulations constantly vary, but for many years ten local families were only able to get in or out of their village via a checkpoint, armed with a special, hard-to-obtain permit, during set hours that were liable to change without warning. They were classic victims of the seam zone – and there are still hundreds if not thousands of families in the same invidious position, all along the West Bank's border.[12]

The school at Azzun Atma had been in the news recently. It was located at the bottom of a steep hill, the top of which was occupied by a heavily walled, 6,000-strong Israeli settlement called Sha'arei Tikva – one of four settlements that surround Azzun Atma on every side. According to news reports, Sha'arei Tikva's residents had been caught dumping sewage over the wall directly into the Palestinians' school playground. If true, it was a neat and flagrant example of the literal weaponization of water of a kind that I was keen to document.

The reports, though, turned out to be false. In the playground, a council official revealed that the settlers had not 'dumped' anything over the wall. Sha'arei Tikva's sewage system had, rather, been overwhelmed by the recent spate of winter rain, causing effluent to seep out wherever gravity took it. A play area planted with trees at the back of the school had undoubtedly been spoiled. The ground was still coated with drying brown sludge that hummed with flies. The official accused the Israelis of letting this happen deliberately, yet there was no proof of malice. It seemed just as likely to me that shoddy urban planning was to blame, compounded by the almost total lack of communication between neighbours – and, no doubt, by the construction of the immense wall between them, which had inevitably interfered with natural groundwater flow. The school, the official finally revealed, had been having trouble with Sha'arei Tikvan sewage for almost thirty years.

It was a storm in a teacup; but that had not stopped the town's worthies from dressing it up and playing to the media gallery. They knew that sewage-dumping settlers would make good copy. Later, when I researched the story more thoroughly, I found that foreign journalists like me had been turning up for years to report on it. I felt as foolish as a dog answering a whistle; because this story, about Jews sneakily subverting Arab water supply, came straight out of the Palestine propaganda playbook.

For example, in the hot summer of 2016, Mohammed Abbas himself complained to the European Parliament that a group of West Bank rabbis had called for the poisoning of Palestinian wells.[13] The allegation was completely unfounded, and Abbas later retracted it, amid Israeli protests that he had repeated an old anti-Semitic canard – which indeed he had. Jews have been maliciously accused of sabotaging wells for centuries; the Black Death that swept Europe in the mid-fourteenth century was some-times blamed on Jewish well poisoners. In Basel and Strasbourg in 1349, hundreds of Jews were burned alive for this purported crime.

I wondered, cynically, what the council would do if the sewage problem at Azzun Atma were ever to be fixed. It was, in one respect, an important asset to their town, because publicity helped to elicit international sympathy and, by extension, aid money. It seemed to me that this was a way to profit indirectly from the occupation, which made the council dependent, in a sense, on the bitter old status quo. The tide of excrement leaking into Azzun Atma's playground, year after year, suddenly seemed the perfect symbol of that sorry situation.

Bassam drove me to Battir, an ancient hill village famed for its terraced irrigation system, a few kilometres west of Bethlehem on the border south-west of Jerusalem. We stopped en route at Abu Dis, a down-at-heel town of 12,000, which lies on the eastern slopes of the Mount of Olives – the dark side of that famous site, seldom if ever seen by tourists, or Jews. We were delayed in the town centre by a giant flood in a dip in the road where rain-water had been dammed up by the border wall, which runs 8 metres high along the western edge of town, blocking out the sun. Five minutes further on, we were delayed again, and almost caught in the crossfire of a shoot-out between a fugitive and the PA police, firing across the road at each other from the windows of their respective cars. We ducked our heads until the bad guy sped off, with the police car in pursuit.

Abu Dis, Bassam explained almost apologetically, has a reputation for lawlessness in Palestine. The town was classified as Area B at Oslo, with its outlying areas designated as Area C. Responsibility for security, therefore, remains with the IDF. Civil policing matters, however, are not a military priority, while the PA police, with whom the Israelis theoretically cooperate, in practice have very limited jurisdiction in the town. So, Abu Dis had long been under-policed, which in combination with its size, its proximity to East Jerusalem, and its accessibility to the rest of the West Bank, made it a favoured hideout for criminals from all over Palestine.

The Kushner peace plan of 2020 proposed, extraordinarily, to make this desperate place the new Palestinian capital, complete with a new US embassy. This was a corollary of America's earlier transferral of their embassy to Israel, in 2018, from Tel Aviv to (west) Jerusalem: a move that effectively endorsed Israel's longstanding claim that Jerusalem, east and west, is Israel's capital: the 'eternal, undivided capital of the Jewish people', as Netanyahu put it. The problem with Israel's claim is that the Palestinians regard East Jerusalem as *their* future capital, pending implementation of a two-state solution; a notion that is endorsed by the UN, as well as by the Oslo Accords. The Palestinians were duly outraged by the US embassy move from Tel Aviv, and all that it signalled about Washington's priorities.

Naming Abu Dis as Palestine's future capital was perhaps Kushner's attempt at conciliation. It appeared, on paper at least, to give the Palestinians what they want, because Abu Dis is so close to East Jerusalem that it is effectively a suburb of it. He even suggested that Arabs might want to consider renaming Abu Dis 'Al Quds', 'the Holy One', the traditional Arabic term for Jerusalem.

The problem was that although the town may be a suburb of Jerusalem, it is emphatically not Jerusalem, with nothing that can be called 'holy' about it, as I had just seen. Part of it is, literally, a dump: for thirty years, half of Jerusalem's rubbish was brought to a notoriously badly managed landfill site on seam zone land expropriated from the town.[14] Kushner's proposal was not even original, but a rehash of an idea first mooted in 1997, when it was rejected by Yasser Arafat. I understood, now, why Kushner's suggestion had prompted such derision in the local media. Even Israeli journalists rolled their eyes at the ignorance it revealed. As one commentator remarked: 'Abu Dis is not Abu Dat'.[15]

In contrast to the grime of Abu Dis, Battir, when we reached it, was the most beautiful village I had yet seen. A well-known tourist attraction, it was so perfectly preserved that in 2014 it was granted world heritage status by UNESCO, a status deliberately sought by its residents to help hold back the eastward tide of settlers and concretization.

UNESCO's decision was immediately controversial. Israeli historians grumbled that Battir was once the headquarters of the Bar Kokhba revolt against Emperor Hadrian in AD 135, and was therefore just as much a part of Jewish heritage as of the Arab one. Israelis have long accused the Paris-based organization of pro-Palestinian and anti-Semitic bias – indeed, Israel quit UNESCO in protest at this in 2011 – and Battir's overnight transformation into a cultural untouchable only seemed to prove their point. It was intriguing to discover that Battir is twinned with Luton, which is not a city often associated with cultural heritage; although it is home to one of England's most active branches of the Palestine Solidarity Campaign.

Whether Arab or Jewish, the village's long tradition of resistance was not in question. Its Arab inhabitants mostly fled during the war of 1948, but a handful stayed on, led by the local hero, Mustafa Hassan. Armed with dummy rifles made of broom-handles, and by lighting candles and moving cardboard cut outs in the windows, they tricked the advancing Jewish militiamen into thinking that the village was still occupied. A military assault was averted and, when hostilities ended, the armistice line was set along the old Jerusalem-to-Jaffa railway line that still runs along the valley at the bottom of the hill. The villagers were later permitted to go on farming their land on the other side of the valley in return for protecting passing train traffic. For many years, this section of the border was not even fenced, a rare arrangement in the seam zone.

Battir's centrepiece is a spring-fed, stone-cut rectangular cistern dating to Roman times, although Nadia Hassan, Mustafa's doughty, elderly daughter, and the chatelaine of a stone-arched cultural centre we visited, claimed it was an upgrade of a cistern much older than that. Irrigation, in any event, was what Battir had always been about. Water from the cistern is still fed through an immaculately excavated maze of canals to the crops and fruit trees on the terraces below – an irrigation technique, Nadia insisted, that had been practised here since early Canaanite times, 4,000 years ago.

An assistant, another aged lady in a traditionally embroidered *thobe*, produced a yardstick made of reed and thorns called a 'sakaron', the means by which Battir's eight farming clans still divvy up the irrigation water in the cistern. The thorns stuck in the side of the reed could be adjusted to match the total amount of water available as it varied from season to season, and from day to day. It was, I could see, a flexible, fair, and deceptively sophisticated system of water allocation. 'There's no need for high-tech meters or electric power,' said the sakaron lady. 'Our way is more trustworthy because it is so simple, and because everyone can *see* it.'

Nadia said that the westward-sloping hills of Judea were once dotted with villages like Battir. The canals on show were only a small example of an irrigation tradition developed over millennia. In Nadia's eyes their continuing function legitimized Palestine's historic claim to the entire region. Her passion for the Battir system – she described herself as another 'cultural defender' – hinted that the connection with water was something visceral. The system amounted to a kind of touchstone for her, an almost sacred interface with the land.

Battir's terraces, I noted, were full of healthy olive trees. This famously longevous plant, which can thrust its roots 6 metres down into the soil, is perfectly adapted to survive in a water-starved land. Its enormous root system creates a strong physical bond with the earth that is mirrored by the deep, almost romantic attachment the fellahin traditionally feel for the land of their forefathers. The olive tree is, therefore, the best-known emblem of

Palestinian nationhood. Steadfastness, or 'samoud', the ability to endure hardship with calm and patience, is considered a vital national attribute. As I once heard the novelist Raja Shehadeh argue, samoud is perhaps the only sane response to the unbeatable military might of the occupation; and Palestinians see this quality reflected in the hardiness of their olive trees, too.

Mustafa Hassan, the hero of '48, explained precisely what olive trees symbolize in a eulogy he wrote in the 1950s called *The Long-Living and Lasting Tree*, an imagined conversation between an olive tree and an autumn tulip. The tree tells the flower:

> I am the daughter of hardship, brutality and animosity as well as the friend of time. I grow amidst misery and I am rejuvenated in hardship, and I give when times are tough and the world is poor, just as you grow in moisture, feel fresh in the shade, and bloom in the dew. Do you not know that these emerald-like tears have a body and soul?

In an overwhelmingly agrarian economy such as Palestine's,[16] the value of olive trees is more than merely symbolic. As recently as 2014, an estimated 80,000 farmers were dependent on the export of olive oil. Until the 1990s, schools and universities routinely closed during harvest season to allow the young to help with the picking. Hardline West Bank settlers, who know full well what olive trees signify, vandalize them so frequently that it has become routine. In 2013, a year of especial Israeli-Arab tension, the UN reported that some 11,000 Palestinian-owned trees were hacked, burned or uprooted.[17]

From Battir, Bassam and I made our circuitous way to Walaja, the neighbouring border village 2 kilometres to the east, the home of a giant olive tree that Palestinians claim is the oldest in the world. It is a symbol of such national importance that the PA pays a man to guard it, a farmer called Salah Abu Issa, whose family has owned the land it stands on for generations.

Salah was a bespectacled man with a thick greying beard that matched the black and white stripes on his tracksuit. Well used to visiting journalists, he had played host to a film crew from Al Jazeera that very morning. He explained that the original village of Walaja, on the other side of the green line beyond the railway line, was evacuated during the Nakba, and eventually demolished. Not a stone of it remained, he said. But the villagers had refused to abandon the area, and had built a new Walaja here on the Jordanian side of the armistice line, on the third of their land that remained to them.

After years of stasis, however, the seam zone was expanding, and the border was advancing again. A new fence had recently cut the village off from Ain Haniye, its traditional spring down the hill, which had been turned into a picnic spot for Jewish day-trippers from west Jerusalem; and now the Israelis were seeking to extend the fence even further. New Walaja was at grave risk of encirclement, and if that happened, Salah thought, the village would soon go the same way as the old.

He skipped ahead of us down a steeply terraced orchard, pausing as he went to turn a two-handed valve wheel set into the ground, opening a sluice from a spring above. 'Ain Jowezi spring,' he specified. 'We used to have twenty-five springs in Walaja. This is the only one left.'

We followed the trickle down. The orchard ended abruptly at a strong mesh fence that snaked to our left and right, above and alongside a smart new asphalt road – entirely empty of traffic – cut into the hillside. Salah explained that it was constructed for the exclusive use of motorized IDF patrols.

The famous olive tree occupied the whole of the bottom terrace, so close to the wire that its branches almost brushed it. It was, literally, a bulwark against Israeli encroachment. Salah presented us to it with exaggerated reverence, as though we were entering the presence of a king. It was, certainly, a monarch among trees. Dendrochronologists from Italy, he claimed, had declared the tree to be 5,500 years old.[18] At 12 metres high, with a canopy 25 metres across, it was an organism of many gnarled trunks that grew in a circle, forming a stockade big enough for six men to squeeze into. The tree produced half a ton of olives a year, Salah said, and it was still growing: Salah showed us a green shoot rising from the base that he stroked tenderly with the back of his knuckle, as though tickling a cat. 'This sprouted seventy days ago,' he said. 'It is the same age as my son Ibrahim.'

We drank tea in the shade of the canopy from a flask that Salah produced. Afterwards, he went a little distance away in order to pray. He seemed wholly at peace in his garden, as zen as a Buddhist priest, although his life could hardly be described as blissful. Like the Bedouin I had met in the Jordan Valley, his family had once been shepherds, with a flock of more than a hundred. But he had been forced to sell off his flock for lack of grazing on this side of the fence, and now he only had six sheep left. For now, he survived on his tree-guarding stipend from the Palestinian Authority, and by selling olive oil and honey and – he added pointedly – 'by making lunch for visitors'.

Salah exhibited great samoud, although not everyone's resistance to the occupation was entirely passive. Walaja's Arabs, he said, organized regular demonstrations along the route of the proposed fence extension. The protests were temporarily on hold because the route had been put out 'for consultation'. On a scrap of wall by the orchard path I spotted the stencilled, stylised face of a well-known martyr called Bassel al-Araj, alongside his most famous slogan, *Our weapons will not rust*. A one-time native of Walaja, al-Araj was an educated man, a pharmacist and tour guide as well as an activist, who was imprisoned by the PA in 2016 for planning armed attacks on Israel. On his release he went on the run, but was killed in 2017 following a two-hour shoot-out in Al-Bireh with the IDF.

In January 2019, Palestine applied to UNESCO to expand the heritage status already granted to neighbouring Battir to include 'Palestinian Olives and Vines – Cultural Landscape of South Jerusalem'. The Israeli right perceived this as effrontery. Shimon Samuels, the Wiesenthal Center's observer at UNESCO, accused Palestine of 'aggression against interfaith harmony', and called the World Heritage Committee 'a Palestinian instrument for ID theft of [Jewish] narratives'.[19]

This enchanted spot by the ancient olive tree was not as peaceful as it appeared. The Palestinian embrace of samoud perhaps keeps a lid on it, but the possibility of violent conflict remains, lurking just beneath the surface, forever threatening to burst at the seam.

CHAPTER SEVEN

The Road to Rawabi

An Alternative Palestine

T HE WEST BANK, perhaps even more than Gaza, was a puzzle. I had witnessed Arab hardship almost everywhere I went, the frustration and anger of an occupied people compounded, often, by poverty; a condition of unhappiness that felt all the more unjust when compared to the neighbours, the occupying power from next door. I had seen how Israel extended its territory at Palestinian expense. I had also proved, at least to my satisfaction, that Israel's exploitation of a flawed water settlement, agreed at Oslo, remains critical to its strategy of territorial domination.

I still struggled, though, to see the bigger picture, of where Israel thought or hoped their strategy might lead. There seemed little risk of a third intifada, at least for the time being. The overwhelming majority of Palestinians I met had no fight left in them for that. Ahmad Yaqubi, among others, described his people as 'beaten'. Yet the human misery caused by the occupation is hardly good for Israel's security. The region's long and unforgotten history of uprising and war points to what could easily happen again. I kept circling back to the same question: is there really no acceptable alternative, for Israel, to keeping Palestine in a permanent state of suppression? Just as important, what do Palestinians want for themselves? In a fair and peaceful

Israel-Palestine, what might they become? Do they not have the potential to lift themselves out of poverty and despair?

Poor farmers like Salah Abu Issah in Walaja conform to a Western idea of Palestinians as a collection of long-suffering peasants. I had already seen plenty to dispel that stereotype, but nothing negated it so emphatically as my visit to Beit Falasteen, 'the House of Palestine', the private palatial home of Munib al-Masri, perched high on Mount Gerizim overlooking the West Bank city of Nablus. Its billionaire owner set out to demonstrate what Palestinians are capable of when he built his house; and everyone who sees it for the first time is obliged to recalibrate what they thought they knew.

Beit Falasteen is an almost perfect copy of *La Rotonda*, a hilltop villa near Vicenza designed by Andrea Palladio in the sixteenth century. Its opulence is in the sharpest contrast to its location: Nablus, the West Bank's second city, is synonymous in many minds with poverty, discontent and political violence. Al-Masri's gardens overlook the jumbled rooftops of Balata, the West Bank's largest refugee camp, where PA policemen once fought gun battles with militants from the Martyrs' Brigades. During the Second Intifada, Nablus produced more suicide bombers than anywhere else.[1]

The Duke of Nablus, as al-Masri is nicknamed, made his fortune in the oil business. He went on to co-found and chair Padico, the Palestinian Development and Investment Company, with personal holdings said to account for a third of the entire Palestinian economy – 'the richest Palestinian in the world'.[2] He was attending a conference in the Middle East when I emailed to ask for an interview, but he generously invited me to visit his home anyway; a housekeeper would show me around.

My tour began in the basement. When the foundations for the villa were being laid in the 1990s, the masons uncovered the remains of a fifth-century Byzantine monastery, the mosaic floor of which al-Masri preserved and incorporated into a museum. The former presence of Byzantine monks was no great surprise because Mount Gerizim is a holy place, still considered sacred by Samaritans, who hold that this is where God asked Abraham to sacrifice his son Isaac, rather than at Temple Mount in Jerusalem as Jews traditionally believe; a tiny community of Samaritans, one of only two surviving in the world, clings on in a village nearby.

The monastery's location was dictated – of course – by the presence of groundwater. Al-Masri's masons had discovered and then excavated a sizeable well in the grounds of the old monastery; a dry one, since the local water table had dropped long ago. I descended a wooden staircase to its sandy bottom, brushing my fingers across the smooth curved brickwork of its sides, still perfectly aligned despite the passage of 1,600 years.

In keeping with its antecedents, the main body of the house was cruciform, with a soaring, cathedral-like rotunda above its intersection, presided over from the very centre by a statue of Hercules in a lion skin. The four grand salons leading off it were no less impressive. I tiptoed into the library. Motes of dust swirled in a shaft of sunlight released when the housekeeper cracked open a shutter, revealing a delicate pair of French spiral stairs that led up a wall of manuscripts and first editions, filling the air with their scent of vellum and old leather.

Outside, I wandered through a maze of balustered white stairs and collonaded terraces, and down an avenue of cypress trees. There were statues of lions and rampant stallions, a gothic temple, a dovecote from the south of France, and a small amphitheatre that overlooked the whole of Nablus. Behind the gardens in all directions lay groves of olive trees, 5,000 of them according to the housekeeper, as numerous as the books in his employer's fabulous library.

I didn't quite know what to make of Beit Falasteen. The house was, in its way, a splendid symbol of defiance against the occupation, an in-your-face display of the Palestine that might have been, and perhaps could yet become. A room in the basement next to the museum was full of murals illustrating Palestine's struggle, alongside a list of the hundreds of towns and villages destroyed or lost to Israel since 1948. In almost every interview I had read, al-Masri justified his palace by insisting that it was built not only for him, but for all his countrymen.[3] Yet its extravagance sat uneasily in such proximity to the squalor and poverty of the city below. Balata refugee camp was visible from every seat in al-Masri's reproduction amphitheatre.

I remembered a disparaging observation of Abdulrahman Tamimi's, that Israel wanted to 'recreate a piece of Europe in the Middle East'. Al-Masri, it seemed, wanted to beat the Israelis at their own game – although he had not, in fact, slavishly copied a gem of European culture when he built his palace, but subtly Arabized it. The grand salons, for instance, were named after different Palestinian cities; and the cupola itself, built 10 metres taller than the Vicenza original – an improvement, in al-Masri's reported opinion – was embellished with roundels bearing the different names for Allah picked out in gold. It was as though he, like Israel, wished to reclaim Palestine's place in the family of Mediterranean nations. The fantastic marriage of styles was perhaps a means of breaching the separation barrier, of negating the isolated otherness of Palestinians, of demolishing the wall in its owner's mind.

But there were obstacles to al-Masri's project if this was indeed his intention, not least of which was the question of his palace's water supply. His gardens contained a descending series of swimming pools – built of stone imported from Andalusia, the housekeeper boasted – but they were not looking their best today because they were empty. The garden's centre-piece overlooking the pools, meanwhile, was a wrought-iron glasshouse reminiscent of London's Kew Gardens. Built in the 1860s, it was once given by Napoleon III to the Italian contralto opera singer, Marietta Alboni. It was hot inside but not humid, as greenhouses are supposed to be, and its ornate shelves were almost bare. At one end I found a scalloped marble basin with a delicate brass tap for pot plants, but nothing came out when I turned the handle.

It felt an apt metaphor for the whole place. Water has always been the basis of human civilization – in Byzantine times, in the Belle Époque, and in the present – yet it seemed that not even al-Masri could quite overcome its shortage here. Mount Gerizim was not the Venetian countryside. The view through the glasshouse windows was of dun-coloured desert hills. Water was naturally scarce, and there appeared to be no generous connection to the mains to make up for it, as there was for Israeli hilltop settlers.

Al-Masri's ambition was magnificent, but in the end the dislocation of this piece of classical European culture to a holy desert hilltop did not feel comfortable. Despite the Arabic twists in its content and design, the

House of Palestine looked and felt to me as out of place as the marooned aquarium-ship in Ramallah.

There were other and arguably better visions of the sort of country Palestine could become. Al-Masri had a kinsman, Bashar, whose wealth and influence are almost as fabulous as his cousin's, and who had used them to pursue a different kind of project. Since 2010, Bashar al-Masri has been building an entire city, called Rawabi, the first planned city in Palestine, intended eventually to house 40,000 people.

A short taxi ride north of Ramallah, a kilometre or two beyond the university campus at Birzeit, I found a cluster of new tower blocks and construction cranes topping a promontory among the sheer barren hills. For twenty years, the West Bank's high ground had been the exclusive preserve of Israeli settlement builders. Rawabi – 'The Hills', in Arabic – represented another attempt to beat them at their own game. Like many Israeli settlements I had seen, this pop-up city in the wilderness seemed as incongruous as a colony on the moon. Indeed, its detractors – and Rawabi has a few – dub it 'the Palestinian Modi'in', a planned Israeli city of 93,000 considered so very typical of the new settler architecture that even Israelis poke fun at it.

Rawabi seemed better than that, however: a brave endeavour to show the world an entirely new version of Palestine. The Kushner peace plan of 2020 spoke repeatedly of 'unleashing the economic potential' of Palestine. Rawabi came the closest I had yet seen to demonstrating what that potential might be.

The architectural style was unmistakeably Arab. The approach was dominated by the giant concrete shell of an unfinished mosque, where the desert sun flashed through empty windows and the superstructure of a crane. In a glitzy visitor centre I met Hadeel, an attractive twenty-something manager in a pencil skirt, who had been dispatched by head office to show me around. She had led such tours too often before – 'we love to share our passion for the project' she began, robotically – but enthusiasm soon burst through, because her pride in Rawabi was genuine.

A chauffeur slowly drove us around in a liveried green car with swish leather seats as Hadeel reeled off the statistics. Rawabi so far comprised four architecturally distinct 'neighbourhoods', with the fifth under construction. Eventually, in eight to ten years, there would be twenty-two. Occupancy was at 70 per cent, and 90 per cent of the 1,200 units built so far had been sold. 'We are deliberately targeting the middle classes,' she said. 'The design criteria for the fifth neighbourhood has changed. Palestinians traditionally like the prestige of big apartments, but the new generation understands that if you're working, these big places just turn into places where you go to clean the china. So we are building more studios and one-bed units now, in response to demand.'

There were few people around. The ghost-town atmosphere reminded me of Poundbury, the Prince of Wales's experimental new town outside Dorchester. The shopping mall in the centre was filled with enticing fashion franchises familiar from airports – Wrangler, Hilfiger, American Eagle – but most of the shopkeepers were lounging by their entrances, bored of the wait for customers. 'That's because the residents are all away at work,' Hadeel said brightly. 'Of course it's quiet in the mornings. It's much busier in the evenings.'

The typical occupants, she said, were young families in which both parents commuted to work in Ramallah, or Nablus, or even to jobs beyond the barrier, in Jerusalem or Tel Aviv. 'The emptiness isn't ideal. But Rawabi is a work in progress. Our aim is to turn it into a centre for high tech. We think we can create 10,000 jobs here. We don't want this to be another dormitory town.'

Bashar al-Masri, it seemed, was intent on copying his Israeli neighbours, who over the last thirty years have converted an agricultural economy into a world-leading digital one. Hadeel insisted it was no pipedream. Google and Facebook, she said, had 'already agreed to come'. Rawabi, she went on, was an energy-efficient city, with solar power, smart water monitoring, rainwater harvesting, wastewater recycling – all the latest technology found in urban Israel. She pointed out the new medical centre they were building, and three schools, one of them already open, a private academy for 250 students who studied English to GCSE level following a curriculum from Cambridge.

Rawabi's centre was circular, and known as 'the Q Center' in homage to the project's main foreign backers, the Qataris. The shopping mall ended in the tail of the Q, a tapered walkway cantilevered over a vertiginous valley. Rawabi's workers, said Hadeel, compared the walkway to the prow of the Titanic, as seen in the famous movie love scene between Leonardo DiCaprio and Kate Winslet. I crept out to the end. In the gulley beneath my feet, buzzards wheeled. The cliffs beyond were connected by a zipwire that led to a drop-off point for bungee jumpers, part of a half-built adventure playground called 'Rawabi Xtreme'.

The tour ended around the corner at an amphitheatre set into the mountainside. It was a 12,000-seater designed to host rock concerts, far bigger than the toy one at Beit Falasteen. It hadn't taken off yet as an international tour venue, although Coldplay's Chris Martin had apparently reconnoitred it, and declared the backstage facilities to be 'the best he had ever seen'. Hadeel recalled how the amphitheatre was inaugurated in 2016 by Mohammed Assaf, the Palestinian winner of *Arab Idol*, before a crowd of 13,000 who then sang along with the Tunisian singer Saber Rebai.

'That's the beauty of working here,' Hadeel murmured earnestly. 'I will never forget the cameras, the tears. Saber sang a very famous song: *I'll write the name of my country on the sun that never sets*. I was going to move on from Rawabi, but this place changes the way you think.'

Rawabi seemed a triumph of hope over experience: the perfect inversion of the Palestinian stereotype of downtrodden victimhood. It was also, perhaps, a model of what Israel hoped Palestine might become, a place full of peace-loving and economically productive middle-class families, married to the principles of security and stability: the mirror image, in fact, of the Israeli settler city of Modi'in. How could Israel possibly object?

The first obstacle the Palestinians encountered was Ateret, an Israeli settlement down the hill, whose residents were opposed to Rawabi almost out of principle. Al-Masri's managers, keen to identify their project as a symbol of the new Palestine, took to flying a huge national flag, black, white, green and red, above the Visitor Centre: the largest such flag in the world. The Ateret settlers snuck up the hill at night, and tore it down. The Palestinians replaced it. The flag was stolen again. The Palestinians won this war of attrition in the end, though. A flag still flew. 'We just bought more flags,' Hadeel grinned. 'We've still got a whole truckload of spares.'

The quarrel wasn't quite as petty as it sounded. Some Israelis view the Palestinian flag, which was adopted by the PLO in 1964, as an incitement to revolt; right-wing politicians have been trying for years to make it illegal to wave in Israel. They have not succeeded – or at least, not yet – but that has not stopped Israeli police from confiscating flags, as they did, for example, at a demonstration in November 2018 in East Jerusalem, following Donald Trump's decision to recognize Jerusalem as Israel's capital.[4]

A row over Rawabi's water supply, however, proved a much more serious threat; so serious, indeed, that it almost destroyed the entire project. Rawabi depends on a nearby spring, Ain Umm Safa, which is connected by a 25-centimetre pipe operated by Mekorot, but which runs through Area C under the control of the Civil Administration. As Rawabi began to grow, so too did the requirement for water. In 2015, however, Mekorot declined to increase supply without authorization from the Civil Administration. But the CA said it was unable to provide this without the agreement of the Joint Water Committee – which had, of course, been boycotted by the Ramallah government, and so was defunct.

'Construction stopped for eighteen months,' Hadeel recalled. 'Hundreds of workers were laid off. It was so sad. So much euphoria and good will was lost. Rawabi turned into a real ghost town. The whole project nearly went bankrupt.' Hadeel took me to a penthouse office to meet the big boss, Bashar al-Masri himself. A British- and American-educated property tycoon with a net worth of an estimated US$1.5 billion, he looked younger than his fifty-seven years, slim and relaxed in his yellow trainers and billowing city shirt. From the sun-blitzed deck outside his office it was just possible to make out the Mediterranean, 48 kilometres to the west beyond the haze of Tel Aviv.

When I asked him about Rawabi's water shortage in 2015, Bashar began by playing it down. The crisis had been resolved eventually, thanks to foreign pressure that forced Netanyahu to step in and order the Civil Administration and Mekorot to crack open the taps. As the project's chief executive, as well as its main conduit of foreign investment, al-Masri understandably had no wish to re-open old wounds that might threaten Rawabi's future. At present, he said, Rawabi received 620 cubic metres of water per day, 37 per cent more than their previous allocation (and more than double what they received in 2015). They would, of course, like more. They had been forced to shelve a plan to add a waterpark to the Rawabi Xtreme programme, and the turf of a new football pitch was struggling. But the next three-year phase of construction work was not in jeopardy: 620 cubic metres, he said, was enough for now.

Bitterness, though, did not lie far beneath Bashar's urbane surface. 'The Civil Administration is just the "nice face" of the army. It is a modern way of brutalising the people, and very smart. Why did they refuse us water? Because they were worried about the precedent it might set. And they were using it to legitimize their settlements. We kept hearing, "You can't have more water until all the settlements have got what they need." Yet I've never heard of a settlement that didn't have enough water. Ateret uses the same supply pipe from Umm Safa as we do, but it has a tenth the number of people as us. There was no real shortage for them. Settlements are the cancer eating up Palestine.'

Israel initially blamed the impasse on the PA's decision to boycott the Joint Water Committee, but Bashar did not blame Ramallah. 'I told them not to compromise for our sake,' he recalled, 'because this was an issue bigger than Rawabi.'

Instead, he began lobbying for more water directly with the Israelis, as well as further afield. At one point, a delegation of twenty US senators visited Rawabi, and went away voicing their support. 'I didn't bother with the politicians, because they only ever say "wait until after the next election." Instead, I spoke to what I call "the Jews of the world" . . . I tried to convince them that Rawabi is a step towards security and stability, and that is a win-win, of benefit to Israel as well as to us.'

Rawabi has its detractors on the Palestinian side. This new city was designed to attract people who were already well off, a tiny, middle-class stratum of society. Of what use was such a project to the impoverished masses? 'Are we to spend our lives in servitude, running around in donkey carts?' al-Masri retorted. The people, he insisted, were proud of Rawabi, a symbol of an alternative future. And they had benefited materially, too, from one of the largest building projects in the West Bank that provided thousands of construction jobs.

Building it had nevertheless required al-Masri to cooperate with his erstwhile enemy, which laid him open to the charge of 'normalizing' the occupation – although al-Masri was having none of that argument, either. 'Rawabi exists in defiance of the occupation, not because of it,' he said fiercely. The water pipe from Umm Safa on which his city depended, he pointed out, could still be cut at any time.

'It's not just the water. They can cut us off by road, too, with their check-points, whenever they like. This is how all of us live in Palestine – even in cities as big as Nablus, as big as ancient Jericho. There is no good or bad occupation: there is only one occupation. But when that occupation is sugar-coated by democracy? That is evil. An ideological evil.'

I saw his point. The policy of suppression and obstruction I had witnessed in the West Bank and Gaza was often cruel, but it made sense, mostly, as a tactic. Rawabi was different. It was the clearest possible example of Palestinians attempting to help themselves, in a way that could surely only benefit Israelis too. Yet Israel nearly scuppered the project by denying it water. Why? Is Israel incapable of pursuing the path of enlightened self-interest? What kind of Palestine, in the end, does Israel really want: a neigh-bour that aspires to the same middle-class values that most Israelis do, or a suppressed, unhappy and impoverished nation almost permanently on the edge of violent rebellion?

As I left Rawabi, Hadeel pointed out a roundabout, the centrepiece of which was a cube of rock with its sides slickened by a trickle of piped water. 'It is called Hope Roundabout,' she said, all earnest again. 'The rock stands for our samoud. And the fountain is a reminder that water is a basic human right, that must be equally available for all to share.'

This was trite, but true. In 2020, even the Kushner peace plan recog-nized Palestine's 'mutual water rights' – and Netanyahu heartily endorsed the Kushner plan, which he called 'a great plan for Israel, a great plan for peace'. Yet so much of what I had seen in Palestine, from the blockade of Gaza to the settlements of Samaria, in the Jordan Valley and all along the separation barrier, pointed to an opposite Israeli intention: a seemingly innate determination to ignore Palestine's water rights, and to snuff out Palestinian ambition and progress through the constriction of supply. Was

Netanyahu serious about the Kushner plan, or was he merely paying lip service to it?

The success of any two-state solution, it seemed to me, will depend on Israel's willingness to uphold Palestine's claim to natural water rights. Yet for twenty-five years, Israel has steadfastly refused even to consider such a thing, even though, thanks to desalination, it now has more water than it needs.

Where, ultimately, does this aversion to sharing the natural resources of the land stem from, and why does it persist? What does water really signify to the Jewish nation, historically, culturally, economically? It was time to cross back over the green line to find out.

1. Benjamin West's rendition of Joshua leading the Israelites into the Promised Land. The River Jordan in 1400 BCE was uncrossable without God's help: 'So it was … as the feet of the priests who bore the ark dipped in the edge of the water … the waters which came down from upstream stood still, and rose in a heap' (Joshua 3. 14–16).

2. On the Madaba map, a sixth-century CE church floor mosaic in Jordan – the world's oldest surviving cartographic representation of the Holy Land – the lower reach is shown teeming with fish so fat that their sides almost touch the banks. Such fish would struggle to swim at all now.

3. The lower Jordan as it should be, near Alumot, just south of the Sea of Galilee. This idyllic stretch is just 3 kilometres long, however – and it is an artificial creation, dependent on dams at either end.

4. Qasr al-Yahud, the supposed site of Christ's baptism by John, is a major draw for international pilgrims. The river here is also artificially regulated, yet still narrow and shallow enough to wade across. In some summers, the only fluid it contains is said to be agricultural run-off from settlements upstream.

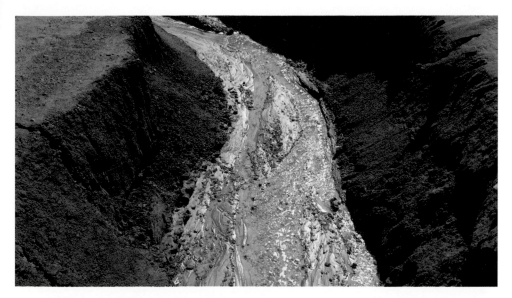

5. The Jordan as it soon becomes: decades of diversion and over-extraction have decimated the basin's natural flow, turning the river of biblical legend into a fetid ditch.

6. An abandoned jetty at a resort on the Dead Sea, the Jordan's terminus. The Sea is now 48 kilometres long, 32 less than half a century ago. Its surface, the lowest point on Earth at 436 metres below sea level, is still dropping by a metre per year.

7. Demonstrators in Bethlehem vent their frustration on an effigy of AJ Balfour, the British Foreign Secretary in 1917, whose declaration of support for a Jewish 'national home' in Palestine is still widely regarded as the root cause of the Arab-Israeli dispute.

8. Yasser Fahmi, head of one of the last six families in the West Bank farming village of Yanoun. He is unable to harvest the olive trees over his shoulder without permission from the Israeli Defence Force.

9. The mausoleum in Ramallah of Yasser Arafat (1929–2004), chairman of the Palestine Liberation Organization and founder of Fatah. The Mukata'a, Arafat's former headquarters, is now a museum, and still a centrepiece of the Palestinian Authority regime.

10. An alternative Palestine? Cranes tower over Rawabi in the West Bank, the first ever 'planned city' built by and for Palestinians. The $1.4 billion project, designed to house 40,000 people, was nearly wrecked in 2015 following a dispute with Israel over water supply.

11. An overground section of the National Water Carrier, which has brought water from the Sea of Galilee to the populous centre of Israel since 1964: for 40 years, the country's primary source of fresh water.

12. Intensive agriculture in the lower Galilee. Self-sufficiency in food production is practically a tenet of Zionism, which helps explain why a sector that contributes just 2.3 per cent of Israel's GDP nevertheless uses 55 per cent of all the water available in Israel to sustain it.

13. Sorek seawater desalination plant, south of Tel Aviv, is the largest of its type in the world: one of five constructed along the coast since 2003. As much as 80 per cent of Israel's domestic water supply is now manufactured.

14. The beachfront at Tel Aviv. Israel's population has doubled since 1987, to some 9.5 million. Before 1906, Tel Aviv did not exist. Today it forms the centrepiece of 'Gush Dan', a coastal conurbation 50 kilometres long.

CHAPTER EIGHT

The Secret Cisterns of Jerusalem

O NE FRIDAY EVENING before Shabbat, in the square before the famous Western Wall by Temple Mount in Jerusalem's Old City, I observed a group of perhaps a hundred young women, all IDF conscripts in olive-green fatigues, engaged in a joyous folk dance in celebration of the start of their military service. They danced in the segregated women's section beyond a low barrier that led to the Temple Wall, and so were doubly separated from the non-Jewish tourists, who looked on with the reverence of anthropologists, while stealing forbidden photographs.

The women sang as they span, a fluting counterpoint to the rumble of men praying in the enclosure next door. The dance itself, the women all holding hands in an ever-contracting and expanding circle, looked ancient: a medieval tradition, I assumed, imported from Russia or central Europe, lovingly preserved as it was passed from mother to daughter through count-less generations. But I was wrong.

The dance, I learned, was called 'Water, Water' – '*Mayim, Mayim*' in Hebrew – and it was modern, created from scratch in 1937 to celebrate the discovery of water, after a seven-year search, at Kibbutz Na'an, the first kibbutz to be established entirely by domestically-born Jews. 'Mayim Mayim' is an

Israeli standard, the words and dance moves known to every schoolchild. The lyrics are taken from the Book of Isaiah:[1]

Ushavtem mayim b'sason mimainei hayeshua
With joy you shall draw water from the wells of salvation

My time in Israel was full of moments like this. The further I travelled, the better I came to understand that water supply is no prosaic matter of civic infrastructure to Jews, but an integral part of Israeli self-perception, almost mystically linked to their unique sense of nationhood. Levi Eshkol, a prime minister of the 1960s who oversaw the construction of modern Israel's water system, likened water to 'the blood flowing through the arteries of the nation.' I began to see that asking or expecting Jews to share it with non-Jewish goyim was not as simple a matter as I had assumed. The preconceptions about water rights that I had formed in Palestine were consequently challenged.

Many of the Jews' most important myths revolve around their ability to control natural water flow, or else their unique arrangement with a deity who could do it for them. The Bible is full of examples. The exodus from Egypt in the thirteenth century BC began with the divine parting of the Red Sea; God repeated the trick forty years later when he parted the River Jordan to allow Joshua to lead the Israelites into the Promised Land.

The tribes were sustained in their desert wanderings in other miraculous ways. At Kadesh Barnea, in the wilderness close to the modern Israeli-Egyptian border, Moses was commanded by God to strike a rock with his staff, whereupon 'water came out abundantly, and the congregation and their livestock drank';[2] the miracle is celebrated in the famous Cwm Rhondda hymn, with its lyrics 'Open thou the crystal fountain / Whence the healing stream shall flow'.

That Moses story appealed to the hydrogeologist in me. When ground-water becomes pressurized in a confined aquifer, it sometimes breaks through the earth's crust where it is thinnest, a phenomenon known as an artesian well.[3] It doesn't take much to break the crust if it is really thin, and if it is under enough pressure, the water will sometimes even spout out like a geyser. Did Moses perhaps have a water diviner's nose for moisture when he struck the rock? Or was he a fellow amateur hydrogeologist, with an ability to read the contours of the land, learned and sharpened by years spent wandering in the desert – an ability that might well have seemed miraculous to any thirsty follower who was not so skilled?

The story has an interesting wrinkle. Moses angered God by tapping the rock not once, as instructed, but twice, which God took as a sign of doubt; God later punished Moses for this by denying him entry into the Promised Land. The miracle at Kadesh Barnea thus plays a role in the most important Jewish foundation myth of all. Israel's latter-day exploitation of the region's water, the means by which the modern state was developed, owes as much to technology as to faith; but it still does not feel fanciful to draw a line from Moses at Kadesh Barnea, through the vital first well at Kibbutz Na'an, to those youthful conscripts I saw in Jerusalem, singing about water to celebrate their allegiance to the Land of Israel.

The Levant is famous for its ancient ruins. I visited several in Israel-Palestine, and was constantly amazed by the sophistication of the irrigation tunnels and reservoirs that once sustained them. The fortress-palace of Herodium in the West Bank, for instance, the final resting place of Herod the Great, is built around four underground cisterns still reachable via a staircase down a shaft dug out of the rock. The underground cistern at the Greco-Roman settlement of Sepphoris, a cavern about 200 metres long and 10 metres high, is even more impressive. I found it empty, its walls ringing with the clatter of startled pigeons' wings, but in its day it held more than a million gallons, brought there via a network of tunnels and aqueducts 12 kilometres long. The size of these systems, and the effort put into their construction, show that they were not afterthoughts, but central to the planning and design of the places they served. They demonstrate that water supply has always been one of the keys to political power in this region, as it still is throughout the Middle East.

In the era of siege warfare between city-states, a reliable and defensible water supply was essential to survival. Jerusalem, parts of which are six thousand years old, has been besieged an astonishing twenty-three times. It survived those sieges thanks largely to its geology. Built on an outcrop of porous limestone, the Old City is still riddled with ancient subterranean cisterns, the private emergency reserves of citizens of the past. Their sides were plastered in order to trap the winter rains leaching down from above, and where the plaster has survived, these cisterns still hold water. They are the gems of a 'hidden' Jerusalem, much visited by tourists led there by guides in the know.

The Coptic Church of St Helen, close by the Church of the Holy Sepulchre, sits above a vast, water-filled cavern that is famed for its acoustics. This was rediscovered in the twelfth century by Crusaders who went excavating for it, believing it to be where, in the third century, St Helen – the mother of Constantine, the first Roman emperor to convert to Christianity – found fragments of the True Cross. For a few shekels, visitors today are invited to descend a narrow stone staircase, dark and clammy with percolating moisture, to a fenced-off platform where they can test the cavern's acoustic qualities for themselves. 'Sing your hymn and enjoy your echo-sounding,' reads a notice by the entrance. 'It is fabulous indeed.'

Private cisterns, however, never contained enough water to withstand a really determined siege. Jerusalem's survival owes more to another water source, the Gihon Spring, which rises in a cave in the nearby Kidron Valley, connected by a shaft and a secret tunnel built in 701 BC by Hezekiah, the King of Judah, in preparation for a siege by the Assyrian ruler Sennacherib.

The tunnel, 540 metres long and 150 metres deep, is an engineering wonder of the ancient world. It is still open, and still flowing with water from the spring that, over millennia, has polished its floor and narrow walls to the smoothness of marble. Tourists equipped with torches are permitted to wade through it, up to their knees in the cool waters of Gihon, all the way to the Pool of Siloam, the collection reservoir at the tunnel's end. Halfway along, I ran my fingers over an inscription, carved into the rock by one of the tunnel diggers to mark their 2,700-year-old achievement. Its words are reminiscent of the moment, in October 1990, when French and British engineers first made contact as they dug from opposite sides of the English Channel, and convey something of the same excitement:[4]

While the labourers were still working with their pickaxes, each toward the other, and while there were still three cubits to be broken through, the voice of each was heard calling to the other, because there was a zdh [crack?] in the rock to the south and to the north. And at the moment of the breakthrough, the labourers struck each toward the other, pickaxe against pickaxe. Then the water flowed from the spring to the pool for 1,200 cubits. And the height of the rock above the heads of the labourers was one hundred cubits.

Sennacherib had conquered forty-six other towns and citadels in Judah, but he failed at Jerusalem. The story of the siege is documented in detail in three different books of the Old Testament,[5] which naturally puts Hezekiah's success down to his unbending faith in Yahweh. Clad in sackcloth in sign of his humility before God, as well as the anguish he felt for Judah's suffering, he was advised by the Prophet Isaiah himself, who assured him and the citizenry that the idolatrous Assyrians would be beaten because they had 'only the arm of flesh'.

No doubt faith did play a role in the outcome – but possibly not one as major as an early decision to stop up all the district's wells and springs, including the old outlet from the Gihon Spring, in order to deny the besiegers a supply of their own. The townspeople understood the importance of this detail of the defence preparations even if the godly Hezekiah perhaps did not, and were willing volunteers in this mammoth task. Their survival depended on it: Sennacherib's palace at Nineveh was decorated with bas-reliefs celebrating the capture of Lachish, Judah's second city, whose defenders were impaled on stakes. In other campaigns in Mesopotamia, Sennacherib's warriors measured their martial prowess in collections of severed heads.[6]

The anxiety the Jerusalemites felt as the Assyrian army approached, an invasion force reputedly numbering 185,000, is still audible in the verses of 2 Chronicles 32:

And when Hezekiah saw that Sennacherib was come … He consulted with his leaders and commanders to stop the water from the springs which were outside the city; and they helped him. Thus many people gathered together who stopped all the springs and the brook that ran through the land, saying, 'Why should the kings of Assyria come and find much water?'

The details of what happened next are unclear. The Bible records simply that 'the Lord sent an angel, who annihilated all the fighting men and the commanders and officers in the camp of the Assyrian king.' Did they die of thirst? Or was the immense siege camp swept by typhus or some other infectious disease, the spread accelerated by hunger, heat, or that other inevitable consequence of water shortage, the lack of sanitation? Whatever the reason, the surviving Assyrians suddenly withdrew to Nineveh, and Jerusalem was saved.

Since Jerusalem owed its survival to its water supply, it is perhaps no surprise that the city's water infrastructure, its very plumbing, has tradition- ally been attributed with spiritual significance. Indeed, it still is – and not only by followers of Judaism. Christian traditionalists believe that Mary washed Jesus's swaddling clothes in the Gihon Spring; Christ also healed a blind man by the Pool of Siloam, according to the Gospel of John. When I at last emerged there, soak-shoed and blinking in the unfamiliar light, I found two pilgrims from Guatemala, one a padre, the other a novitiate, quietly immersing each other on the very spot of that miracle. The church they belonged to back home, they said, was called the Church of Siloam, a branch of a large Central American mission called Christ's Hospital.

Water is mentioned a total of 722 times in the Bible – more often than bread, fire, faith, hope or love.[7] It appears variously as a symbol of life, of rebirth, of divine revelation, of Paradise itself. Its mystical power is at the same time very often rooted in the prosaic here and now, in the dust and dirt of the real earthly city of Jerusalem. The Book of Revelation, for example, tells us:

> Then the angel showed me the river of the water of life, sparkling like crystal, flowing from the throne of God and of the Lamb *down the middle of the city's street.*[8]

Deep beneath the golden Dome of the Rock, at the heart of Temple Mount – Haram al-Sharif, to Muslims – lies a mysterious cistern-like cavern known to Islam as the 'Well of Souls'; Jews and Christians know the spot as the 'Holy of Holies'. Its architectural purpose, if it ever had one, is unknown.

It may have been designed as a simple water cistern, although the absence of rope grooves around its top suggests that it was never used as such.[9]

The cistern is covered over by the famous Foundation Stone, which the Talmud, the primary source of Jewish religious law, describes as the centre of the world, the spot where God gathered dust to create Adam, as well as the altar on which Abraham attempted to sacrifice his son Isaac; all Jews turn towards it in prayer. It acts as a kind of mystical manhole cover over the Abyss, which contains the waters of the Flood, no less – a body of water said to be raging still, and maybe only temporarily receded, despite the passage of so many years.[10] This surreal concept predates Judaism by millennia: it has its roots in the traditions and beliefs of ancient Sumer.

Muslims also put the Foundation Stone at the centre of the world, and venerate it as the earthly launch pad of Mohammed's 'Night Journey' to heaven in 621. According to one tradition, the stone does not rest on the ground, but floats just above it like a permanently hovering flying saucer. According to another, the stone is supported by the branches of a lofty palm tree growing out of the River of Paradise, the mother of all oases flowing far below at the bottom of a measureless pit. The details may be different, but the concept is the same: the Well of Souls is where the three Abrahamic religions come together in veneration of the very notion of running water, which, to the faithful, literally lies at the foundation of all human existence.

Armageddon provided another demonstration of the ancient link between water supply and political power. It was a joy to discover that this Old Testament metaphor for the End of the World is a real place, a chariot fortress on a hill near Nazareth, from where it once dominated the Via Maris, 'the Way of the Sea', the trading trunk route that connected the empires of Egypt and Mesopotamia. Just as at Jerusalem, its defensibility depended on a secret water supply, a deep shaft and tunnel leading to a hidden underground spring.

Tel Megiddo, as it is properly called, is a site of unusual antiquity, even for Israel. Archaeologists have identified twenty-six layers of demolition and reconstruction on the tel, the lowest of them dating to 7000 BC. It was controlled, turn and turn about, by Assyrians, Egyptians, Philistines, Israelites,

Arameans. Although eventually abandoned in the sixth century BC, the tide of history has not ceased its ebb and flow around Megiddo. In 1949, a group of Holocaust survivors from Hungary and Poland built a kibbutz nearby, on the ruins of a depopulated Arab village called Lajjun, which had itself been built on the ruins of a camp of the Roman 6th legion; Lajjun was a corruption of the Latin *Legio*. Countless battles have been fought in the area, including in 1918, when Field Marshal Allenby defeated the Ottomans here; he later styled himself Viscount Allenby of Megiddo. The Christian fundamentalist tradition that the final battle at the End of Days will be fought here, Christ versus the kings of the Earth, is thought to date to 609 BC, when the pious king Josiah of Judah was killed in a battle with Pharaoh Necho II.

The Christian fundamentalists were out in force at the time of my visit. Many of them were from Bible-Belt America, and indeed were carrying bibles; some of them were organized into tour groups with matching coloured baseball caps. I caught snatches of intense theological debate as I overtook them on the path that winds to the top of the tel. According to researchers in Washington, 23 per cent of all Americans believe in the Second Coming of Christ, and that this will 'definitely' happen by 2050.[11] So the excitement of these visitors was unsurprising. Of course Armageddon was a highlight of their Holy Land itinerary. I recalled Mark Twain's cynical description, in *The Innocents Abroad*, of:

> ... a fantastic mob of green-spectacled Yanks, with their flapping elbows and bobbing umbrellas', who 'entered the country with their verdicts already prepared ... The veneration and the affection which some of these men felt for the scenes they were speaking of heated their fancies and biased their judgement.[12]

Armageddon had certainly heated these visitors' fancies. They were, perhaps, unwitting bit-players in the wider Israel–Palestine drama, as emissaries from the voter base of Donald Trump, who pandered to their belief in the coming apocalypse so assiduously that *Rolling Stone* magazine once dubbed him 'the End-Times President'.[13]

To be fair, Armageddon heated my fancy, too; because if a Final Battle really is to take place, there are surely few better spots for it. The Plain of Jezreel, stretching into the distance beneath the lookout point on the tel's palm tree-dotted summit, seemed just as suitable for a modern tank battle as it once was for chariots. The plain is home, furthermore, to an Israeli air force base. Twice in the course of my short visit, pairs of fighter-bombers streaked by, the thunder of their engines rolling across the hazy flat fields so loudly that we tourists flinched. The jets, I suspected, were heading for Gaza, mounting retaliatory strikes against Hamas, which the previous day had launched yet another volley of homemade rockets over the fence into Israel.

The Israeli Parks Authority had done their best to present Armageddon in its historical context. The remains of the stables were embellished with the silhouettes of horses and chariots constructed from iron and wire. More interesting to me, though, was the fortress' water supply, an underground spring that lay just beyond the walls – a location that, as at Jerusalem, made it vulnerable in times of siege. In the ninth century BC, therefore, the external entrance to the spring was blocked up and concealed, and a new, secret one excavated from within.

This excavation, known as Ahab's Water Works, was the largest single surviving feature of the entire complex, a wide, conical crater, 35 metres deep, with a narrow staircase cut into its side. A sign explained that it led to the entrance of a tunnel that ran for 80 metres beneath the bedrock to the spring. The staircase was closed for maintenance, but when no one was looking I hopped over the rope and descended into the bowels of Armageddon.

The tunnel was tomblike. The only sound was my footsteps clanging on the metal grill of a walkway. By the feeble light of my mobile phone I saw that the striated ceiling must once have been slick with dripping ground-water, but it was dry now, as was the spring-fed collection pool at the tunnel's end. It felt portentous. The Old Testament Prophets, Joel and Jeremiah and Isaiah, all predicted that Judgment Day would be preceded by a period of devastating drought.

Judah mourns,
And her gates languish;
They mourn for the land,
And the cry of Jerusalem has gone up.
Their nobles have sent their lads for water;
They went to the cisterns and found no water.
They returned with their vessels empty;
They were ashamed and confounded
And covered their heads.
Because the ground is parched,
For there was no rain in the land,
The plowmen were ashamed;
They covered their heads.
Yes, the deer also gave birth in the field,
But left because there was no grass.
And the wild donkeys stood in the desolate heights;
They sniffed at the wind like jackals;
Their eyes failed because there was no grass.[14]

Water scarcity, for sure, was the greatest obstacle facing the first Zionist settlers of the late nineteenth century. This much I learned at Rishon Lezion, a city just south of Tel Aviv. Established by a handful of wannabe farmers from Ukraine in 1882, fully twenty-seven years before Tel Aviv proper, the name meant 'the First to Zion', in recognition of its status as one of the two oldest Zionist communities in the country. It was the birthplace of the national flag, the first Hebrew-speaking school, the first national orchestra, even Israel's first iron plough. Today, Rishon Lezion is the fourth-largest city in Israel, with a population of 250,000. Yet, as every Israeli schoolchild knows, the community very nearly failed at inception for lack of a decent well.

The city's small museum was closed for lunch when I arrived, but the caretaker agreed to open up, and ushered me into a pitch-dark auditorium to watch a cheaply made costume drama that told the Rishon Lezion story. The founding *bilu'im*, as the early Palestine pioneers were known, didn't much worry about details when they set out for their new life. They were not farmers but town dwellers, many of them students from Kharkov who were escaping the anti-Semitic May Laws of 1882.

Their religious and political motivation was no doubt impressive, but they were clueless when it came to the practicalities of settling a desert land. There was a pond on the plot that they naively bought from the local Arabs, but the water it contained was soon found to be brackish and malarial, forcing them to buy in clean water from the previous owners who, according to the film, demanded extortionate prices while giggling at them over their hookah pipes.

So, the newcomers decided to dig a well. Being unversed in the rudiments of hydrogeology, they began their excavations at the top of a hill. Idealism was partly to blame for this disastrous decision: the pioneers had planned to use gravity to supply water in precisely equal amounts to the dwellings round about.

The first dig naturally failed to find any water. But then a young boy observed that plants grew better at the bottom of the hill – which the film presented as a Eureka moment, akin to Newton's encounter with an apple – and persuaded his elders to try again there. With the help of a special augur paid for by Baron Edmond de Rothschild, the bilu'im dug down 25 metres where they at last found what they needed, and the community was saved. To this day, the city's motto, displayed on the municipal orange flags that I saw hanging from lamp-posts in the central shopping district, is 'We have found water!' which is also the punchline of Genesis, Chapter 26, the story of Isaac's settlement of Beersheba; Rishon Lezion's pious founders evidently saw themselves as heirs to that biblical tradition.

The auditorium lights came up, dramatically revealing the well itself beyond the front row. 'Careful,' the caretaker said as I approached the edge to take a photograph. 'I've seen two phones dropped down there already.'

Rishon Lezion was just the beginning. As the Zionist project got into its stride in the 1900s, a new generation of migrants dreamed of building not just farmsteads but whole cities, presenting a water supply challenge of a different order. The most famous dreamer, perhaps, was Theodor Herzl, a Viennese journalist and playwright whose vision of the future was published in a utopian novel, *Altneuland*, 'Old-New Land', in 1902. 'This country needs nothing but water and shade to have a very great future,' he wrote.

Herzl reasoned that if his Zion were to attract the Jewish citizens it needed, it would have to be at least as comfortable as the great urban centres of Europe the migrants were leaving behind. The future city he describes is 'thoroughly European ... One might easily imagine [one]self in some Italian port. The brilliant blue sky and sea was reminiscent of the Riviera.' Achieving this dream would require, above all, good utility planning.

'Under our streets,' explains David Litwak, the young hero of *Altneuland*, 'tunnels have been provided for the reception of all kinds of pipes and cables (present and future) for gas, water, sewage ... When we drew up our plans, we knew just what utilities a modern city required.'

The novel became a kind of urtext for the new city builders. Akiva Aryeh Weiss, the Zionist activist-architect from Belarus who founded Tel Aviv in 1909, followed Herzl's Europe-in-Palestine vision almost literally to the letter: the very name Tel Aviv is a poetic rendering of *Altneuland*, from *tel*, an ancient mound, and *aviv*, Hebrew for the season of spring. 'In this city,' wrote Weiss in a promotional pamphlet in 1906, 'every house will have water from wells that will flow through pipes as in every modern European city, and also sewerage pipes will be installed for the health of ... its residents.'[15]

For all the milk and honey promises of the Bible, building a modern urban state from scratch in a place like Palestine struck many at the time as a project doomed to fail. In 1917, the Yishuv community numbered a sustainable-sounding 80,000. By 1948, however, it had reached 800,000, a figure that far exceeded the expectations of the pioneers. How were the new citizens to be fed and watered?

The same question had occurred to Palestine's British imperial overlords. As early as the late 1920s, British economists were warning that the region's scant natural water resources would soon be overwhelmed if Jewish immigration was left unchecked. They were of the view that the entire geographic area of Palestine could hold a maximum of 2 million people.[16]

The provision of water, moreover, was not the only challenge faced by the expanding numbers of Yishuv. Although the local Arabs rubbed along with their new neighbours to begin with, they grew restive as the number of incomers surged. Finally, in 1936, Arab nationalists staged the Great Revolt, seeking an end to uncontrolled Jewish immigration and land purchases, as well as the Arab independence they believed the British had promised them at the end of the First World War.

The British were deeply alarmed. The eastern Mediterranean was the gateway to the Suez Canal, a vital connection to India, the jewel of the British Empire. Throughout the 1920s, moreover, Britain had spent huge sums turning the port of Haifa into a hub for the refining and shipping of oil from Iraq. Unrest in this part of the world was not something they would willingly tolerate.

The Great Revolt took three years to suppress, and the deployment of as many as 50,000 British troops. In 1939, Neville Chamberlain's government, spooked and anxious to avoid a repeat, published a White Paper that sought to limit future Jewish immigration to Palestine to a mere 15,000 a year for the next five years. And they justified this number, to themselves as well as to the Yishuv, by recalling the earlier calculations by British economists who insisted that Palestine had enough water for no more than 2 million people.

The British restriction on immigration presented an existential threat to the entire Zionist project. The Yishuv's first response, therefore, was to try to prove those economists wrong. They found an important ally in an American soil scientist, Walter Clay Lowdermilk, who was sent to survey the region on behalf of the US Department of Agriculture in 1939, and who declared himself 'astonished' by the progress the Zionists were making in restoring a land exhausted by centuries of Ottoman 'mismanagement'. He was equally impressed by the Yishuv's burgeoning water infrastructure, urban as well as rural. Unlike the British, he was of the view that the 'absorptive capacity of any country is a dynamic and expanding conception. It changes with the ability of the population to make maximum use of its land.'

Lowdermilk published his findings in 1944 in a book called *Palestine, Land of Promise*, in which he argued that the progress he had seen could act as 'the leaven that will transform the other lands of the Near East'. His book became an unlikely but influential bestseller in the US, which undoubtedly helped to change the official American view of the Zionist project. A copy of Lowdermilk's book was given to every member of Congress. It may also have been the last book that President Roosevelt ever read: a copy was found open on his desk when he died in 1945.[17]

Lowdermilk was, of course, correct about Palestine's 'absorptive capacity'. Today, the area of Palestine is home to more than 9 million people in Israel, with another 5 million in the West Bank and Gaza.[18] The key, the early Zionists realised, was water distribution. By far the biggest natural reservoir of fresh water in the region, the Sea of Galilee, was in the sparsely populated north of their Promised Land. The Yishuv, however, were clustered around the new city of Tel Aviv in the centre of the country. This region contains several small rivers, such as the Yarkon that flows to the sea just north of the city, but the quantities available were always a tiny fraction of the water to be had in the Galilee.

Most domestic and irrigation water in the central region was drawn from where it had always come – shallow wells drilled into the local aquifer – a source and a system that the Zionists soon realised could not be sustained. But what if, instead, the waters of the Galilee could be brought to the south where there was most need? That would remove a powerful brake on Tel Aviv's development. As Israel's first prime minister David Ben-Gurion foresaw, it might even enable farmers to exploit the Negev Desert, the sparsely populated tracts of land to the south. 'Make the desert bloom' remains one of the best-known slogans of his era.

Ben-Gurion wasn't the first regional administrator to grasp the benefits of a networked water supply. The Romans built more than fifty aqueducts in their Palestinian province.[19] They understood better than anyone that farmers prospered when they could irrigate their crops. Well-supplied town-dwellers were healthier and happier, too. A good water supply meant a richer, more stable, taxable and governable empire: a means of pacifying the natives, in short – a point inadvertently made by Reg, the absurdly ineffectual Jewish nationalist played by John Cleese in Monty Python's 1979 satire, *Life of Brian*, when he remarks: 'All right, but apart from the sanitation, the medicine, education, wine, public order, irrigation, roads, a fresh water system, and public health – what have the Romans ever done for us?'

By Ben-Gurion's time, however, the infrastructure built by the Romans was dilapidated. The Ottomans had done their best to maintain and regulate Palestine's ancient irrigation system, and water still flowed through the old village qanats, but many of the grander pieces of infrastructure – such as, most famously, the mighty aqueduct built by Herod and Hadrian to serve the important port of Caesarea – lay in picturesque ruins.

The decay the Zionists found at the beginning of the twentieth century is still the subject of propaganda, as a popular Israeli story about the etymology of the Mamilla Pool, an important Roman-era collection reservoir in Jerusalem, neatly demonstrates. The pool still exists, hidden away behind an overgrown Muslim cemetery just west of the Old City's Jaffa Gate. Although dry and disused today, water somehow continued to trickle into Mamilla Pool long after the Romans left. According to Israeli lore, this mystified the local Arabs, who reasoned simply that it was a miracle; hence the name Mamilla, from the Arabic *ma'* (water) and *min Allah* (from God). Perhaps, in Ottoman times, the idea that water could be systematically transported over long distances, in quantities great enough to service entire cities, really did seem the stuff of miracles. Other explanations for the Pool's name, however, do not so impugn Arab intelligence. Scholars have advanced several theories: 'Mamilla' may derive from the Hebrew word for a 'filler', *m'malle*; or from the name of its original Roman sponsor, Mamilla or Maximilla; or from a church that once stood nearby, dedicated to a saint of that or a similar name.

Ben-Gurion, in any case, dreamed not just of replacing what had been lost, but of creating a modern distribution system that would surpass the old Roman one. He turned for help to his most brilliant water engineer, an émigré from Warsaw called Simcha Blass, who, by 1935, had successfully created the Yishuv's first true irrigation network, which linked several farming communities in the western Jezreel Valley.

Ben-Gurion asked him to reimagine that project on a national scale – what he called a 'fantasy water plan' – and in July 1939, Blass presented the first draft. He would spend the next twenty years revising and refining his plan, but all of the essential elements were present from the start.[20]

His plan's centrepiece was a scheme for the maximum exploitation of the most obvious source of fresh surface water available in Palestine: the Sea of Galilee. Inspired by the diversion of the Colorado River, an engineering project begun in the 1920s in order to supply Los Angeles, Blass proposed to siphon the Galilee into a National Water Carrier, a 130-kilometre system of pipes and canals that would pump water westwards from the Galilee and then south to the populous centre of the country, and ultimately, all the way to the Negev Desert beyond. It was a plan of extraordinary scope and ambition for the Yishuv, a community that in 1939 numbered no more than 450,000.[21] It was, nevertheless, the blueprint for what was to become the first unitary national water system in the modern Middle East.

CHAPTER NINE

Water Not for Drink

The Sea of Galilee and the National Water Carrier

THE GALILEE NAME alone brought to mind Bible stories I had first heard in childhood. Rounding a corner in my hire car on the steep road that winds down from the rocky hills to its west, the Sea was suddenly revealed in its entirety, its waters sparkling for miles to either side: the fabled source, at last, of the River Jordan. This was where Jesus calmed a storm, walked on water, fed the 5,000 – all the best miracles. It was one of the central motifs of Christianity itself. Elated to be so near the end of a long day's journey, I found myself whistling a half-forgotten carol about pigeons and cuckoos, and descended on Tiberias, the shoreline city I had selected as a base from which to explore the region.

The Galilee is not, of course, a sea, but a freshwater lake spread over 166 square kilometres: by some margin, the largest body of natural fresh water in the Near East.[1] Such abundance so pleased the first-century historian Josephus that he called the area 'the ambition of Nature'. It has always attracted settlers: the remains of mud huts found at Ohalo on the eastern shore are thought to date to 21,000 BC, making Ohalo the oldest known permanent human settlement in the world.

The Galilee has always been the key to control over the region. The second crusade ended in disaster here in July 1187, when an army of 20,000 led by Guy de Lusignan marched to the relief of besieged Tiberias, following the same route that I now drove. Saladin blocked their path, and in the savage heat of summer, the crusaders were soon desperately short of water. They, like me, must have looked down on the glittering waters below, and been tantalized. Broken by thirst, the army was annihilated at the Battle of the Horns of Hattin, paving the way for the Muslim reconquest of Jerusalem.

The Galilee has been called many names in the past: Minya, Ginosar, Gennesaret, or more simply, in Arabic, *Buhayrat Tabariya*, the Lake of Tiberias. Israelis, though, generally call it Kinneret, its name in the Hebrew Bible; the word is possibly a corruption of *kinnor*, the Hebrew word for a harp, which the shape of the lake roughly suggests (and which, happily, was also a musical instrument played by the Jewish patriarch King David). It has naturally always been one of the Chosen People's most strategic jewels.

I checked into a grubby boarding house in the town centre, and went for a walk along the waterfront. Old Tiberias, a city named after the Roman emperor when it was founded two millennia ago, seemed a tawdry place, full of cheap eateries and shops selling plastic beach gear and cut-price booze. It was still only March, so the waterslide adventure park and many of the shops and restaurants had yet to open. It felt as sad and tired as Clacton or Cromer in the off-season.

'Squalor and poverty are the pride of Tiberias,' wrote Mark Twain, as dyspeptic as ever when he visited. 'Its people are best examined at a distance.' He was no more impressed by the Galilee, whose solitude he found 'dismal and repellent', a 'solemn, sailless, tintless lake, as expressionless and unpoetical as any metropolitan reservoir in Christendom.'[2]

The winter of 2018 had been the rainiest for six years, yet the water level was evidently still much lower than normal. No water lapped at the tall stone breakwater along the boardwalk. Gangplanks led out over mud to pontoons where fishing boats and tourist cruisers were moored, but even some of these were grounded on the near side.

'You should have seen how low it was last month,' said a waiter, cheerfully touting for passing trade outside a fish restaurant. 'We were worried then, but the lake is fine now.' I looked out at the slimy foreshore, wondering at the waiter's insouciance. The recovery of the lake on which his livelihood depended looked pretty fragile to me. I sat down at one of the many empty tables, and ordered the St Peter's Fish, a local species of tilapia that Bible scholars believe was used by Jesus in his miraculous feeding of the 5,000. It tasted of mud.[3]

Further along the boardwalk after my supper, I found the waterfront's most famous landmark, the National Water Level Indicator, a harp-shaped sculpture with a digital water meter set into it. As the primary source of fresh water when Israel was founded, the health of the lake remains a national preoccupation, akin to the British obsession with the weather. Israeli newspapers traditionally print details of its water level alongside the weather forecast. Every schoolchild is taught what it should be – 209 metres below sea level – although the meter now indicated 212 metres below sea level.

The indicator struck me as a modern version of a nilometer, the calibrated stone shaft that the priests of ancient Egypt used to 'predict' the extent of the annual flooding of the Nile, the deified river on which their society's agricultural economy depended. Just about 30 kilometres west of here, among the astonishingly well-preserved Roman ruins of Sepphoris, I had seen a depiction of precisely such a nilometer, the centrepiece of a large floor mosaic garlanded with horsemen, fruit and ferocious beasts: further proof, if any were needed, that the obsession with water supply in this part of the world is nothing new.

Low as it was, the lake's surface was in fact rising, as the waiter said. Thanks to winter rains, it had recently gone up by 2 metres. The level of the previous summer – 214 metres below sea level – was close to the all-time record low for the lake, set in 2001, of 214.87 metres. As all Israelis know, 214 metres below sea level is called the lake's 'black line', below which the water starts to thicken with salt, and nutrients push up from subterranean springs, leading to potentially permanent alteration of the lake's fragile lentic ecosystem. A few months previously the Israeli Water Authority (IWA), which minutely monitors the lake's chemical make-up, had been forced to pump 17,000 tons of salt out of the lake just to keep things stable. It seemed that the rains had come in the nick of time.

Simcha Blass's National Water Carrier, known as the NWC, took twenty years to complete, and did not come fully on line until 1964. For the next forty years, the Sea of Galilee became Israel's primary source of fresh water. Billions of gallons of water have been pumped out over the years, so it is tempting to blame the present ecological crisis in the Jordan Valley, as many Palestinians do, on over-extraction.

Water that would otherwise have flowed into the Jordan was prevented from doing so even before Blass began to siphon it off via the NWC. As early as 1932, Yishuv engineers built a dam at Degania, which still stands at the southern end of the lake where it enters the lower Jordan. Before 1932, the Jordan carried 1.3 billion cubic metres of water down to the Dead Sea each year, but has since lost 98 per cent of its flow. The Dead Sea itself, as I had seen, is still dropping by a metre a year. It was understandable, therefore, that Palestinian farmers in the Jordan Valley thought that all their problems would be solved if the dam were removed.

But I already knew that the problem was not so simple. For one thing, Israel is not alone in diverting the River Jordan's headwaters. Lebanon, Jordan and Syria have all done the same for many years. Under the 1994 treaty that brought peace between Jordan and Israel, Jordan gained control of 75 per cent of the flow of the Yarmouk, the River Jordan's principal eastern tributary, which enters the mainstream below Degania. Under the same treaty, Israel is obliged to provide their water-stressed neighbours with an additional 50 million cubic metres of water every year, and in practice often provides considerably more than that, under other arrangements.

Much more significant, though, is that Israel no longer pumps out anything like the amount of water that it used to via the NWC. Thanks to the desalination plants that Israel has been building on its Mediterranean coast since 2002, the country passed the point when it relied on the Galilee as its primary water source long ago. As recently as 2004, some 527 million cubic metres were drawn off from the lake.[4] Since 2015, however, Mekorot has extracted no more than 25 million cubic metres a year, an amount that they call a 'maintenance levy', the bare minimum needed to prevent the NWC's pipes and canals from drying out and cracking, and the ageing pump machinery from permanently seizing up.

I was to learn much more about the desalination revolution, and its incalculable importance to Israel's water security. Throughout the twentieth century, water supply was the greatest constraint on the growth of the state. Water shortage remained a major problem until a decade ago, but Israel now produces so much water that, since 2016, it has actually enjoyed a surplus. Desalination has proved the key to this transformation – today, an astonishing 80 per cent of Israel's domestic tap water is not 'natural' at all, but manufactured – although other innovations are important too, notably the development of water recycling plants. These days, as much as 86 per cent of all domestic 'grey' water – that is, the relatively clean waste from baths, sinks, and washing machines, which is not to be confused with domestic 'waste' water from toilets – is reused in agriculture.

I heard more raw statistics from Doron Markel, the former head of the Israeli Water Authority's Kinneret management department. Recently appointed as chief scientist to the Jewish National Fund, the venerable state institution responsible for land development, he was the voice of water officialdom.

'Water supply is no longer finite, and therefore no longer a zero-sum game,' he enthused. 'Israel produces 600 million cubic metres of desal per year, and with more plants coming on line it will soon produce more. The Water Authority's master plan for 2050 speaks of 1.5 billion cubic metres per year. The only limit is the amount of land available to build the plants on. And even then, maybe we could float them offshore.'

Israel, he made clear, had long outgrown the Sea of Galilee, which is far too small to supply its 9 million citizens – a population, he noted, that is forecast to double by 2050. The IWA estimates the total amount of natural fresh water available to Israel, surface as well as groundwater, at 1.17 billion cubic metres per year. Yet the demand for drinking water *alone* stands at 1.7 billion cubic metres per year, a figure projected to rise to 2.45 billion cubic metres by 2050 – a rate of consumption that, if the Galilee were the only source, would completely empty it in less than two years. So why, if Israel was no longer sucking the Galilee dry, was the lake's water level so manifestly unstable?

The reasons are hotly debated within Israel's water management community. The demand from the NWC is far from the only one placed by Israel on the Galilee basin. For an extensive area around, the surface streams that naturally feed the lake, along with the upper Jordan that flows down from the Golan Heights, have long been diverted for local agricultural purposes, or to service growing towns or cities such as Tiberias. Increasing amounts of groundwater have been extracted via wells for irrigation, too. In 2018, researchers from Ben-Gurion University blamed this for the lake's alarming depletion, and accused the IWA of mismanagement.[5] The debate intensified in July 2018, when Tiberias was rocked by a mysterious 'swarm' of earth tremors, which lasted for five days. Seismologists suggested that this, too, was linked to overpumping of the surrounding aquifer, which they speculated had 'unclamped' the Jordan Valley's tectonic faultline.[6]

The IWA denied there was any connection, and still insists that the real cause of the lake's problems is reduced rainfall in its 1,000-square-kilometre catchment area, together with evaporation caused by rising temperatures: the effects, in short, of climate change.[7] In the 1970s, according to IWA figures, net inflow to the lake was around 500 million cubic metres per year. It now averages 290 million cubic metres per year, and it is still falling: by 2040, the IWA predicts a net inflow of 200 million cubic metres. Critics of the IWA accuse it of erroneously 'climaticizing' the debate – perhaps, even, of deliberately exaggerating the drying effects of climate change in order to absolve itself of responsibility for basin mismanagement.[8]

It is true that climate change might suit certain Israeli agendas and business interests – the desalination industry, for example – while assisting Israeli right-wingers who sometimes argue that Israel cannot afford to raise the annual allocation of water it grants, under the Oslo Accords, to Palestine (or, indeed, to Jordan, under the 1994 treaty). However, it is not in doubt that 2018 was the fifth year of the worst drought in Israel-Palestine since records began in the 1920s; and nor do many climatologists dispute that the entire Middle East has been experiencing a widening pattern of climate change, a deepening cycle of temperature and weather extremes, for the last thirty years.

The first piece of NWC infrastructure l wanted to see was the old pumping station on the Galilee shore. If Israel was a body, and water its blood, as Levi Eshkol remarked, then the National Water Carrier was its aorta, and the pumping station was once its beating heart. Not for nothing was it named after Pinchas Sapir, the 1960s minister of finance known as the Father of Israel's economic development. Without it, the modern state of Israel might never have developed at all.

I had reckoned, though, without the dead hand of Israeli bureaucracy. It was weeks since I had applied to Mekorot for permission to visit Sapir. I was close by now, but despite my almost daily badgering phone calls and emails the permission had still not come through. Early next morning, therefore, I drove 16 kilometres up the lakeshore from Tiberias to try a different approach – a knock on the front door.

The pumping station wasn't hard to find. Sandwiched between the road and the water's edge near the ancient settlement of Tabgha, it was surrounded by wire and surveillance cameras, with spikes in the approach road to deter ram-raiders. Sapir was still considered strategically and symbolically important enough to be a potential target for terrorists. Part of the reason for the delay with Mekorot, I understood, was the need to vet my press credentials. I tried chatting up the guard on the gate but it was futile. There was no way past without an appointment, and clearance from head-quarters in Tel Aviv.

If Sapir was a modern miracle, its location was appropriate: Tabgha is where Christ fed the 5,000 on bread and tilapia. The road was already busy with tourist buses heading for the Church of the Multiplication of the Loaves and Fishes, or up the hill to the Mount of Beatitudes, the site of another church which marked the spot where Jesus delivered the Sermon on the Mount. I joined the convoy, wondering what to do with my day now that I had been rebuffed.

The church on the hilltop, 500 metres above the lake, was a big Italianate affair, built by Franciscans in the 1930s. I looked back down the hill for signs of the mighty pressure pipes leading up from Sapir – the route had to be nearby – but it was half a century since they had been laid, and the pipes had disappeared beneath the steep green fields.

It was early morning, but the chapel grounds were already thick with pilgrims. Some were deep into Bible classes, squeezed together on benches beneath awnings, from where the occasional *Hallelujah!* disturbed the enraptured hush. I wandered a path through the pretty gardens, and photographed a reedy water feature embellished with a stone-carved Bible, the pages of which bore words from the gospel of John 7:37:

> Let anyone who thirst, come to me and drink. Whoever believes in me,
> as Scripture says, rivers of water flow from within him.

Next to it, hilariously, was a sign with a crossed-out water tap and the instruction, in Hebrewised English, WATER NOT FOR DRINK.

I drove west from Tiberias, looking for a better vantage point from which to see the NWC. The water flows in underground tunnels for most of its length, but I knew this was not the case in the first, northern section, where it passes along an open canal via a reservoir to the Beit Netofa Valley, and from there to the enormous Eshkol treatment plant, where it disappears below ground for good on its long journey southwards.

Eventually, I found a gravel slip road off the Route 65 motorway, from where I gazed down a broad green valley filled with acacia trees through which a canal wound like a great grey snake between tall wire security fences. The canal was far from full, but there was water there, glittering in the late afternoon sun. Along the track was a simple stone building housing the tomb of the Old Testament Prophet Habakkuk. I took my shoes off before stepping inside, to the outrage of the suspicious Hasidic caretaker, who yelled at me above the noise of passing traffic. His words were in Hebrew, but I could guess at my mistake: shoe removal was a mark of respect reserved for mosques.

The caretaker no doubt resented the intrusion of the NWC into his valley, but to most Israelis the carrier is still an icon, a source of great national pride. Thousands of workers were involved in its construction, and the cost was huge, accounting for as much as 5 per cent of GDP between 1950 and 1970.[9] At adjusted prices, this was six times more per capita of population than the United States spent on the Panama Canal.

When the NWC finally opened in 1964, according to the author Seth Siegel, it was regarded as 'more than an infrastructure project. It was ... the embodiment of the idea that the interests of the nation were superior to that of any one part ... [the] planning and usage of water thereafter was national in outlook. This contributed to the development of an Israeli identity.'[10] The nation's investment in its success was emotional as well as financial, no doubt. Much of the money that paid for it came, controversially, from a war reparations fund set up by Germany in recompense for the Holocaust. Until 1995, a section of NWC pipework was depicted on the back of Israel's five-shekel banknote, with the project's prime ministerial overseer, Levi Eshkol, on the front.

The NWC was an engineering marvel in the tradition of the Gihon tunnel at Jerusalem. For the water to flow to the coast under gravity, it first had to be pumped to a point above sea level, a differential totalling 374 metres. The energy required to do this was said to amount to a third of all the electricity generated in Israel at the time. Nor was the planned route westwards simple: it had to traverse two wadis, one of which, the Nahal Amud, has almost vertical sides and is 150 metres deep. The engineers overcame this obstacle by building a siphon that pushed the water through 700 metres of pipe laid at the bottom of a steep V, with the top of the eastern side precisely one metre higher than the other. The water thus flowed to the western side under natural hydrostatic pressure according to the principle of communicating vessels, a method in use since Roman times.

The Amud siphon, when I went to inspect it, resembled an outsize version of a laboratory demonstration from my student days. The pipes were encased in sections of pre-cast concrete that had been lowered down the sheer face of the wadi before being fixed into place, an operation that must have been as dangerous as it was difficult. The concrete sections were stepped, which made the siphon resemble an inverted Babylonian ziggurat, or perhaps an ancient Mexican pyramid, raised by the Mayans in honour of their rain god, Chaac.

The following day, I headed to the south end of the Galilee for a look at the dam at Degania. The dam was invisible from the road because its top *is* the road, so that I crossed over without realising at first, and had to double back. It takes a sharp eye to spot the 1930s-era concrete rotunda that houses the old sluice gates. Apart from a few days in May 2013, following an exceptionally wet spring, it was half a century since the gates had been fully opened.

The sluices evidently were kept partially open, however. Immediately below the dam, the River Jordan appeared as nature intended, a broad stretch of clean, green water that rolled and gurgled among clumps of reeds, beneath a canopy of palms and noble eucalyptus trees. Dragonflies skimmed, and waterfowl scooted among the roots and foliage along the banks. This was the Jordan of illustrated children's Bibles, a dreamscape as pretty as an Aubusson tapestry.

The reason for its pristine state became apparent 100 metres downstream, where I turned my car through the entrance to the baptism spot known as Yardenit. Until 2011, when the historically correct site on the West Bank was opened to Christian pilgrims, this was where the Israeli tourist office sent them. It is still a very popular calling point on the so-called Jesus Trail. The car park is vast, with a gift shop the size of a small supermarket. I passed along aisles of jewellery, menorahs and other assorted Judaica through sliding electric glass doors to an expanse of timber decking beyond. Steps with handrails for the infirm led down to the water's edge, where white-clad pilgrims from Wichita Falls whooped and wept. The gospel classic, *Down to the River to Pray*, was playing through loudspeakers on a loop.

I got back in the car and followed the satnav to Alumot, 3 kilometres further downstream. The river was narrower here but looked just as lovely, with sandy, shaded banks dotted with picnickers and anglers. Smoke rose from a barbecue. A group of children splashed deliriously in the shallows, or swung out over the water on a tire hung from a tree branch. But here also was another small dam, below which the Jordan reverted to its more familiar state: a dirty ditch, almost narrow enough to jump across. Water gushed in from a rusty pipe to one side, next to a sign explaining that this was a 'salt conduit' bringing unwanted brackish water from springs around the Galilee. Alumot was the limit of the river illusion. From here on south, the Jordan was useful to Israel mostly as a drainage channel for agricultural run-off.

I spent the next two days criss-crossing the area, and the more I saw the more I understood how completely the waters of the Galilee had been manipulated and exploited. The farming here was of the most intensive kind. In all directions stretched vineyards and orchards under neat rows of polytunnels, and extensive, lush plantations of banana under nets, all copiously irrigated from pipes that often ran parallel to the roads.

This garden of plenty had been planted at the very beginning of the Zionist project, long before the NWC or even Degania dam had been thought of. This region at the top of the lower Jordan was one of the crucibles of the Second Aliyah of 1904–14, a wave of inward migration that proved pivotal to the Israeli national narrative. It was a heritage landscape, dotted with museums and trails and special brown placards signposting the earliest days of Zionism, all catering for Jewish tourists nostalgic for their heroic past.

I stopped at the Kinneret National Farm, a square-shaped, Ottoman-era farmstead, now a museum surrounded by painted horse-drawn harrows and other lovingly conserved agricultural relics. An exhibition explained how the World Zionist Organization had converted the farmstead in 1908 into an agricultural training centre for would-be farmers, although it soon became something more, a kind of social laboratory that led to workers' collectives and the birth of the kibbutz movement.

There was a curious shrine-like quality to the museum, evincing the almost cult-like respect with which modern Israelis still view the early pioneers. The founders of this farm were some of the original and best exponents of a fundamental Zionist ideal, the physical re-connection to the land. They included men like Aaron David Gordon, a forty-eight-year-old estate manager from Troyanov in what is now Ukraine, who refused the clerical work offered him when he first made aliyah, 'and instead took up the hoe, labouring in the fields by day and writing by night'. His puritanical embrace of the simple rural life helped to shape what became known as the 'religion of labour', the socio-cultural mind-set that drove – and arguably still drives – the Zionist project.

A.D. Gordon is buried nearby in Israel's first kibbutz, called Degania A, which a sign at the entrance boasted was established in 1910. It is still going strong, farming everything from bananas to cows, with a lucrative sideline making jewellery and knick-knacks for sale to the pilgrims at Yardenit. I drove in for a look. An old grey tractor from the 1950s, repurposed as the centrepiece of a flowerbed by the entrance, set the tone. I saw bungalows, cowsheds and a pre-war concrete grain silo, the classic (and to Israelis, iconic) symbol of kibbutz architecture. A collection point for the community's worn-out appliances had been turned into a kind of art installation, with herbs and cacti growing out of old kettles, washing machines, lavatories.

I drove south along Route 90, parallel to the River Jordan towards the northern edge of the occupied West Bank. Before the border, I turned west and followed a switchback up to the spine of Mount Gilboa, Route 667 on my tourist map, to a viewing point near the top of the mountain from where I looked down into the West Bank, out over the upper Jezreel Valley. I could just make out the separation barrier, its position betrayed by a tan-coloured patrol road winding across the middle distance. To the south-west lay the shimmering suggestion of Jenin, and in the haze beyond it, the Dothan Valley that I had visited with Bassam. It seemed a lifetime since I had been there.

At my back, to the north, lay a wide green valley of immaculate orchards and fields that seemed to belong to a different world. The abundance of water here was immediately apparent, not least from the river in the fore-ground, the Harod, an important tributary of the Jordan. The Harod no longer looked like a river. Its waters had been dammed and channelled into a tidy chain of ponds and reservoirs that filled the near horizon, all the way to the edge of Beit She'an, the largest town in this region.

The ponds were fish farms, the centrepiece of a thriving aquaculture industry that began with the importation of carp in the 1930s. Even by the time of independence in 1948, there were more than ninety fish farms in Israel, producing so much carp and bass for the table that by the mid-1960s the country had a problematic surplus of them.[11]

Had the harnessing of the Harod contributed to the lack of adequate water supply downriver? Perhaps not, if the flow was only temporarily trapped in the fishponds. But the aquaculture business of Beit She'an is nevertheless controversial in the West Bank. I had met Jordan Valley farmers who viewed it as a primary source of pollution in 'their' river; and anyone with access to Google Earth, or just to an ordinary map, can see for themselves the scale of the operation. Older Palestinians no doubt remember with bitterness that, until 1948, the ancient settlement of Beit She'an was an entirely Arab town. No Arabs at all live there now.

Fish, a symbol of plenty in all the Abrahamic religions, have always been associated with the River Jordan. On the Madaba map, a sixth-century floor mosaic in a Byzantine church in Jordan – the world's oldest cartographic representation of the Holy Land – the river is shown teeming with fish so fat that their sides almost touch the banks on either side. Fish like that, if they ever existed, would struggle to swim far in the river now. In any case, West Bank fishermen are unable to get to the river to catch any fish, not even tiddlers.

The fish farms on the Harod replaced what had been lost to Israelis from the Jordan, but there was no such substitute for Palestinians. None of the Jordan's tributaries that flow through the Occupied Territories is large enough to sustain a fish farming operation like Beit She'an's. Tilapia were once raised in irrigation ponds in the West Bank, but the practice was abandoned in the 1990s when even Palestinian farmers began to switch to drip irrigation, and the traditional but wasteful pond system fell out of use. By 1997, according to a study, the average per capita consumption of fish in the West Bank had dropped to just 2 kilograms per year, compared to 12 kilograms for Israelis.[12] It was no wonder if some Palestinians saw the fish farms as yet another aggravating example of how Israel always took all the best for themselves, and never gave anything back.

I returned to the River Jordan. The 35-kilometre stretch between the Sea of Galilee and the northern edge of the West Bank still forms an international border, so the riverbank is still a closed military zone, mined in parts and fenced off to the public, just as I had found further south. Only one place was truly accessible: the confluence with the River Yarmouk, which flows in from the east where it forms the border between Jordan and Syria. Naharayim, or 'Two Rivers', as the confluence is called, was also once a border crossing point between Jordan and Israel.

In the 1930s, Naharayim was chosen as the site of a giant hydro-electric plant, the brainchild of Pinhas Rutenberg, an engineering genius from Ukraine who became known as 'the old man of Naharayim'. The sluice gates erected in 1932 at Degania were designed not only to secure water for irrigation but also to allow it to be diverted here via a special canal. Theodor Herzl anticipated that the new Israel would be powered by hydro-electricity. This was where the pioneers first put Herzl's vision into practice, a clean and green energy project years ahead of its time.

The plant had long ceased operating – partly because there was no longer enough water in the Galilee to power it – but I was keen to see what remained of it. In 1994, as a part of the Israel-Jordan peace treaty, the Amman government agreed to lease a stretch of the Jordanian riverbank here to Israel, for conversion into a 'peace park' to symbolize the new spirit of cooperation. Aimed at ecotourists, school groups and students of international relations, the park was centred on an artificial island, the so-called 'Island of Peace,' that was created by the diversionary canals that served the old power plant. The twenty-five-year lease agreement was due to expire in November 2019, however; and it had recently been reported, to the surprise of the Israeli government, that Jordan's King Abdullah wanted the land back, and was refusing to agree to an extension.[13] The expiring leasehold gave me another reason to visit Naharayim, because once the park was gone, there would most likely be no public access to this section of the river at all.

At the end of a bumpy track, I found the way to the island blocked by tall rusty gates, chained and padlocked and topped with razor wire. It had been many years since Naharayim functioned as a border crossing. A hut for passport control lay derelict, its windows smashed in. Close by was a small café surrounded by flowerbeds and neat lawns leading to a hillock with easterly views towards Jordan, the usual dun-coloured hills turned an improbably vivid green by the recent rains. Beyond the fence lay Jordanian territory, and the ruins of the old hydro-electric plant.

There were no customers in the café apart from a group of Israeli soldiers, swigging Coke Zero in the shade on a break from their morning border patrol. From the way they teased the café owner, who was also the Island of Peace gatekeeper, it was clear they were regulars here. Their sergeant, a burly older man with darker skin, was the only one who didn't speak English. One of the others made lewd jokes at his expense, for my benefit. 'I'm the active one, and he's the passive,' he said, wiggling his hips. 'Isn't that right, sergeant?' There were laddish chortles all round as their uncomprehending officer nodded.

Access to the island was supposed to be by appointment only, and was usually only granted to groups on guided tours, but the gatekeeper took pity and agreed to let me through for half an hour on my own. 'You're in luck,' he said as he fiddled with the padlock. 'The Yarmouk is in spate. It's usually just a trickle but it's been raining a lot in Syria. Shout when you're ready to come out again.'

The gates creaked shut behind me, and I was left alone in a secret world. I followed a path through waist-high yellow chrysanthemum towards the forlorn ruins of machinery. It still bore the date and place of its manufacture: *Ransomes and Rapier Ltd. Ipswich, England. 1931.* The Yarmouk thundered over a concrete waterfall down a sluice towards the confluence. Wires drooped from broken telegraph poles. An overgrown railway embankment, part of a spur of the famous Hejaz railway that once connected Haifa to Damascus, now terminated in a cliff over the water, the sole remaining buttress of a bridge.

Naharayim evoked the transience of all human endeavour, perhaps even its ultimate futility. Between 1932 and 1948, most of the electricity consumed in British Mandate Palestine was produced by this plant, which took 3,000 workers five years to build. Nature, however, was now firmly back in charge. Every man-made edge and angle was softened by thick greenery; everything concrete and metal had been eroded by the action of water and oxidization. It wouldn't be long before this landscape reverted to its former state, leaving nothing of Rutenberg's gift to Israel but memories.

Not all of these would be benign ones. The opening salvo of the Arab invasion of Palestine in April 1948 was launched at an Israeli police fort here. The power plant itself, an obvious and vulnerable symbol of Jewish technological superiority, as well as an actual engine of economic development and Zionist expansionism, was occupied and looted the following month by forces from Iraq. The Iraqis' further advance was averted only by the quick thinking of Israeli engineers who cranked open the sluices at Degania and flooded all the surrounding canals.

For all the good intentions behind the park, Naharayim seemed a very uncertain symbol of peace. In the Israeli public imagination, indeed, it was associated with the precise opposite. That was because in 1997, a crazed Jordanian border guard, Ahmad Daqamseh, massacred seven Israeli schoolgirls on a field trip here. The caretaker pointed to the spot where it happened, a grassy hillock 100 metres from his café where the girls had been picnicking. The pretty garden he tended was dedicated to the schoolgirls' memory. Their photographs, a row of smiling thirteen-year-olds, were displayed on a plaque that was fading in the sun. They were the same age when they died as my own eldest daughter back home.

The caretaker gamely insisted that the massacre hadn't damaged the cause of peace because, he said, it had helped focus minds on the need for better understanding. King Hussein, he recalled, had tried to make amends by visiting the bereaved families in person and falling to his knees in apology. Daqamseh, meanwhile, was caught and sentenced to twenty years with hard labour. 'Israelis knew then that Hussein was sincere,' said the caretaker. 'The Arabs normally treat their terrorists like heroes.'

And yet the car park here was empty, the tour groups few and far between; and soon, with the expiration of the 1994 lease, Naharayim would revert into another fenced-off border zone, and the public would not be able to visit at all. 'I hope the lease can be extended and the park can continue, but we will see,' the caretaker said. 'In the end this is Jordanian land, not ours.'

It took many more days of lobbying to get through the doors of the Sapir Pumping Station on the Galilee. Mekorot was world-renowned for its water management expertise and the boldness of its vision, but its public relations strategy had not kept pace. 'Maybe they're scared that what you write will be used politically,' said my contact at the Israeli Water Authority, when I complained to him about their slowness. 'The Right says that Mekorot gives Palestine too much water. The Left says they give too little. Either way, they can't win.'

Ashley, the press handler eventually assigned to me, was a long-time émigré from the south of England. He was not a press officer but a scientist by background, who stuck firmly to a prepared script of Mekorot's corporate history. He would not be drawn on any matter that he considered even remotely controversial or 'political'. Any questions I might have about that, he said, would have to be put to head office. I wasn't so surprised. Mekorot, which enjoys a near-monopoly over its sector, is a parastatal utility company, with little need or incentive to explain itself to anyone.

Photography anywhere within the Sapir pumping station compound, Ashley crisply informed me, was forbidden. He showed me a concrete collecting-pond, only partially full, and the pipe at its bottom that fed it, drawing lake water from a point half a kilometre offshore. He pointed out a pair of white pipes that rose inshore along the awkward contours of a steep, rocky hill: the very start of the 130-kilometre NWC. Eventually he led me through some gates and down a tall, wide tunnel carved into the side of the hill at the centre of the compound. The tunnel opened into the engine hall, an enormous, dank cavern, with walls streaked with grime from pigeons nesting in the shadows at the top.

In the centre of the hall were the pumps: the mighty mechanical heart of the NWC system. They were enormous machines, three of them, built in the 1960s by the Swiss engineering firm, Brown Boveri Ltd. Their pleasingly curved flanks, like the bolts and pipes and tubes that encased them, were covered in many coats of shiny green paint. 'They're as good as new,' Ashley said. 'They're like a vintage car. They work perfectly so long as you look after them and run them occasionally.'

They were, however, silent; the only sound in the machine hall was the occasional flap of birds' wings. Since 2015 the pumps had only been switched on for a few hours a night, when power from the grid was cheaper. Despite the machinery's state of readiness, this curious cavern felt like a museum piece, a relic of another era. Ashley explained that its subterranean location was designed to defend the pumps from air attack. It reminded me of a villain's lair in a James Bond movie, although the security arrangements weren't paranoid: Israel's water network had been attacked in the past. One of the first armed operations ever mounted by the PLO, in 1965, was an attempt to sabotage a newly opened NWC water tunnel near the Palestinian village of Eilaboun. The saboteur, Ahmad Musa, was caught and killed as he attempted to flee to Jordan. Fatah still consider him the first martyr of their cause, and commemorate 'Martyr's Day' every 7 January, the date of his death.

Sapir and the NWC still occupy a special place in the imaginations of the security conscious. For instance, the plot of *Dark Waters*, a thriller published by the American author Chris Goff in 2015, turns on a bid to sabotage the pump engines, and the notion that this would force Israel to divert water from the upper Jordan instead, thus provoking renewed regional war. This fanciful idea was out of date even in 2015: if the pumps were put out of action, Israel even then could easily have made up the shortfall with desalinated water. Yet the fixation on water security, and the conviction in particular that the NWC is Israel's Achilles heel, persists.

The pumping station shared its compound with the Kinneret Limnological Laboratory, the lake's water-monitoring centre where Ashley had once worked. The entrance was fashioned from a section of water carrier, a hoop of concrete 3 metres high. Inside, we found a crowd of white-coated scientists who greeted their former colleague with shaloms and backslaps. Surrounded by retorts and racks of test tubes, a middle-aged lady in goggles explained how her team examined 100,000 water samples each year, forever on the look-out for increased turbidity, perhaps caused by algal bloom, the first sign of eutrophication which, if left unchecked, could irreversibly damage the lake. 'Nutrient levels are definitely higher than usual this winter,' she confided. 'We counter it with "burst" chlorination in the substations. It's a constant balancing act, trying always to stay one step ahead of nature.'

One step ahead of nature: that approach seemed to encapsulate much of the Zionist project. It was constantly astounding to me how this successful modern state had established itself, in hostile desert terrain, against all the political odds, and in defiance of the experts who said it couldn't be done.

I wondered, even so, why Israel was so anxious to keep the old NWC system going. The Sapir station was much more of a museum piece than I had expected. If the Galilee had been replaced by desalinated seawater as Israel's primary water source, why had the pumps not simply been decommissioned?

I heard the clearest explanation from Doron Markel, the former regional chief of the IWA. 'Since 2015, the city of Haifa, 400,000 people, has depended for drinking water on a single desalination plant at Hadera,' he said. 'But what if the plant fails? We have to keep Sapir going as a back-up system.'

This was rational; but it was also, I thought, profoundly unfair on Palestine. The Galilee had been demoted to a secondary Israeli water source. Yet to Palestinians, the lake, as the main feeder of the lower Jordan, was still very much a primary one. I had not forgotten the anger and passion on the face of Ali at the eco-hotel by Al-Auja, who dreamed of rehabilitating the river by demolishing the dam at Degania with a bulldozer. But when I repeated that conversation to Doron, he dismissed the suggestion as 'nonsense'. With rain-fall patterns as they were, he insisted, removing the dam would by itself make almost no difference to the long-term health of the river. 'In the modern Middle East, it is in any case almost a crime to discharge fresh water into the saline Dead Sea,' he observed.

He was right, no doubt; but his lofty tone bothered me. It did not seem likely to me that the water-starved Palestinians, if given full access to the natural flow of the Jordan, would waste it on the Dead Sea. In any case, was it not up to them to decide what to do with the resource – especially now that it was no longer critical to Israel's water security, thanks to the surplus of water produced by desalination? In fact, why could not all the restrictions on the exploitation of natural water in the West Bank be lifted?

'Personally I think the Palestinians should have more water,' Doron said. 'We get ninety litres per capita per day, they get ten to twenty, and it shouldn't and needn't be like that.' He acknowledged that the water quotas allocated at Oslo were out of date and needed revising. Yet he stopped well short of blaming Israel for the impasse in the peace process, and he did not seem to think that Israel took more than its fair share of natural water – or if he did, he would not admit it to me.

'But what about land rights?' I persisted. 'Shouldn't Palestinians have the right to pump water from their own aquifers in the West Bank?'

'Look,' he shrugged. 'We are water workers – and the Water Authority obeys government policy. I can't talk about politics. What matters more is to find ways to produce more water, in agreement with the other side.'

His best hopes for the future all rested on new water management schemes, designed to mitigate or even reverse the decline of the Jordan Valley hydrologic system. The first was a twenty-year-old project known as 'Red-to-Dead', a scheme to provide Jordan with desalinated water drawn from the Gulf of Aqaba, while sending the brine northwards in a separate pipe for the replenishment of the Dead Sea. Doron had been involved with Red-to-Dead for years; although, as he admitted, it is currently stalled, partly because of security concerns over the infrastructure.

More promising, in his eyes, was a new, billion shekel (US$280 million) plan to start refilling the Galilee using desalinated water from Hadera, the nearest plant on the Mediterranean. Construction work on the necessary pipework, he said, had already begun. 'There is something similar in California – the Southern Conveyor – but that water goes into an artificial reservoir. No one has ever tried to replenish a natural lake with desal like this.'

The cleverness of the new 'reverse pipe' plan was that it would mostly utilize the existing infrastructure of the old NWC, making it relatively cheap to construct and operate. Doron explained how, according to Blaise Pascal's Laws of Hydraulics, any water can be forced uphill when placed under pressure in a sealed pipe. In those places where the NWC ran not in sealed pipes but in open canals, such as the Netofa Valley, new locks and pumps were being installed to push the water up and over the final hill until gravity took over and decanted it into the lake. I remembered the acacia-filled valley by Route 65 where I had first seen the NWC canal, and a pair of yellow bulldozers that I had spotted rumbling in the distance, their yellow flanks flashing in the fading afternoon sun. Their activity was no longer a mystery.

The reverse pipe, Doron went on, would eventually bring 120 million cubic metres per year to the Galilee; and unlike natural inflows that are subject to the vicissitudes of the seasons, this extra water could be guaranteed and supplied whenever it was needed. 'That is something you can start to plan with. We will be able to sustain the lake at the right level. We might even be able to open the dam at Degania eventually, for the long-term rehabilitation of the Jordan. Israelis are still obsessed with black and red lines around the Galilee, but it is all nonsense. The National Water Level Indicator is not important anymore. It's an irrelevance.'

It sounded fantastical, but Israel was aiming at mastery over nature itself – and not for the first time. Over the Golan Heights, where the upper Jordan rises, the Israeli air force had for years been seeding storm clouds with silver iodide, by which technique, Doron said, 'you can enhance precipitation by 10 per cent.'

It was impossible not to admire his confidence, optimism and ambition. Most public Western discourse on the environment, and on climate change in particular, assumes that it is already too late to restore the balance of nature, and that the best mankind can hope for is to allay or delay the fallout. The Global Commission on Adaptation, launched by the UN in 2018, predicts that by 2030, water shortage will affect some 5 billion people, causing unprecedented competition for water and, in turn, apocalyptic levels of conflict and migration.[14] But what if human ingenuity can find a way to fight back against climate change? Could Israel's reverse pipe project really right the wrongs of half a century of resource exploitation in the Galilee? If so, what did that imply for the Israel–Palestine peace process; and what lessons might be drawn for the resolution of all the other deepening water crises around the world?

There remained, however, a difficulty with Doron's inspiring vision of the Jordan Valley's future – and that was the Palestinians, who had no say in it, and had never been consulted. The question of honouring the rights of any of Israel's Arab neighbours while the new strategies were developed – whether to land, to groundwater, or to any other natural resource – was for politicians to puzzle over, not him; but there seemed to be no doubt, in his mind, that Israel and its interests should always come first. The air force's raincloud seeding operation that he described was a case in point. Did he worry at all – had he even considered the possibility – that when Israel made it rain over the Golan, it might be taking water that could otherwise have fallen on neighbouring Syria, or Lebanon?

'Mm ... that would be very difficult to measure,' Doron replied. His outlook was, of course, distinctively Israeli. Our meeting took place not in Tiberias but, at his invitation, in a popular restaurant called the Camilla, in a service station on Israel's busiest north-south motorway, Route 6, which runs parallel to the western edge of the West Bank. The restaurant turned out to be less than 2 kilometres from Qalqilya, the walled-off Palestinian town whose desperate govenor I had interviewed not long previously. Doron looked astonished when I told him. 'I've never been there,' he said eventually. 'We just can't.'

As with other Israelis I had met, Palestine to him was the 'other', an alien universe that existed in parallel to but entirely separately from his own world, out of sight and therefore very often out of mind. Route 6 might as well have been a shoreline, so definitively did it delineate the edge of the country he inhabited; and he looked towards the West Bank as one might gaze out at an empty sea.

I wondered at the intellectual and imaginative contortions required to sustain this illusion. The Camilla restaurant, with its prosperous laid-back clientele, its pleasantly shaded terrace and its Euro-generic menu, all gnocchi and schnitzel and boeuf bourguignon, was typical of the comfortable Israeli modus vivendi. Yet not even this place could be described as truly safe. Four days after our meeting, a long-range missile from Gaza injured seven in Mishmeret, a moshav 3 kilometres away.[15]

The dialogue of the deaf between Israel and Palestine continues as loud as ever. For a quarter of a century, Israel has been focused on finding technical fixes to the water shortage, while Palestinians speak only about the restitution of their rights and the land they have lost. It is Palestine, though, that suffers most from this miscommunication. For all the brilliance of the solutions Doron outlined, the peace process remains stalled, the Jordan River is still a dirty trickle, and Palestinians everywhere lack the water with which to live as they could or should.

CHAPTER TEN

The Golan Heights

Who Needs Italy?

I DROVE NORTH from Tiberias into the Golan Heights: the final leg of my journey up the River Jordan.

The Golan has a dour reputation abroad as a permanently tense military zone: a bloc of strategic high ground, captured from Syria during the Six Day War of 1967 and occupied by Israel ever since, in contravention of numerous UN resolutions.[1] So I expected an Afghan-style desert mountain, barren, windswept and heavily fortified with minefields and artillery positions. There would no doubt be bleak army bases guarded by sentries in dugouts and pillboxes, and IDF armoured patrols and checkpoints at every turn.

What I found, in March 2019, resembled the pre-Alps in spring. A fast, smooth road led upwards between sparkling waterfalls and lakeside groves of eucalyptus to a grassy moorland plateau ablaze with wildflowers. I passed herds of grazing cows, tidy lines of beehives: this was, literally, a land of milk and honey. Not all the occupiers here, evidently, were soldiers.

On the northern horizon loomed the snow-capped peaks of Mount Hermon, the tri-state border with Syria and Lebanon, and the ultimate source of the Jordan. At one point, driving too slowly in order to admire the lovely views, I was overtaken by a tootling car with skis on its roof, en route to Israel's only winter sports resort for the last gasp of the season. With the Sea of Galilee at my back, it reminded me of the approach to the Mont Blanc massif on the road from Lake Geneva.

The Golan, though, was not the Shangri-La it first seemed. Skull-and-crossbones signs on the roadsides warned that much of the pretty moorland was indeed mined. I thought that might explain the flowers: as I learned in the Jordan Valley, flora as well as fauna flourish when they are undisturbed by people. Here and there I passed designated crossing points for tanks, just like on Salisbury Plain where public roads intersect a British Army training ground. The Golan's defences may have been half a century old, and the military presence more felt than seen, but I didn't doubt that the IDF were ready for immediate deployment if required.

Successive Israeli governments have treated the Golan not as occupied territory, but as an integral part of their nation. In 1981, under Menachem Begin, the Knesset passed the Golan Heights Law, which brought the Golan under mainstream national administration: a de facto annexation, in short. The United Nations swiftly condemned it as illegal. The US, too, has traditionally viewed the Golan's occupation as an obstacle to peace.

The old status quo, however, is changing. In the very week that I visited, in a move widely interpreted as a gift to Netanyahu's electoral campaign, President Trump announced a sudden reversal of half a century of American policy. 'After 52 years,' he tweeted, 'it is time for the United States to fully recognize Israel's sovereignty over the Golan Heights.'[2] Netanyahu was overjoyed, and tweeted back: 'At a time when Iran seeks to use Syria as a platform to destroy Israel, President Trump boldly recognizes Israeli sovereignty over the Golan Heights. Thank you, President Trump!'

Trump's move attracted predictable criticism. Robert Malley, a former Middle East adviser to Barack Obama (and now President Biden's Special Envoy to Iran) called the decision 'gratuitous' and – presciently, it turned out – 'ominous . . . at a time when voices in Israel calling for the annexation of the West Bank are growing louder'.[3] Netanyahu, however, was undeterred. To mark his gratitude, he later announced that a new settlement in the Golan, 110 housing units on a hill just east of the upper Jordan, would be named Trump Heights: the first time a sitting US president had been so honoured since the renaming of Kfar Truman in 1950. The occupation of the Golan Heights, in short, was as controversial as ever, and emphatically back in the news.

Israel's decision to occupy the Golan in 1967 was driven, at least in part, by a hydrological imperative. It has always been a wet area, the source and principal catchment area for the only major river in the region. Snowmelt from Mount Hermon feeds two rivers, the Dan and the Banias, which drain west to the upper Jordan, where it is joined by a third river, the Hasbani, entering from Lebanon. The Jordan then flows due south to the Galilee, swollen en route by seasonal rains that cascade down countless east-west streams and rivulets.

By 1967, Jews and Arabs had already been skirmishing over this rich resource for twenty years. In 1953, when Israel began building an intake pipe for the NWC on the upper Jordan 16 kilometres north of the Galilee, Syria responded by shelling the construction site from artillery positions in these hills. The Arab States knew what water meant to the new Israeli polity, and the NWC, especially once it came online in 1964, was the greatest *casus belli* of all. 'The establishment of Israel is the basic threat that the Arab nation in its entirety has agreed to forestall,' ran a communiqué issued by the Arab League in Cairo in January 1964, 'and [. . .] the diversion of the Jordan waters by it multiplies the dangers to Arab existence.'

Arab suspicions that Israel sought control of the entire Jordan basin system were not without foundation. As long ago as 1919, the Zionist leader Chaim Weizmann, who would become the first President of Israel, listed control of the 164-kilometre Litani River – which flows entirely within the territory of modern Lebanon – among the 'minimum requirements essential to the realization of the Jewish National Home'. Ben-Gurion also proposed occupying land as far north as the Litani valley in the 1940s. As late as 2006, a year of conflict with Hezbollah, Israel's intentions were again questioned when Israeli airstrikes knocked out irrigation canals in the Litani valley, as well as a pumping station on the Wazzani River, which feeds the Hasbani.[4]

In 1964, the Arab states reacted to the opening of the NWC with a diversion plan of their own, and began to build dams on the Banias and the

Hasbani, a scheme calculated to reduce the NWC's intended intake by a third. Israel responded, in 1965, by destroying the construction sites with tanks and artillery, and then with airstrikes deep over Syria. It was the start of a phase in the conflict that led to the Six Day War, the very last Israeli gambit of which, tellingly, was the complete takeover of the Golan catchment area.

Israel no longer depends on natural fresh water as it did but, as Doron Markel explained, the Galilee is still important to the country's water security. Was this why Israel persisted with its occupation of the Golan, in the teeth of half a century of international condemnation? Doron suggested that this was at least part of Israeli thinking. 'Control of the Golan is important not just for the quantity of water it provides, but for the quality,' he told me. 'In Syrian times the upper Jordan and its tributaries were often polluted with agricultural run-off and sewage. If we didn't control the run-off as we do now, with monitoring stations and supervision of cattle farms and settlements, the [Galilee] would soon be in trouble.'

In 1990 the Egyptian foreign minister (and later UN secretary general) Boutros Boutros Ghali predicted that 'the next war in the Middle East will be over water, not politics'. He was echoed in 1995 by the Egyptian academic Ismail Serageldin, a former vice-president of the World Bank, who warned that 'the wars of the next century will be about water'.[5]

Global risk analysts, spurred on by an immense academic literature on the subject, have been debating whether the Egyptians were right or not ever since. The naysayers argue that, historically, states more often cooperate than fight over contested water resources – which is, in fact, what happened in 1994, when Jordan and Israel agreed to share the River Jordan's tributary, the Yarmouk. They also point out, correctly, that a captured reservoir or river system is not the kind of war booty that you can put on a truck and take home with you; this, too, tends to lead to cooperation agreements.[6]

In the Golan, however, the invading army never went home. Through de facto annexation, Israel has turned its water resource into an exclusive national asset. Their strategy, moreover, has arguably been successful, since there has been no major inter-state violence over the territory for more than forty years. Yet, with demand for water increasing everywhere in the Middle

East, the pressure on natural resources is only going one way. For all Israel's insistence that their occupation is permanent, the Golan is still coveted by Syria, and therefore remains a potential flashpoint for another war, in which the desire to control its waters could easily be an important motivating factor. Can Israel really maintain its occupation forever? And if so, at what cost?

Here, in the meantime, it was obvious that Israel's attachment to the Golan ran deeper than mere military or hydrological expediency. The region, I soon discovered, was a major tourist destination. Wherever I drove, there were brown signposts directing me to trailheads, parks, archaeological sites, look-out points. Israelis are a nation of nature-lovers, and the Golan, clearly, was one of the places where they came to indulge their passion. The entire landscape seemed set up for romantic appreciation.

Many other parts of rural Israel have been turned into nature parks. What is striking about the Golan is how many of its attractions revolve around water. Kayaking and white-water rafting are available along the upper Jordan. Higher up, every waterfall, lake and pool seems to boast a car park, a snack bar, and a visitor centre doling out maps. I wasn't sure I liked the effect. The brown signs made the landscape feel manicured and over-tamed.

The natural environment of the Golan has, in fact, been much manipulated by Israel. The Hula Marshes through which the upper Jordan once flowed were not even mapped until the 1860s, when the Scottish explorer John MacGregor penetrated them in a homemade canoe. In those days, the marshes were a malarial wilderness filled with panthers and wolves, and inhabited by Bedouin who built homes out of papyrus. In the 1950s, however, the Jewish National Fund drained the swamp, which created much useful farmland and got rid of the mosquitoes, but also devastated the ancient ecosystem. Several species, such as the reed cat, *Felis chaus*, were driven to extinction; and the Marsh Bedouin were moved on, never to return.

Concern for the Hula Valley led to the creation of SPNI, the Society for the Protection of Nature in Israel, the overlords of modern Israel's mighty conservation lobby. Some of the wetlands were subsequently restored and turned into a nature reserve, which has since become a world-renowned bird-watching site on the migration route between Europe and Africa. What SPNI did for migratory birds was admirable, but the Hula is still a wilderness lost for good.

I drove to the far north of the Golan to inspect the River Banias, an important tributary of the Jordan, and the northernmost leg of my long riparian journey. The Banias flowed through another well-appointed nature reserve, of course. In their shorts and sandals, the tourist horde passed from a car park through a turnstile down into a thickly wooded gorge, a lovely glade a world away from the urban mayhem of central Israel. The river was in spate, its blue-white waters roaring like a Scottish burn in winter. The visitors took turns on a metal walkway cantilevered across the plunge pool of a waterfall, grinning and whooping in the moisture cloud that filled the air, and calling out to each other above the thunderous din.

Waterfalls have been mesmerising people for a long time at Banias. The spring from which the river rises, in a limestone cavern on the flanks of Mount Hermon, was once a shrine to the goat-footed god Pan. The Herodian kings of the first century built a town around the cave, Caesarea Philippi, from where they once administered the entire region. Then, as now, the Golan's cool sylvan hills offered welcome respite from the summer heat of the desert south, rather as the British rulers of nineteenth-century India retreated to their hill station at Shimla. Watching the tourists beneath the waterfall, it was as though the cult of Pan was still alive.

I gained a similar impression at Gamla, yet another national park set around a ruined fortress, and the site of another celebrated waterfall. The car park was so busy that the rangers were about to close it and turn newcomers away. I set off along a well-trodden moorland path, a designated 'bloom trail', joining a string of weekend day-trippers from all over Israel: honey-mooners, young families with prams, schoolchildren with picnics in their backpacks, pensioners tottering arm in arm. Some were taking selfies, or scenic shots through the spring flowers – anemone, wild mustard, cyclamen, iris – that everywhere erupted through the scrub and grass.

The waterfall at the trail's end was the tallest in Israel, a grey mare's tail in a fenced-off cleft of basalt, 50 metres high. The overlook was crowded with people reverently cooing. The sky was full of lark-song. It was a forty-minute walk from the car park, yet it felt like the completion of a kind of pilgrimage.

The ruin on the other side of the visitor centre, perched on a conical hilltop, was a national icon. 'Rediscovered' by archaeologists following the 1967 occupation, Gamla town was besieged for months by the Romans during the Great Jewish Revolt of AD 66–73. The story of its heroic but futile defence still fires the national imagination. Located in the very south of the Golan, Gamla was a natural gateway to the lands below. The towns-people calculated, correctly, that detaining the legions there would slow their advance on Jerusalem. Thousands died, in an action sometimes described as 'the northern Masada'.

In modern times, Gamla's eyrie-like position made it a useful location for Syrian artillery batteries. The Galilee itself was clearly visible to the south, with a hazy suggestion of Tiberias beyond. Israel's insistence on controlling these Heights was not without military justification.

National security has always been an election issue in Israel. Netanyahu liked to style himself as Israel's 'Mr Security' (a moniker first used by Yitzhak Rabin; today it is used by Netanyahu's rival, Naftali Bennett). Gamla's story was perfect for the security pedlars: in his 2009 election campaign, Netanyahu made much use of an old Israeli catchphrase, 'Gamla will not fall again'. Overlooking the ruins, I found a war memorial to Jewish residents of the Golan killed by 'terror' or while doing their military service. 'This memorial,' explains a sign for anyone missing the point, 'symbolizes the link between the Gamla residents of the Second Temple period and today's residents.'

The crowds at Gamla presented a chance to find out what ordinary Israelis thought of Trump's recent declaration of support for their sover-eignty over this place. I expected naked triumphalism from the day-trippers I spoke to, and I heard some, from a middle-aged Russian couple visiting from Haifa who weren't even aware of the news. 'Really?' said the wife, 'Trump has done what? But that's *good!*'

Other views, however, were more nuanced.

'In my opinion,' said a father of two young children, a settler from further north, 'Gamla is the most beautiful place in Israel, and I am pleased that my children can see it. If it was returned to Syria, it would be ruined.' He drifted away, busy with a recalcitrant four-year-old, but returned a minute later, a thoughtful expression on his face. 'Look,' he said, 'Trump is just playing politics: he wants to help Bibi in the election. Most Golani people will be pleased, but I am against. I am for peace. And if the price of that is the return of the Golan to Syria, so be it.'

Perhaps Israeli populism played better with right-wing conservatives; perhaps hikers and outdoor types like this young father belonged to a different demographic. It was clear, nevertheless, that not every Israeli was impressed by Trump and Netanyahu's manoeuvrings.

It was apparent to me that the tourist authority's free hand here, the assiduous brown-sign glorification of the land and its history, was part of a conscious policy of 'Israelification'. A new narrative was being imposed, physically, with signposts, designed to persuade not just sceptical foreigners but Israel's own people that the Golan was Jewish, not merely through military conquest, but intrinsically, by historical right.

Turning the Golan into a nature park was another prong of the same strategy. Perhaps the government genuinely saw itself as the dutiful curator of a national treasure. But they must have known that playing to Israelis' famed love for the outdoors in this way was also likely to bolster their support for the occupation. At Gamla, the two great Israeli obsessions, nature and nation, intertwined and overlapped. Its presentation seemed part of a clever illusion, a political sleight of hand.

Elsewhere, if one looked, it wasn't hard to see how the trick was done. The small archaeological museum at Katzrin, for instance, was clearly pedalling propaganda. It contained artefacts from every imperial culture that had swept the Heights over the millennia: Seleucid, Roman, Ayyubid, Mamluk. The abundance of water in the Heights had always attracted conquerors and settlers; I was interested to learn that Hippos, a Roman settlement east of the Galilee, was supplied by water from the Golan via an aqueduct 50 kilometres long. Yet the museum's emphasis, its true focus, was all on Jewish achievement in the area. Its centrepiece was an impressive scale model of a sixth-century synagogue which, a sign explained, was one of thirty-five such buildings known to have existed in the Golan in past times, the precise locations of which were revealed on a large wall map.

I chatted to the middle-aged woman manning the reception desk. I was the museum's first, and possibly only, visitor of the day, and she was glad of the diversion. She spoke good English. Her daughter, she said, was an optometrist in Stockport. 'It is my policy never to talk about politics,' she said genially, 'but look at that map. It is very important. Maybe that is why we Jews are here. The Golan *is* Israel.'

Her assertion was questionable. The synagogues on the map were all ancient ruins. In 1967, the Golan's population was almost entirely Syrian. At least 80,000 Syrians fled or were driven out during or after the war. Jewish settlement here – or resettlement – was a recent event, and much more shallow-rooted than it appeared. In the 1970s, the government planned to settle 54,000 people here, but public take-up failed to meet expectations. The Jewish population, even now, amounts to just 22,000. Katzrin itself, the self-styled 'capital' of the Golan, is really just another planned urban community, founded in 1977, with a population of only 7,000. It is not even the biggest town in the Golan: that distinction belonged to Majdal Shams, at the base of Mount Hermon, which is populated not by Jews but by Syria-facing Druze, who have lived there since the late sixteenth century.

'You have a British passport?' the receptionist went on. 'You are lucky. You can go anywhere. Israel is so . . . small, sometimes.' This remark, delivered with a sad inward shrug of her shoulders, perhaps pointed to another reason why the Golan mattered so much to Israelis. As an Israeli, she said, it was hard, if not impossible, to visit any of her country's immediate neighbours, with the exception of Jordan. On the wall behind her was another map, this one showing the whole of Israel, on which the outline of greater Los Angeles had been imposed. Israel did indeed look tiny: the ghost Los Angeles extended right across the country, from coastal Tel Aviv to a point several kilometres beyond the border with Jordan. The Golan covers some 1,800 precious square kilometres, an area equal to one-twelfth of the total area of Israel. Its amenity value increases with every passing year, as this urban nation becomes ever more crowded; it is one of the few places that its citizens can escape, breathe, and immerse themselves in a landscape matching the mythic homeland of their imaginations.

The Golan is, in the end, a very weird place; its serenity, if not its underlying beauty, is an illusion. Nowhere is this more obvious than on Mount Bental, a vertiginous hilltop on the eastern extremity of the plateau. The tourist authorities here are at pains to keep alive the memory of the Yom Kippur War of 1973, when the Syrians tried to recover what they had lost in 1967. The hilltop is still riddled with the trenches and bunkers from which the IDF heroically repulsed them. When I arrived, the trenches were swarming with groups of tourists and schoolchildren on field trips, peering far out across the Syrian plains below.

Hundreds of Syrian tanks were destroyed in their bid to force the Quneitra Gap, a rare depression in the Golan's eastern basalt wall, and a place known ever since as the 'Valley of Tears'. Later, when Israeli engineers went down to salvage the wrecked hulls, they discovered the blackened corpses of crews who had been handcuffed to their guns.

The hilltop was dotted with dark metal cut-outs of Israeli troopers, their rifles silhouetted against the snows of Mount Hermon. Our imaginations, however, needed little prompting, because another round of carnage, the Syrian civil war, was still in progress. The fighting, indeed, was so close that I could hear the faint thump of an artillery barrage.

There was no arguing with the sound of guns. On Mount Bental, maintaining a buffer zone between the mayhem of Syria and the populous centre of Israel suddenly seemed not just reasonable but a necessary thing to do. Syria's war, which in March 2019 was just entering its ninth year, had cost more than half a million lives, with no end to the carnage yet in sight. All that separated us from it was a narrow, demilitarized strip of land patrolled for more than forty years by blue-helmeted UN peacekeepers. Damascus itself, according to a helpful signpost on the hill, was just 60 kilometres away. Israel's neighbourhood was dangerous as well as small. To stand on Mount Bental in 2019 felt like teetering on the edge of the civilized world.

It reminded me of the platforms that used to be erected along the Berlin Wall for the benefit of Western tourists. It was fun, in those Cold War days, to wave across at the taciturn East German guards with their guns and binoculars, smug in our certainty that they couldn't harm us. The presence on Mount Bental of so many chattering schoolchildren, with their earphones and backpacks and picnic lunches, somehow also reminded me of an outing to a zoo. But, however the sounds of war struck us, we all knew that we were the lucky ones. Beyond the Golan lay chaos and danger, an alien enemy to be kept out and away from Israel forever, by any means, at any cost.

The artillery barrage continued to rumble, far off across the plain towards Daraa, the city where Syria's present catastrophe began in 2011. The catalyst, an Arabist diplomat friend once told me, was a dispute over the supply of water from Daraa's reservoirs. This was supposed to be allocated to local farmers on a strict rotation basis, but the Governor of Daraa, a corrupt Assad placeman, reportedly ignored the rota system in favour of his political allies. The farmers protested. Some of their teenage children sprayed anti-Assad graffiti on the city's walls. But the teenagers were caught, and imprisoned, and then tortured, some of them to death. The whole city rose in outrage, and Assad dispatched soldiers to quell them. The revolt spread, the war began. And Syrians were, by the sounds of it, still killing each other around Daraa. I thought: states might not go to war over water so much, but people could certainly tear themselves apart over it.

Several small reservoirs were visible down on the Syrian plain, glinting in the sun. Doron Markel, who I guessed had access to satellite imagery of the area, and perhaps even the ability to measure water volumes from space, told me that drawdown from these reservoirs had visibly diminished as a result of the war. The recovery of these reservoirs was no cause for celebration, though. It indicated, rather, that the farmers who once used them as a source of irrigation had fled, as millions of their compatriots have done. In many cases, furthermore, the displaced Syrians had merely carried their water crisis with them. Beyond Daraa, over the River Yarmouk in Jordan, lay Zaatari, home to some 80,000 refugees, the fourth-largest 'city' in that country. Located in a part of Jordan that was suffering from drought even before the Syrian war began, the challenges of providing these uprooted people with enough water are still legendary among international aid workers.

Back in the car park, I was approached by two middle-aged women who had spent the day hiking the border hills with their dogs; they wanted a lift back to their car, which they had parked a few kilometres away at a kibbutz called Ein Zivan. One of them was a senior health administrator who lived on a moshav 32 kilometres away, on the western edge of the Hula Valley, close to the Lebanese border; her friend, a hotel manager, was on a break from Haifa.

Flushed and happy from their walk, their talk was one long eulogy to the beauty of the Golan and the marvellous lifestyle to be had here. They sounded like Tom and Barbara from the 1970s sitcom *The Good Life*. The eastern part of the Heights, said the health administrator, with its rich volcanic soil, was famed for its grapes and apples. She owned a small orchard herself, and told me proudly how she pressed her own apple juice. When, however, I mentioned the orchards I had seen near a village in the northern Golan, called Buq'ata – kilometres of tightly espaliered apple trees topped by a haze of pink blossom – her hotel manager friend pulled a face.

'The Golan is a bit over-used, in my opinion,' she sniffed. 'We Israelis are intense people, and do everything intensely. The trouble is, there's not much room for us all.' It sounded like ordinary middle-class nimbyism; although I wondered, uncharitably, whether the real reason for her disapproval of Buq'ata was because it is a community not of Jewish settlers but of Syrian-Israeli Druze.

Ein Zivan, barely 2 kilometres from the Syrian border, was semi-militarized, with strong wire fences and sliding electric gates at the entrance. The gates, however, were wide open, which I took as a sign of how safe the residents felt, despite their remote rural location and proximity to the war next door. The interior of the kibbutz looked correspondingly detached from reality. Its 350 residents had created a pop-up oasis of Western culture, a mimicked hybrid of suburban California and the Alps. The chalet-style houses were surrounded with well-watered lawns, the plots divided by neat footpaths shaded by fruit trees. Country music, a Dolly Parton number, played from loudspeakers mounted on poles.

Ein Zivan boasted a boutique chocolate factory, run by a couple called Chepalinski who had made aliyah from Argentina. The glossy brown selection of chocolates on sale, marshalled rows topped with delicate twists of crystalline fruit, would not have looked out of place in Paris. Next door, there was a winery. Wine-making, the hotel manager explained, is big business in the Golan. Some settler back in the 1980s had discovered that the local soil and climate were perfect for vines, so now there were wineries all over the Golan, producing 5 million bottles a year, a third of it for export, some of it good enough to win international prizes.

The wine industry was another, occupation-justifying 'fact on the ground'. Israelis here had literally put roots into the soil, harnessing the fertility of the land for profit as well as politics. They were hydrocolonial frontiersmen, executors of a modern economic miracle, the conversion of the Golan's waters into wine.

The hitchhikers and I pushed on through a pair of saloon bar doors to the shop, the cool white walls of which were lined with racks of Shiraz and Cabernet Sauvignon, with variants called Brown, Black and Blue Alabaster, some of them costing US$40 a bottle. The proprietor, Ofer Bahat – a surname that means 'alabaster' in Hebrew – appeared, and proposed a tasting session. The hitchhikers didn't hesitate. He produced a plate of cheese cubes speared with cocktail sticks, and began to slosh booze into miniature plastic cups. The conversation flowed, comfortably and easily, and not only because of the alcohol. I saw that the women recognized themselves in this wine-maker, and vice versa. He was like them, one of a pleased and privileged tribe of escapees from the urban world, living the Golani dream and flying the flag for Israel.

'We make our own cherry liqueur, too,' he said proudly. 'And limoncello. You must try our limoncello. There's no need to go to Italy, you see?' I didn't think he was joking.

I had to cover my glass, eventually. The light was fading, and it was a long drive back to my boarding house in Tiberias. Ofer Bahat sold me a bottle of Alabaster as I said my goodbyes, and I set off southwards. A stretch of my road ran very close to the Syrian border, and when a lay-by appeared, I stopped, switched off the engine, and turned an ear towards the gathering gloom to the east. The artillery barrage, I was sure, was intensifying.

Back in my lodgings, I noticed that the provenance of the wine I had bought was marked, in Hebrew and English, simply as 'Golan Heights'. Product-labelling was no easy matter for settlers like Bahat with an eye to the export market. I discovered online that in 2006, a rival Golani wine producer had exported his product to Sweden, for sale by the state-owned alcohol retailer, Systembolaget, under a label that read 'Made in Israel'. There were loud complaints from Swedish activists. So, following consultation with the Swedish foreign ministry, Systembolaget changed the label to 'Made in Israeli-occupied Syrian territories'; but this prompted furious counter-complaints from officials in Israel. Insisting they had never meant to make a political statement, Systembolaget hastily changed the label for a third time, so that it read 'Of other origin' – a phrase that at last neutralized the row, with discerning Swedish oenophiles perhaps the only real losers in the saga.[7]

Product-labelling is still the stuff of international controversy. Some months after my visit, in November 2020, Mike Pompeo, in one of his last acts as US Secretary of State, paid a surprise visit to Netanyahu in Jerusalem. From here he was driven to the West Bank, where he stopped for lunch at an Israeli winery at Psagot, a settlement near Ramallah, which the EU, as well as the UN, considers to be illegal. 'A significant portion of the grapes from which [Psagot] wine is made come from plundered soil,' warned the activist organization Peace Now.[8]

It was the first time that a serving US Secretary of State had ever visited a settlement like Psagot, although it hardly came as a surprise: Pompeo, an evangelical Christian, said in 2019 that the US, under Donald Trump, no longer regarded settlements as 'inconsistent with international law'.[9] At Psagot, Pompeo announced an important change in US policy: henceforth, he said, products made in West Bank settlements could be sold in America bearing the words 'Made in Israel': a major, and conscious, departure from regulations in Europe, where the European Court of Justice ruled, in November 2019, that products from settlements must be clearly labelled as such.[10]

'Enjoyed lunch at the scenic Psagot Winery today,' he tweeted. 'Unfortunately, Psagot and other businesses have been targeted by pernicious EU labelling efforts that facilitate the boycott of Israeli companies. The US stands with Israel and will not tolerate any form of delegitimization.' The Psagot winemaker, Yaakov Berg, thanked him by presenting him with a new blend of cabernet sauvignon labelled 'Pompeo', beneath a tag in the corner reading '#madeinlegality'.

After Psagot, Pompeo visited the Golan: another first for a US Secretary of State. The Syrian government, predictably outraged, issued a statement condemning the visit as 'provocative', 'criminal' and 'a flagrant violation of the sovereignty of the Syrian Arab Republic'.[11] But that made no impression at all on Pompeo who, following a 'security briefing' on Mount Bental, bluntly affirmed the outgoing US President's earlier assertion of Israeli sovereignty over the Heights.

'This is Israel,' he averred. 'I very much wanted to come here today to tell the world that we have it right. That the United States has it right. That Israel has it right.'[12]

CHAPTER ELEVEN

The Balfour Forest

I WONDERED WHAT my forebear, Arthur Balfour, would make of modern Israel were he to see it now.

As a committed Zionist he would no doubt be impressed and moved by the state's success, and all that his signature on the 1917 Declaration had made possible. Today's Israel, with its motorways and airports, its skyscrapers and its shopping malls, would surely have amazed him.

The groundwork of the new state was already laid by the time of his one and only visit, in April 1925, when he was 76. He received a hero's welcome in Tel Aviv, by then already a city of 35,000, where crowds roared their approval as his motorcade passed by. At the inauguration ceremony of the new Hebrew University on Mt Scopus in Jerusalem, which he attended dressed in the flowing red robes of the Chancellor of Cambridge University, 10,000 people turned up to hear him speak. In 1936 his biographer wrote:

The Hebrew University (barred to no one, whatever his race or religion) seemed about to fulfil all his hopes for a revival and a concentration of Jewish culture. He rejoiced frankly in his own share in the political settlement of Palestine that had made its foundation possible. He knew that when the Jews cheered him there was deep feeling beneath, the feeling of a homeless people, who for the first time in two thousand years were welcoming an honoured guest in their own National Home.[1]

For all the ambiguity of the language of his Declaration in 1917, the Jewish-Arab future Balfour envisioned clearly *was* predicated on peaceful coexistence between neighbours. He was, perhaps, naïve in his expectations; his view of the Jewish nation was romanticised, helped along by the rhetoric of Zionism's greatest advocate in Britain, Chaim Weizmann. But, as a conservative Christian, a product of his Victorian upbringing and Eton and Cambridge education, he also would have explicitly understood how sharing lies at the heart of the Judaic tradition. 'You shall enjoy, together with the Levite and the stranger in your midst, all the bounty that the Lord your God has bestowed upon you,' Moses tells his people in Deuteronomy, 'that they may eat their fill in your settlements.'[2] Balfour's hope – his *understanding* – was that the land, as well as its resources, would be equitably shared in a spirit of mutual neighbourly respect.

(Those resources certainly included water, the importance of which to the Zionist project cannot have eluded him after the Yishuv's proud dignitaries took him to inspect a new hydro-electric plant on the River Yarkon in Tel Aviv. The plant was built by Pinhas Rutenberg, the engineer who went on to build the much bigger plant at Naharayim.)

I suspected, however, that his enthusiasm for Zion was more equivocal than his biographer described. The seeds of Arab-Israeli conflict were already starting to sprout in 1925 – and he cannot have missed them. Balfour's tour took place under tight security. On his arrival in Jerusalem, Arab newspapers were printed with mourning borders, shops closed in protest, and workers went on strike. Later, in Damascus, his hotel was stormed and very nearly overrun by 6,000 Arab rioters, three of whom were killed by the French cavalrymen protecting it. What foreboding must Balfour have felt when he finally departed, by ship from Beirut, back to England?

I found Balfour's ghost wherever I went in Israel. Roads, parks, entire villages are named after him. Even Beit Aghion, the official prime minister's residence in Jerusalem, is located on the corner of Balfour Street, an address so well known to Israelis that the media use it as shorthand for the leader-ship, as 'Number 10' is used in Britain.[3]

I made a point of visiting Balfouriya, a moshav in the Jezreel Valley south of Nazareth. A sign outside boasted that it was founded in 1922, one of the earliest moshavim in Palestine; Balfour himself dropped by in 1925, to give the enterprise his blessing. The security gate was closed, but it opened up for a local in a truck, and I slipped in behind him in my hire car. I stopped at a dusty corner store to ask for directions to the centre, hoping to find a museum, a memorial – anything. 'You're in the centre,' replied the shopkeeper gruffly.

I cruised a grid of empty avenues lined with modest clapboard houses. There were few people about, and little of interest to see, apart from an enormous customised motorbike mounted on a pole on someone's lawn, a skull on the handlebars and its front wheel rearing in the air: the home, I guessed, of a diehard Meat Loaf fan.

Thanks to funding from American Zionists, Balfouriya's first settlers could afford to build big houses, and dairy barns of concrete with shingle roofs, which earned them the nickname 'the millionaires'.[4] The milestones of the community's subsequent development were all about water. A new well was sunk in 1934; the mains arrived, courtesy of Mekorot, in 1959. I knew there was a good story to be had here, a vignette of rural planning, the role of water infrastructure in this community's rise and fall. But I could find no one to explain why or how Balfouriya had turned into such a drab commuter town, despite its illustrious beginnings and early promise.

I drove on to Ginegar, a kibbutz a few kilometres away, another waypoint on the Balfour trail: it sat at the base of a densely wooded slope that was planted in 1928 by the first kibbutzniks, who named it the Balfour Forest.

Although founded in the same year as Balfouriya, Ginegar had begun life earlier, in 1920 on the bank of the Jordan at the southern tip of the Sea of Galilee; the community moved to its present location in 1922 because Israel's first kibbutzim, Degania A and B, were already established there, and it was felt that development of a third would overtax the available land. Ginegar was one of the farming communities that later benefited from the long-distance irrigation network in the Jezreel Valley built by Simcha Blass, the prototype for the NWC. So Ginegar helped fill a gap in the narrative of Israel's water development. But this was not my first interest in Ginegar, which was more personal.

In 1958, in an episode half-forgotten even by my own family, a monument was put up in the forest to my staunchly Zionist great-grandmother, Balfour's niece and biographer, Blanche 'Baffy' Dugdale. Baffy had been a close friend of and adviser to Chaim Weizmann in the pre-war decades when he was lobbying Westminster for support for a Jewish state. The monument was designed by Baffy's architect son, my great-uncle Michael, and unveiled by her daughter, my grandmother Frances, at a ceremony attended by Ben-Gurion himself. No member of my extended family had seen the monument since. They had no photographs, no idea of what it looked like, no certainty even that it still existed. So I went looking for it, armed with a large-scale app map.

The Mediterranean pine saplings planted by Ginegar's pioneers had matured into a sun-dappled forest that was truly lovely, and I had it to myself. The ground was carpeted in green and yellow vetch, red poppies, purple campion, all humming and flashing with bees and the wings of butterflies. A pair of partridges whirred away from a hovering kestrel.

Reforestation was an important part of the early Zionists' agenda. In *Altneuland*, Theodor Herzl envisioned a land 'fructified into a garden and a home for people who had been poor, weak, hopeless and homeless.' Reversing the decay brought on by centuries of over-logging came to be seen almost as a sacred duty, the means by which the Promised Land could literally be recreated.

'The hillsides everywhere were cultivated up to the very summits,' Herzl wrote. 'Every bit of soil was exploited. The steep slopes were terraced with vines, pomegranate and fig trees as in the ancient days of Solomon. Numerous tree nurseries bore witness to the intelligent efforts at forestation of the once barren tracts. Pines and cypresses on the ridges of the hills towered against the blue skies.'[5]

The Balfour Forest was where Herzl's dream first came to pass. Some 400,000 saplings were planted, all paid for by the Jewish National Fund (JNF), a body that began buying up Palestinian land for Jewish settlement in 1901. It was the largest forest in Israel at the time, although it has long since been eclipsed. Today's JNF owns 13 per cent of all Israeli territory, on which it has planted more than 240 million trees. It has also established more than a thousand parks, and built 180 dams and reservoirs. Its assets are worth billions, making it what its founders intended, one of the mightiest engines of the whole Zionist enterprise.

Reforestation sounds laudable to modern ears, but in Israel there is more to it than a wholesome exercise in environmental stewardship; because tree-planting soon became a useful means of covering over the ruins of emptied Arab villages after the Nakba of 1948, thereby ensuring that their former inhabitants could never return. Today, according to Zochrot, a Tel Aviv-based organization dedicated to raising awareness of the Nakba – and which has attracted controversy with its support for the right to return – as many as forty-six JNF forests are planted on the ruins of Arab villages.[6] The forest through which I walked was therefore a tainted paradise, because the Jezreel Valley was where that insidious process of effacement began. Theodor Herzl even predicted it in *Altneuland*: 'Up yonder, in the Valley of Jezreel, you must not expect to see the filthy nests that used to be called villages in Palestine,' says his uber-pioneer character David Litwak, as he guides two new arrivals around a landscape transformed.

Baffy's monument, when I found it, was not in good shape. It was a square-cut pillar, 3 metres high, on a shady promontory that overlooked most of the Plain of Jezreel – great-uncle Michael had chosen the location himself – but only its cement-rendered core still stood. The black marble facings with gold lettering had all been stripped away, replaced by scrawls of Arabic graffiti. Nothing remained to indicate whom or what it commemorated.

I retraced my steps to the kibbutz below. Ginegar had come a long way since the tough early years. It is a community of 700 now, descendants of Polish and Russian immigrants mostly, who live in bungalows with gardens full of trees. Its economic mainstay is a giant plastics factory that specializes in different types of sheeting, mainly for polytunnels. They call these products 'smart cover solutions', which are as clever as they sound. Based on the knowledge that the optimum amount of UV light for plant growth depends on the type of plant, the factory is able to control the translucence of its sheeting by minutely altering its opacity. It then matches its product, via a bespoke agronomy service, to their client's precise needs. It is a very Israeli kind of business, both in the ingenuity of its concept and in its organization and execution. It is highly successful, with subsidiary factories in the US, Brazil and India, and customers in over sixty countries.

I found a woman peeling potatoes on her porch, who directed me towards Nitza Tzur, a retired schoolteacher, and Abes Maoz, the kibbutz's self-appointed historian. Both had been born in Ginegar. Abes, the offspring of Auschwitz survivors, was in his sixties, old enough to remember the monument's unveiling ceremony in 1958, when he and all the kibbutz children were deployed to wave little Israeli flags. They were thrilled when I explained that I was the grandson of the unveiler.

The memorial, Nitza explained, had been vandalized by persons unknown, but suspected to be local Arabs from villages around Nazareth. The trouble had begun in the early 2000s during the Second Intifada. 'As a Zionist monument it was an obvious target, and too far from the kibbutz for us to protect,' she said.

Ginegar, it seemed, had lost its innocence. When she was growing up, Nitza recalled, the boys and girls of the kibbutz used to play a game in the woods called 'hunter and deer' – a version of kiss-chase – while the parents picnicked nearby, smoking and chatting beneath the trees. But the intifada had put a stop to all that. Like so many Israeli settlements, modern Ginegar had become a fearful place surrounded by tall gates and fences. Even the entrance to the track up to 'their' forest, Nitza sighed, was usually locked these days; she confessed that it was a long time since she had ventured up the hill as far as the monument.

Her sigh spoke volumes. With its forced retreat from the world, and especially now that it was separated from the forest that once defined it, Ginegar had entered a darker place. Only the old-timers recognized that their kibbutz was a spoiled paradise: as denatured, perhaps, as the high-tech plastic produced in its factory. The security threat they faced was clearly not negligible. Yet these kibbutzniks were feisty people, accustomed to fighting hard for themselves and their land. In the forest's early days, Abes said, local Arabs crept onto the hillside at night in order to pull up the newly planted saplings. Each morning, the kibbutzniks would doggedly replace them. Later, near the community primary school, Abes took me to a secret cave that the Palmach, the underground Jewish army of pre-state Palestine, once used as a weapons cache. 'For use against you British,' he grinned. 'Sorry about that.'

My great-grandmother has not been forgotten at Ginegar. In 2014, in response to the vandalization up the hill, the kibbutzniks erected a small new memorial to her in the grounds of the school where they could keep an eye on it. I posed for a photograph next to the memorial at Abes's insistence: 'for the kibbutz archive', he said.

Fatheful worker for Israel, said the epitaph; which, apart from the spelling, was certainly accurate. Some early Zionist leaders regarded Baffy as their 'spy' at Westminster. Ben-Gurion valued her so highly that he compared her to the prophet Deborah.

Abes's archive was a treasure trove. It included a photograph from 1928, curled and brown with age, of the first settlers planting the hill behind Ginegar, proving that the land really was barren when they arrived. There was also a picture of my grandmother, Frances, making the speech of her life at the unveiling ceremony in 1958, before a crowd a thousand strong, with Ben-Gurion and Chaim Weizmann's widow Vera looking on. Even the text of her speech was preserved.

'We should be insensitive and unimaginative indeed if this was not one of the most moving days of our lives,' she told the crowd. 'This memorial is a symbol of the continuing admiration and love which I hope generations of our family will always feel for the people and land of Israel.'

I felt a mixture of discomfort and pride. I remembered my grandmother's infectious enthusiasm for Israel, the birthday cards of my youth with which she tried to transmit the optimism and idealism of early Zionism. But I also knew that this land had not been empty when the first kibbutzniks arrived. Ginegar was established on the site of Junjar, a village of Arabs who had lived there since at least the sixteenth century. The JNF had bought the land from the Sursock family, mega-rich absentee landlords from Beirut.[7] 'Filthy nest' it may have been, but it was still home to twenty-five Muslim families in 1921. The ancient well that served them still exists, somewhere beneath the foundations of Ginegar's communal laundry. What happened to them? Where had they gone? Was it their descendants who had scrawled such angry graffiti on the remains of Baffy's monument?

Herzl wrote blithely of the 'beneficent character of the Jewish immigration', of native Arabs and newcomer Jews who would live together as brothers in a 'common fatherland', of a 'New Society' where economic opportunity would be extended equally to all. But instead of living in a common fatherland, the people and culture of old Junjar had simply been expunged, while the Jews who remained had retreated behind security gates, from where they continued to prosper thanks to their high-tech plastics factory. The reality of Israel's New Society is an immense and growing divide between the peoples of old Palestine.

Baffy Balfour died in May 1948, one day after hearing that the state of Israel was at last established. 'You will see. It will all work out,' she is reputed to have said on her deathbed. 'This is my happiest day.'

Yet there was nothing happy about her ravaged memorial on the hill which, Nitza pointed out, had stood unharmed on its shady hillock for more than forty years until the Second Intifada. The damage was a sign of how badly off-track the Zionist project had strayed. Baffy was traduced, and the generous spirit as well as the letter of the Balfour Declaration that once inspired her seemed betrayed.

CHAPTER TWELVE

Tel Aviv

Miracle City

I FOLLOWED THE water, west and south along the route of the National Water Carrier, back towards the crowded centre of the country. Water from the Galilee, flowing through a buried three-metre pipe, typically takes a week to arrive where it is needed most. My journey by road took an hour and half.

Back down the Jezreel Valley I drove, past Armageddon, and through Umm al-Fahm, the Arab-Israeli city that the Israeli Right want to transfer to Palestinian control. Umm al-Fahm was once surrounded by forests, which in Ottoman times supported a thriving charcoal-burning industry – Umm al-Fahm means 'Mother of Charcoal' – but there was little sign of those forests now, the trees all displaced by suburban sprawl.

I joined Highway 6, the impressive new arterial motorway that skirts the West Bank, eight lanes wide in places, passing through many tunnels under Samaria's rocky foothills. I marvelled again at the proximity of Palestine – the hilltops to my left were crowded with Arab towns and villages – and pitied its millions of citizens, who enjoy no such roads.

Tel Aviv soon rose into view, its tower blocks castellating the whole horizon, an immense flowering of concrete that would never have sprouted without artificial irrigation, the diverted waters of the north. The city had changed astonishingly since my first visit thirty years before. The pace and extent of development was disquieting; it made me feel my age. I remembered a small, ambitious, slightly tacky Mediterranean city, albeit with a nice bit of beach. Since then, two dozen previously discrete towns had merged to form the metropolitan area of Gush Dan, the 'Dan bloc',[1] a coastal conurbation 50 kilometres long, criss-crossed by six-lane highways in the style of Miami or Los Angeles.

I looked on the Gush Dan with the jaundiced eye of a hydrologist. If water was the fuel of urban development, I thought, it was obvious that there had been no brake on its supply in these parts. Israel's population has doubled since 1987, to 9.45 million.[2] Renewed waves of migrants, notably from the ex-Soviet Union following the collapse of communism in the early 1990s, as well as high birth rates among the Haredi Orthodox community, mean that numbers are still increasing by about 2 per cent a year;[3] and around half of all Israelis live here in the crowded centre of the country, on land amounting to just 8 per cent of the total area.

None of this development, past or present – Zion itself – could have been achieved without a reliable water supply. Israel's self-sufficiency, via desalination, was a recent thing; this prosperous city was the fruit of decades of surface water diverted from the Galilee and the River Jordan, and groundwater appropriated from the West Bank's aquifers, all brought here by the NWC, the subterranean route of which I was now shadowing, above ground, in my car. The contrast with the poorest parts of the West Bank, and above all with waterless Gaza, was so stark it felt obscene.

Yet there was also something inspirational about Tel Aviv's transformation. It was astonishing to consider that, until 1906, there was, literally, nothing here but marshes and sand dunes. Now there was a genuinely global twenty-four-hour city with a booming high-tech sector, immense glass shopping malls, tall clusters of flats and office blocks punctuating the sky, a glittering nightlife, world-class art collections and restaurants. The construction cranes that stalked the eastern horizon showed that the conurbation was still expanding. It was impossible not to admire the ambition of the first Zionists, and the relentless energy and determination of their heirs to make their vision a reality.

Still, I had questions about the Gush Dan. Away from the glamorous seafront with its clubs and restaurants and golden sands, what was it like to live here? Was it really the urban paradise the first Zionists set out to build? Palestinians, like the Jordan Valley system itself, had paid the highest price for Israel's achievement. So what, actually, had Israel bought with the waters it had taken?

I sought my answers through Daniel, a vape-smoking, pony-tailed, thirty-something PhD student and tour guide, shrewdly recommended to me by Bassam, who had met him once, somewhere out on the tourist trail. They had liked each other, and had shared contact details precisely in order to pass each other their clients, such as me. My experience of Palestine, as well as what I read in the media, a constant drip of stories about occupation-related violence and cruelty, had inclined me to think that there could be no love between Arabs and Israelis; but of course this was not the case. Bassam had many Israeli friends, and Daniel had many Arab ones. Human contact could and often did survive the harsh political narratives imposed upon the region.

Daniel had grown up in the 1990s in the inland Gush Dan suburb of Rosh HaAyin. This was once a small town of 5,000, many of them Jewish refugees from Yemen who settled there in 1950. Located unfashionably close to the West Bank, it was considered a backwater. In the early 1990s, however, when the then housing minister Ariel Sharon launched a policy of building all along the green line, Rosh HaAyin suddenly found itself in a designated development zone. Generous government subsidies were offered to anyone willing to move there. Daniel's parents, formerly residents of the West Bank settler city of Ariel, were among those to take the bait.

The move, Daniel recalled, was a shock. It was policy in those days for Israeli schools to 'integrate' cultural strangers in the classroom. For the first time, he found himself sitting alongside children who were not all white, European Ashkenazi like him, but Mizrahi Yemenites, or more recent Sephardic incomers from North Africa and the Middle East. This Jewish ethnic hodgepodge sounded an interesting place to grow up, although Daniel hadn't liked it. 'As a teenager it was really, really boring,' he said flatly.

He took me to Rosh HaAyin. The backwater had turned into a satellite city of 50,000 since the 1990s, with a second major building programme, intended to provide housing for another 50,000, already under way. We drove the perimeter of the latest section, weaving along clean black asphalt through countless interlocking mini-roundabouts, cricking our necks at the windowless shells of half-completed new-builds. It had been a year or two since Daniel last visited – he lives in a trendy neighbourhood of Jerusalem these days – and even he whistled at the speed with which his childhood town was changing. 'It never stops,' he mused. 'They say the entire coast will eventually be urbanized like this, from Beirut in the north all the way down to Gaza.'

He partly blamed his teenage boredom here on poor urban design, a subject he knew quite a lot about since his girlfriend was a professional town planner. The new high-rise development zones, he said, were all residential, with few shops, offices or businesses. Rosh HaAyin had therefore turned into a commuters' dormer town. The architects arranged their identikit blocks into horseshoe shapes, an inward-facing layout intended to enhance a sense of community, but the spaces in between remained desolate, apart from playgrounds that children didn't much want to use.

'Only teenagers went there, in order to break things,' Daniel remembered, as we passed one of them. 'Look, you see? More horseshoes. They are making the same mistake all over again . . . I saved myself from the life here by joining a pioneer youth club. It got me out of there.'

Rosh HaAyin owes its existence to water. Located at the head of the River Yarkon, which rises from a spring bubbling out of the Samarian foothills, the town's name means 'Fountainhead'. In the 1920s, the British built a pumping station at the spring in order to supply Jerusalem, back up the hills to the south-east: the first time since the Romans that Jerusalemites had enjoyed a truly external water supply. During the war of 1948, Jordanian forces opened their siege of Jerusalem by blowing the pumping station up.

In the 1950s, when Simcha Blass began building the NWC, he did so in two phases, beginning with the southern section which leads from Rosh HaAyin to the Negev, the desert that Ben-Gurion was determined to make bloom; and he initially filled this southern pipe by diverting the River Yarkon, here at Rosh HaAyin. Water from the Galilee did not come online for another ten years.

Today, Rosh HaAyin still marks the NWC's half-way point, a junction where it splits into two, with one branch heading west towards Tel Aviv and the coast, the other running southward to the Negev, eventually to be rejoined by the western branch near Ashkelon, where it splits again, flowing on to the desert settlements along the edge of Gaza, almost as far as the border with Egypt.

Rosh HaAyin's spring, along with the Yarkon River that flows from it to the sea, was strategically important long before the British built their pumping station or the NWC came to town. Allenby, in his northward advance against the Ottomans in 1917, established an offensive west–east line across Palestine from here known as the 'Line of the Two Aujas'.[4]

Daniel, always full of good stories, recounted an old Arab belief predicting that 'a Prophet would one day arrive from Egypt and conquer all'. When Allenby arrived, some Ottoman troops understood his name to be *al-Nabi* – the Prophet – and threw down their arms in the belief that he must be *the One*. 'You Brits did great PsyOps,' Daniel observed.

I had worried that my interest in Israel's water infrastructure was a bit too specialist for a tour guide when I first contacted Daniel, but my concern was misplaced. The quest for water, after all, was central to the experience of exile that underpinned the Jewish national story, and thus integral to Jewish self-identity – which by good fortune was the topic of his PhD. As a guide he was, in any case, well steeped in the lore of his country, which made my subject familiar to him in a different way. He nodded enthusiastically when I explained my project, and immediately reeled off a list of people I should talk to and places to see. He was perfect.

Daniel took me to nearby Antipatris, also known as Tel Afek, a ruined Ottoman fortress that once guarded the spring at Rosh HaAyin. It was another fortified waypoint on the Via Maris, a smaller version of Armageddon, which had been fought over since at least the third millennium BC. The Via Maris had become Highway 6, the traffic along which was audible in the distance, while the fortress had become the centrepiece of another well-manicured public park, created on marshland that had been drained. There was a pretty lake, beside which families were picnicking beneath blossoming pink Bauhinia trees, or feeding bread to the catfish and a species of bream,

Acanthobrama telavivensis, that a sign proudly informed us is found nowhere else in the world.

The park's popularity was another expression of what Daniel called Israel's 'cult of the outdoors'. He said he often wondered at it himself. He described how, on fine spring weekends, urban Israelis ritually decamp to the countryside, sometimes with no other purpose than to inspect a field of newly blossomed wildflowers. Space for urban development, he went on, is increasingly tight in Israel, yet the national reserves and parks – 500 of them, accounting for 22 per cent of Israel's total land area – remain sacrosanct. 'Water is a basic human right everywhere in the world,' Daniel observed, 'but in Israel this right is extended to nature reserves, by law. I was quite stunned when I read about that. We really do live in an era of post-humanism.'

The relentless emphasis on nature was partly about state-building. As Theodor Herzl foresaw a century ago, the progress and success of Zionism would depend on its ability to attract new recruits from abroad. It followed that the lifestyle on offer would have to be at least as good, if not better, than in the countries left behind. This thinking hasn't changed: Israel's planning laws, Daniel said, include strict and generous guidelines for the amount of urban recreational space to be made available per capita.

'Israel's planning ethos has changed. There are no new communities being built in Israel proper anymore. The direction of construction now is up, not out, because green spaces are so precious. It's about building cities instead of towns, with a strong focus on quality of life.'

A desire to offer the citizenry nice parks was only part of the story, however. Daniel explained that the national quest for *yediat haaretz*, 'knowledge of the land', had its roots in German political philosophy of the 1860s. The notion that landscapes have an inherent narrative history was useful to Bismarck and his fellow unifiers of the German nation. The new Germans were encouraged to see themselves as *Landschaftskunde*, literally 'customers of the land', who were bonded to the territory by a common heritage, like sheep hefted to a highland pasture. Bismarck wanted to forge a romantic reconnection to the Germanic peoples' roots as a nation of forest dwellers, a nation that, in prehistoric times, had indeed worshipped trees.

The first Zionists brought these ideas from central Europe and adapted them to their own purposes. They, too, were propagating a narrative of a lost land reclaimed; a land they viewed as Jewish by historical right and, in many cases, by divine right as well. I asked Daniel what he thought of the establishment of new parks and reserves in the occupied territories of the West Bank, on land not formally recognized as Israeli. Wasn't that just another means of extending Israeli hegemony through the expropriation of Palestinian land? 'The reserves in the West Bank are definitely part of a political strategy,' Daniel replied cheerfully, 'but the mind-set that spawned that strategy and makes it possible is already within all Israelis.'

Downstream of Antipatris he took me to another, much larger park, the Yarkon River Park. The lower Yarkon once delineated the northern limit of Tel Aviv, but now bisects one of the densest urban areas in the country. We wandered westwards along its bank towards the old port, encountering picnickers, joggers, Frisbee players, mothers with prams, and squads of electric scooter riders: some of the 16 million people who visit each year. The shaded lawns leading down to the river were edged to the south by the skyscrapers and shopping malls of Ramat Gan, and the most densely populated municipality in all Israel, Haredi-dominated Bnei Brak. Over the river to the north loomed the towers of Ramat Aviv, with the suburb of Herzliya beyond. The last open area in that direction, Daniel said, was not a green space but a small domestic airport, and even that was due to close; bulldozers would soon be moving in to build yet more housing.

Yarkon Park was not always such a pleasant public amenity. Part of it was once an Arab farming village, Jarisha, which was 'depopulated' in the war of 1948; nothing of it remains.[5] The park, which opened in 1973, did not fare well to begin with. Its centrepiece, the river, had all but dried up when its headwaters were diverted into the NWC in the 1950s and 1960s; its natural flow was replaced by urban sewage and industrial run-off during the Gush Dan's furious expansion northwards in the 1980s and 1990s.

Quite how badly polluted became clear in 1997, when a footbridge over the river collapsed during the opening ceremony of the Maccabiah Games, the Jewish version of the Olympics held since the 1930s in Ramat Gan Stadium. Most of the Australian team, who were leading the parade, cascaded into the filthy water. Sixty of them were injured, and one died. The bridge's designer was later imprisoned for cutting corners: an unfortunate example, Daniel said, of *yihye beseder*, a peculiarly Israeli mentality that he translated as 'Meh, don't worry about details. Everything will be fine.'

Israel's embarrassment deepened when three more Australians later died in hospital, and not of injuries sustained when they fell, but from pulmonary infection caused by toxins ingested in the river. Scientists later blamed a rare and notoriously drug-resistant species of fungus, *Pseudallescheria boydii*, which is associated with stagnant and polluted water.

Daniel remembered the disaster well: he was among several hundred teenage schoolchildren inside the stadium, waiting to perform a marching display for which they had rehearsed for weeks. He showed me the bridge, long since rebuilt, and a black marble memorial to the unlucky Australians. 'I remember waiting . . . and waiting. Then the rumours began of something awful happening outside. We never did get to perform our show.'

The disaster had an upside for the environment. Public attention was drawn to the filthy state not just of the Yarkon but of all of Israel's water-courses, and a major national clean-up campaign was initiated. The Yarkon got a new filtrating wetland area, along with a series of mini-dams designed to promote aeration. The riverbed was dredged, the banks reinforced, and new sewage treatment plants constructed. Eventually, in 2011, the popular mayor of Tel Aviv, Ron Huldai, was filmed diving into the river to demonstrate how clean it had become, although not every Israeli was convinced. Huldai, it was observed, did not linger in the water for long. His stunt was reminiscent of John Gummer's, the one-time British minister of agriculture who, in 1990, tried to reassure his public that the national cow herd was free of Creutzfeldt-Jakob disease by feeding his four-year-old daughter a beef burger.

Even so, the Yarkon was evidently much cleaner than it had been. Its headwaters are no longer wasted on irrigating farms in the Negev, any more than the waters of the Galilee now are; and the river is certainly no longer used for the dumping of sewage. Nowadays, all of the Gush Dan's effluent, the waste product of 2.3 million people, is treated at a Mekorot-run plant near Ashdod known as the Shafdan Ponds, the largest sewage plant in Israel.

Daniel took me to Shafdan to meet a water quality monitor, Dubi Segal. I expected a technician in a white helmet and high-viz jacket. Dubi, sixty-something, shuffled around the filtration ponds in open-toed sandals and a floppy sunhat with *Hakuna-matata*, Swahili for 'no worries', written across the front. Daniel was charmed by his style, which was direct to the point of gruffness – the mark, he said, of a settler-pioneer of the old school, overtly secular, independent-minded, a true son of the soil.

The Ponds extended over 500 acres, the contents of each a varying shade of brown. The filtration process that Dubi described tested Daniel's translating abilities to the limit: there was talk of anaerobic thermophilic digestion, primary clarifiers, flocculent capture, ammonia-stripping. The main point, though, was that none of the effluent treated at Shafdan, 130 million cubic metres of it every year, is discharged into the sea. Instead, it is sent via three pipelines to the Negev, for use by farmers, two-thirds of whose irrigation water, Dubi said, is now recycled sewage.

We trudged under a hot sun along the muddy edge of a lagoon to a small monitoring station, a humming knot of different-coloured pipes, where Dubi busied himself with his monitoring job, tapping dials and adjusting aeration taps with practised ease. The water that left Shafdan was easily clean enough to drink, he said. The only reason Mekorot did not, in fact, add it to the national domestic water supply was a religious one. 'There is no faecal matter left in our treated water, but apparently it still cannot be declared kosher,' he explained, with the tiniest raise of an eyebrow which I took to mean that he thought such scrupulousness absurd.

Daniel gave a quiet chuckle: he clearly agreed with Dubi. A great many Israelis, he explained later, are 'extremely relaxed' about Jewish religious dietary requirements. This is especially the case in liberal Tel Aviv. Daniel recounted how he was once hired to guide a party of American orthodox Jews around the Holy Land. Fresh from the airport on their first night, they asked Daniel to book them a table at a good 'mehadrin' kosher restaurant. Such establishments, in which food preparation is supervised to the strictest standards by a certifying rabbi, are common in New York. They were naturally astonished when Daniel informed them that such restaurants barely exist in Tel Aviv.

Dubi was only a subcontractor of the state water utility. For the last twenty years he had been employed by Netafim, an irrigation equipment firm founded by Simcha Blass. His age and connection to Blass and Netafim confirmed him as one of Israel's originals, a member of that heroic older breed who had helped build the country from scratch. 'Mekorot don't take enough care,' Dubi complained. 'Water quality downstream of here has been declining recently. I wanted to put in a new monitoring filter – very cheap – but they said no. They are bureaucratic and sclerotic, a part of the problem, not the solution.'

His turf war, though, was of little consequence to the bigger picture. The Shafdan Ponds were a paragon of order compared to the fetid lagoons I had seen in Gaza, from where sewage gushed entirely untreated into the sea. Israeli city dwellers, if they thought of it at all, doubtless viewed Shafdan as the dark underbelly of their urban idyll. But for all its unsightliness there was no environmental scandal to expose here, nor even much miasma to complain of. Indeed, the plant is so advanced and efficient that in 2012 the United Nations cited it as a global model of excellence. An extraordinary 86 per cent of all Israeli effluent – 'grey' water as well as human 'waste' water – is recycled for use in agriculture: a proportion that puts the rest of the world to shame. Spain, the world's second-best performer, manages 19 per cent; in the United States, the figure is just 1 per cent.[6]

Netafim, Dubi's employer, was headquartered an hour's drive away at Kibbutz Hatzerim near Beersheba, the principal city of the Negev. Daniel secured an invitation there from a kibbutz resident, Talia, who turned out to be his aunt. Hatzerim is an unusual kibbutz, one of only 50, out of a total of 274 in Israel, which still operate on the traditional, fully collective model.[7] This meant, among things, that my lunch in the self-service canteen was on the house. We ate under the beady gaze of a black and white crested hoopoe, Israel's national bird, which tapped on the window of the noisy dining hall as Aunt Talia recounted the kibbutz's history.

Hatzerim was founded by a pioneering youth organization in 1946. In those pre-independence days, at the tail end of Mandate Palestine, the British, still determined to restrict Jewish migration, had banned the construction of new settlements, and bulldozed the efforts of anyone who tried. There was, however, a loophole in the prohibition. According to an old Ottoman law, which still applied in Palestine at the time, no new dwelling could be demolished once its roof had been put on, unless it was a safety hazard.

Kibbutz Hatzerim began as one of eleven settlements in the northern Negev that literally popped up overnight: 'the Night of the Eleven,' in Zionist mythology. The operation was carefully timed to coincide with Yom Kippur, a national holiday (and, by good fortune, a Saturday) when the youth pioneers knew that the British military would be off their guard. By the Sunday morning, the prefabs were in place, complete with roofs and settlers to live under them. The eleven teams were each accompanied by a water truck, but this was obviously no more than a stopgap. The NWC, which would bring water from the River Yarkon and eventually from the Sea of Galilee, was still at the design stage. Some other source of water would have to be found if the new settlements were to be sustained.

Their secret weapon was Simcha Blass, who was sure that water could be found in the Negev if wells were drilled deep enough. He had already secretly been prospecting for water in the region, and had struck lucky in the coastal aquifer at Nir Am, 45 kilometres north-west of Hatzerim, hard by the modern Gaza border. His problem, then, was how to transport the water to the new settlements. Pumps and pipes were scarce in Israel in the straitened post-war years. Blass found what he needed in London, where a special network of pipes laid to tackle house fires during the Blitz was no longer needed. The cost of buying and importing this materiel was so huge that the link-up from Nir Am was nicknamed 'the champagne pipeline'. But the toehold in the Negev that it represented was worth it to Ben-Gurion.[8]

A socialism-in-sandals ethos survived in the dining hall, but little else remained of the early kibbutz that Aunt Talia described. Modern Hatzerim was a slice of suburbia, with comfortable-looking villas, wide emerald lawns, and a busy car park shaded by tall eucalyptus and palm trees. Looming over everything was a large, ochre-coloured factory, the main manufacturing plant of Netafim, a proportion of which company the kibbutz collectively owned.

Netafim was in the business of drip irrigation, a process that Blass, its founder, invented, or rather discovered, in the early 1930s. From humble beginnings in a backyard workshop, Netafim had grown into a company worth US$2 billion. It was a classic success story, a part of Israeli folklore, almost, that showcased characteristics of which Israelis are rightly proud: self-assurance, courage in adversity, a flair for resourcefulness and innovation. Thanks to Netafim, Talia and her 500 lucky co-kibbutzniks were also extremely rich.

According to one version of drip irrigation's discovery, Blass was passing a neighbour's farm when he noticed that one tree was twice the height of all the others in the same row. His curiosity piqued, he went to investigate, and found that a tiny leak in a nearby underground hosepipe had saturated the tree's root ball. The fruit tree had outperformed its neighbours, he realised, because it had no need to expend energy pushing out roots to find water, which in its case had been delivered directly to the root ball. The energy thus saved had naturally been directed into above-ground growth instead.

Blass began tinkering in his workshop, and developed a prototype dripper that had many other advantages over the traditional sprinkler irrigation method. Because the water was applied underground, none of it was lost to evaporation, an important consideration in a country as hot as Israel. The dripper also allowed him to apply exactly the right amount of water needed, according to environmental conditions and, even, to the species of plant. It could be used to apply fertilizer directly to the roots, too. The amount of water and fertilizer farmers could save with such a system was enormous, and was soon shown to increase yields by up to 200 per cent. Its utility ultimately became Netafim's company slogan, still emblazoned across the front of the factory: GROW MORE WITH LESS.

We were shown around by the factory's chief engineer, Danny Retter, a senior citizen on a mobility scooter who had held the job from the firm's very beginning in the mid-1960s. Danny remembered Blass well: 'A genius, no doubt about it,' he said. 'I liked him, but he was very tough to work for. Always shouting. Like a megaphone.' Even Blass, he recalled, initially doubted that his invention was commercially viable. 'He thought we were crazy,' Danny chuckled. 'The dripper line in those days was really just a hosepipe with pinpricks in it. I remember we went to the banks in Tel Aviv with a business plan that predicted we would eventually employ twelve people. But look at us now!'

He pointed with a flourish to a poster listing Netafim's successes. The company employed over 5,000 people in plants and subsidiaries abroad. Laid end to end, the pipes Netafim sell each year would encircle the planet 130 times. The company's products conserve tens of billions of gallons of water each year, while helping to feed nearly a billion people in 150 countries.

The shop floor was mesmerising, a triumph of automation. Danny had his favourite robots: at one point he stopped by a machine spitting black plastic drippers like bullets, his face suddenly boyish despite his age, and plunged his hands into the enormous collection hopper. He was as gleeful as Willy Wonka in his Chocolate Factory and indeed, the dripper was as ingenious, in its way, as an Everlasting Gobstopper. The shape and size of a razor head, it contained a miniature labyrinth of interlocking teeth, which forced the water into an accelerated spiral as it exited the nozzle.

'We own the trademark on its design,' he laughed. 'We call it "Turbonet". The system is self-cleaning: the nozzle would get clogged up with dirt right away without it. It is the Cadillac of drippers.' His factory, he added, produced 7 million of these miraculous widgets every day.

It wasn't hard to understand why he smiled so much: the company to which he had dedicated his life is so obviously a net contributor to the good of the planet, and even to the sustainability of life on earth itself. Netafim is, I thought, an example of Israeli innovation at its very best – and I frankly envied Danny Retter.

On the coast just south of Tel Aviv, at Sorek, Daniel showed me another and even more important example of Israel's water system supremacy: the largest seawater desalination plant, of its type, in the world. It works on the principle of reverse osmosis, or 'RO', in which seawater is forced through a semipermeable membrane that catches the salt crystals and other impurities. The process was once prohibitively expensive, but costs are falling all the time thanks to the development of membranes made of graphene, the early twenty-first-century *Wundermaterial*. The technique has certainly come a long way since 1748, when Jean-Antoine Nollet 'sweetened' seawater by forcing it through the bladder of a pig.

There was none of Dubi Segal's informality at Sorek. Opened in 2013, at a cost of US$400 million, this was a modern and clinically clean facility, where plastic white helmets were obligatory. The plant was enormous, yet there were few workers around: Sorek is so highly automated that it employs no more than twenty people.

An enthusiastic Water Authority official, Uri Schor, led us along a gantry above the immense collection tanks, where he pointed out a school of small fish, unluckily sucked up by the intake pipe a kilometre out to sea. We proceeded to the desalinating shed, a building as big as an aircraft hangar that echoed to the sound of dozens of huge whirring pumps, and eventually to a tap-water point at the end of the process. 'Twenty minutes ago, that was seawater,' said Uri triumphantly as I drank from a paper cup. 'I've been here hundreds of times, but I still find it amazing.'

There was a messianic quality to what followed, a well-rehearsed talk and slideshow in a purpose-built auditorium inside. Uri's presentation even invoked the story of Moses tapping the rock for water at Kadesh Barnea, complete with a melodramatic illustration from a nineteenth-century Bible. 'We don't have Moses's power,' said Uri solemnly, 'but we do have some technology. And the Bible teaches us to prepare for drought. In Exodus, the seven years of fat in Egypt are followed by seven of lean.'

It was overdone, but I did not think the self-congratulation was unjustified. Sorek *was* amazing. The conversion of seawater into something potable seemed a modern miracle, like Jesus's water-into-wine trick but on an industrial scale: the plant can produce 624,000 cubic metres of drinking water every day, enough to fill 250 Olympic swimming pools. And it is only one of five Israeli coastal plants, which collectively produce enough drinking water to meet an astonishing 80 per cent of national demand, one of the highest rates in the world.

Desalination has its critics. Despite recent advances, it is still a very energy-intensive process, expensive for the environment as well as for consumers. The lack of natural minerals in desalinated drinking water requires additives to avoid health problems. And the unwanted brine that the process produces, millions of gallons of it, has to be disposed of somewhere. At Sorek it is simply pumped back out to sea along a pipe almost 2 kilometres long, with consequences for Mediterranean sealife that are still being disputed by environmentalists. Yet the upside of desalination, Uri Schor argued, outweighs all that. Desalination, he contended, offers the best chance to save not just Israel and Palestine but all the world from spiralling demand and the drying effect of climate change.

'Cape Town has 4 million people, with a climate like Israel's, and similar problems with drought,' he went on, 'but they do not manufacture water. Last year, they were down to 50 litres per person per day: enough for a shower lasting two and half minutes. It is absurd that there is no desalination in South Africa. Climate change is here to stay. You have to prepare.'

Desalination, he made clear, was not the whole answer to water scarcity, but merely one strategy among many. His slide show also referred to recycling, to regulatory and tariff reform, to the importance of pipe maintenance to avoid leaks, and to the importance of public education. 'It isn't enough to be aware of climate change. People also have to respond to it, with action,' he said.

A year-long televised information campaign in 2018 – which starred the actress Renana Riaz, the creamy skin of whose beautiful face was digitally transformed into the cracked and desiccated surface of a desert – had helped to reduce household water consumption by 18 per cent, an amount equivalent, Uri said, 'to the annual output of two large desalination plants'. Israel's approach to water management, in other words, is holistic, a combination of interdependent strategies – although there is no doubt that desalination is its centrepiece.

I saved my most awkward questions until last. The domestic surplus that Israel has enjoyed since 2016 is all well and good; and it is true Israel exports its water management know-how for the benefit of the world. Yet Israel's achievement was founded on many decades of oppression of their neighbours. A people had been cruelly displaced, and their land expropriated, along with their rivers and the groundwater beneath their feet, an accrual of resource that made Israel's present water surplus possible, and without which the technological water revolution would never have happened.

Sorek itself was built on land that once belonged to an important medieval Arab village called Nabi Rubin; its citrus and banana-growing inhabitants were expelled at gunpoint in 1948.

So, I asked, what about the Palestinians, who despite the proximity of Israel's bounty still do not have enough water; who, since the Oslo Accords, have enjoyed access to only 20 per cent of the water in the West Bank, while Israel controls the rest? What about the unfolding disaster in Gaza? Did desalination spell salvation for them?

'Palestinians have more water per capita than they would in any other Arab country,' Uri replied, 'and they could easily get 40 per cent more if they treated their sewage and fixed their infrastructure. Israel stands ready to provide Palestine with the water it needs, but their network is so leaky it could not handle it.'

'But Palestine isn't allowed to repair its network without Israeli permission, which is almost impossible to get,' I said.

'I deal in facts, not fairy tales,' he countered sternly. 'When Israel withdrew from Gaza, the Arabs dug 6,000 illegal wells and the aquifer was wrecked. The same would happen to the West Bank if Israel allowed it.'

There was an uncomfortable pause. Tricky questions about Palestine, I could tell, didn't come up very often at Sorek. From my understanding, his fact was wrong: the number of 'illegal' wells in Gaza, by which I assumed he meant unregulated, privately dug ones, was closer to 4,000 than 6,000. It was true that Hamas had failed to grip that problem, but it was also the case that over-extraction of the aquifer had been going on long before they came on the scene, including during the Israeli occupation. The headline problems in Gaza were thirst and overcrowding, for which Israel was ultimately responsible, both as the past perpetrators of the Nakba and as the enforcers of the present blockade. I was in the mood for an argument; but Uri looked appalled, and ended it before it could really start.

'Look,' he said firmly, 'water should be a bridge for peace, not a cause for war. But sometimes that's not enough. We try to help the Palestinians. They come to Sorek to learn, sometimes. Their water officials are fine. The problem is the politicians, on both sides.'

It was a familiar lament, in Israel just as in Palestine.

CHAPTER THIRTEEN

The Negev Desert

How the South Was Won

I T WAS TANTALISING, this notion that Israel could redeem itself – and even find peace with Palestine – through the application of new water technology. Whether Israelis would ever truly share the fruits of their know-how with Palestinians was moot; the old argument, rights versus technology, went around and around. But, in the meantime, there was no stopping Israeli progress. That became clearer than ever when Daniel and I set out on a grand tour of the Negev, the triangle of desert that forms the Israeli south, hanging down from the centre of the country like a giant fang. This was the part of Israel that Ben-Gurion dreamed of turning green: the original point, and the final destination still, of the NWC.

Through the car windscreen, all was bleak, brown and dusty: a forbidding, sparsely populated badland. I thought of T.E. Lawrence who, with the archaeologist C. Leonard Woolley, surveyed and mapped the Negev on behalf of the Palestine Exploration Fund in 1914. Lawrence and Woolley paid particular attention to the region's water holes, in part because archaeology was a smokescreen for the real purpose of the expedition, which was military reconnaissance: British High Command in Cairo knew that water holes would be tactically critical in the event of an Ottoman invasion of Egypt.[1] Lawrence's findings were later published in a much-celebrated book, *The Wilderness of Zin* – the same wilderness once traversed by Moses and the tribes, who survived much of the thirteenth century BC on manna from heaven and water miraculously spouting from rocks.

The impression of barren emptiness was false, however. As we barrelled along the dead straight road that bisects the flatlands south-west of Beersheba, what appeared to be a second sun rose over the horizon. 'That's Ashalim!' grinned Daniel, as I squinted and rubbed my eyes. 'The locals call it the Eye of Sauron. You'll see. It's pretty cool.'

Indeed it was. The light source, when we drew level with it twenty minutes later, was a solar tower 260 metres high, with a top that glowed so brightly that it hurt to look at it. Arranged all around was an enormous circle of mirrors, more than 50,000 of them, all angled at the tip of the tower like a horde of pagans bowing before an idol. The mirrors were computer-controlled heliostats, constantly adjusted to track the movement of the sun; the solar receiver at the top of the tower was a boiler that heated water to 600 degrees centigrade, producing steam that drove a turbine at the tower's base, generating enough power for 110,000 homes, or 2 per cent of Israel's electricity needs.

Innovation, perhaps above all in the sphere of environmental engineering, is Israel's best secret weapon, with a track record so long and successful that it has come almost to characterize the state. The country's ambition is to produce 17 per cent of its electricity from renewable sources by 2030,[2] and this modern-day Burning Bush is lighting the way. The achievement was, literally, dazzling. What Israeli could not feel proud of such prowess?

Harnessed to the desalination process, solar power has the potential, at least, to drive down production costs to a point where fresh water could be had almost for free – and that has important implications for the peace of the region. Sorek and the other desalination plants are mostly private enterprises, not public ones. Although desalinated water is becoming cheaper to produce, the plants are still powered by expensive fossil fuels; and consumers have to pay for the end product. Price, arguably, is as great an obstacle to equitable water provision in Israel-Palestine as the politics of the occupation. But what if the process was powered by sustainable solar energy rather than fossil fuels, so that desalinated water became genuinely cheap?

Israeli entrepreneurs are already exploring this intriguing possibility. A Tel Aviv start-up firm called Tethys Solar Desalination has piloted a design that uses direct solar heat to evaporate water, which it then makes potable through distillation. Tethys claims its prototype 'weather box', which uses no photovoltaic cells or, in fact, any electricity at all, can produce 10,000 cubic metres of drinking water per day, while cutting the usual energy costs by 90 per cent.[3]

Clever water technology, Daniel said, is nothing new in the Negev, where brains were applied from the outset of the Zionist project. The Netafim dripper factory that we visited at Kibbutz Hatzerim was just a foretaste. The solar tower at Ashalim added to my growing impression that the Negev was a kind of giant laboratory for Israel's environmental engineers.

Daniel, in full tour-guide mode, took me to Mitzpe Revivim, one of the pre-state Yishuv's first desert settlements, now preserved as a museum. He explained how Ben-Gurion, on one of his visits to the US, was inspired by the go-getting, can-do spirit of the nineteenth-century pioneers who conquered the American West: the place where he conceived his ambition to 'make the desert bloom'. Revivim – a hopeful name, meaning 'rain showers' – began life in 1943 as an agricultural research station, the Yishuv's first concerted effort to make Ben-Gurion's vision a reality.

The station resembled Fort Zinderneuf in *Beau Geste*, a white-painted courtyard with a lookout tower surrounded by thick stone walls. In its day, it was the Yishuv's southernmost outpost, in remote country used by no one but Bedouin nomads. Its founders were a dozen *halutzim*, pioneers from the centre of modern Israel, who had no choice but to find their own irrigation water. Simcha Blass's 'champagne pipeline', the forerunner of the NWC that supplied other early Negev settlements like Kibbutz Hatzerim, was still three years away.

The displays in the museum made much of the hardships faced by the first occupants, and the fortitude and ingenuity it took to make the place a success. These were familiar characteristics. Revivim was as much a shrine to the new mythology as it was a museum: a Zionist version, perhaps, of the Spencer Tracy Hollywood epic, *How the West was Won*.

A preserved hut, small and crudely furnished with a camp bed, a paraffin lamp and other period bric-a-brac, contained a cardboard cut-out of its former occupant, an engineer from Caesarea called Dov Kublanov, who built canals and dams to trap seasonal flood water: dogged efforts that kept the venture alive. The pioneers eventually struck groundwater 100 metres down, and pumped it out using a modified tractor.

Revivim's remote location made it vulnerable to attack. Eight of its garrison were killed in battles with Egyptian forces during the war of 1948. Its defence in the early years was organized by the Haganah, the underground military arm of the Jewish Agency, pre-state Israel's government in waiting. As elsewhere, Revivim's Haganah commander double-hatted as a sergeant in the British colonial police, a role that allowed him to smuggle in illegal weapons hidden in the false bottom of a police van.

Of course, the fort was not only about agricultural research. Its other purpose was to establish a Jewish foothold on territory that Palestine's British overlords firmly viewed as Arab. In this respect, too, Revivim was a stunning success. In 1947, a delegation from UNESCO toured the Negev, charged with setting the new border between Israel and Palestine. Revivim, the Jewish Agency argued, proved that the Yishuv, and only the Yishuv, had the capacity and technical know-how to exploit and colonize the empty desert; the Negev should therefore be given to them.

The first thing the UNESCO delegation saw on the morning of their arrival at Revivim was a garden of fresh pink gladioli. The pioneers, apparently quite by chance, had watered the gladioli the night before, causing them to burst into bloom as though choreographed. The bright colours against the dun-coloured land made a great impression on the delegates, who were accompanied by the press; a colour photograph of the flowers appeared in the English-language *Palestine Post* the following day.

The officials went away convinced that the Negev should be granted to Israel, and in November 1947 – in a vote from which Britain pointedly abstained – the UN General Assembly agreed. It was a pivotal moment for the nascent Israeli state, the geographic area of which was instantly increased by 13,000 square kilometres, or 55 per cent of Israel's total land area. Irrigation technology was literally how the South was won.

The scale of the achievement was clear from the top of the lookout tower. Beyond the shell of an old Dakota cargo plane that had supplied the fort in 1948, the desert was no longer barren. Since the eventual arrival of the NWC, the research station had evolved into a kibbutz of 1,100 people, whose 8,000 acres of farmland were filled with olive groves. Modern Revivim is also home to the most productive dairy farm in Israel. Down the road later on we found a fish farm, and even, at nearby Neve Midbar, a spa and water park.

The region is still a work in progress, undergoing a water-driven transformation that the modern Negev's patron saint, Ben-Gurion, could not have foreseen. Daniel said that the ancient city of Beersheba – the so-called capital of the Negev, a bare 32 kilometres north of of Neve Midbar – had doubled in size in his lifetime, to become a conurbation of 650,000. Water was the city's first raison d'etre: Beersheba in Hebrew means Well of the Oath, a reference to a 3,700-year-old truce over a disputed well.[4] The civic centrepiece of modern Beersheba, said Daniel, is also about water: a vast new riverpark, in the style of Yarkon Park in Tel Aviv. The municipal authorities aimed to rebrand Beersheba as Israel's 'Water City'; their riverpark incorporates fountains and a man-made beach on an artificial 22-acre lake, the second-largest lake in Israel after the Galilee.

Despite the impression given by the museum at Revivim, the gladioli-growing pioneers were not the first frontiersmen in the Negev. Whatever the arguments put forward by Zionists, the Negev has never been truly 'empty'. Other peoples made this desert bloom long before Israelis did.

Daniel took me to the ruins of Shivta, a settlement that thrived for centuries before its abandonment in the eighth or ninth century. A hot desert wind blasted across the empty car park, scouring us with sand. Unlike Revivim, we had Shivta entirely to ourselves. A battered information panel explained that it was once a waypoint on an ancient trading route, built by the Nabateans, the creators of Petra. For 700 years, incense-laden camel trains passed from Oman, via Petra, through the Negev to the ports on the Mediterranean coast – including Gaza – from where their loads were shipped onwards to Greece and Rome.

Nabatean Shivta was no mere caravanserai. By the Byzantine era it had evolved into a proper town, large enough to contain three churches, the main one as big as a small cathedral; we sheltered from the east wind in the well-preserved remains of its apse. Archaeologists had also excavated the remains of winepresses, which they calculated were capable of producing 2 million litres of wine a year. This was despite Shivta's location in one of the driest parts of the desert, where rainfall does not exceed 10 centimetres a year.

The Nabateans' secret was rock-hewn cisterns, which were filled with run-off captured on terraces up to 2.5 kilometres away, and channelled to town via an extensive network of canals. In the 1960s, agronomists calculated that 10 centimetres of rain was enough to keep Shivtans in all the fruit and veg they needed: enough not just to grow grapes or olives but peaches, pomegranates, pistachio nuts. They had even proved their calculation by reconstructing Shivta's orchard, using the original irrigation system, just outside the ruined town.[5] It seemed that Dov Kublanov, the engineer hero of Revivim, was not quite the innovator that UNESCO once took him for.

In any case, the true heirs of the Nabateans were, arguably, not Yishuv or Israeli Jews but Bedouin nomads, who called the Negev home long before any Israeli did. Much land was expropriated by the military following the war of 1948, when the nomad Bedouin who lived on it were forced to move. They scattered everywhere, to the Galilee, to Gaza, or to the Jordan Valley, as the Jahalin clansmen I encountered there had done. But many remained; and today, despite the space available, the Negev is as hotly contested as every other territory of old Palestine.

A government resettlement programme was launched in the 1960s and 70s, when nomad Bedouin were 'encouraged' to move to seven government-built townships; the government argued this was the only way it could provide them with the jobs and services they needed. Rahat, founded in 1972, is the largest of the Bedouin-majority townships, with a population of 70,000; it is officially recognized as a 'city', and is said to be the largest Bedouin city in the world.[6] But many Bedouin retort that they were not 'encouraged' but pushed from their grazing lands, and then corralled, for the convenience of the Israeli state. Some 90,000 Negev Bedouin never moved to the townships, and continue to live in scattered camps and villages, in their traditional way.

They pay a high price for their stubbornness: Bedouin villages unregistered with the Israeli authorities – of which there are around fifty – are the victims of the same remorseless military bureaucracy that I witnessed in the West Bank, including frequent court-ordered demolition orders. The case of Al-Araqeeb, a village built on land just north of Beersheba expropriated by Israel in 1951, is particularly notorious. In November 2022, the village, the home of twenty families, was demolished by the IDF – and immediately rebuilt by the Bedouin – for a record 209th time.[7] In June 2018, at which point Al-Araqeeb had been demolished a mere 130 times, a spokesman for the community, Aziz al-Turi, said: 'No matter how aggressive and destructive the Israeli authorities are, we insist on staying in our homes and land and hold on to every grain of dust from our dear homeland, and we will not let go.'[8]

We stopped at Sde Boker, the kibbutz that Ben-Gurion joined when he temporarily retired from politics in 1953, and where he was buried when he died twenty years later. The asceticism of the simple kibbutz life greatly appealed to him. 'The desert,' he wrote, 'provides us with the best opportunity to begin again. This is a vital element of our renaissance in Israel. For it is in mastering nature that man learns to control himself.'

Irrigation was, naturally, critical to his redemptive vision. He specifically linked and compared the nurturing of plants to the cultivation of Israeli nationhood, writing:

> When I looked out of my window today and saw a tree standing before me, the sight awoke in me a greater sense of beauty and personal satisfaction than all the forests that I have crossed in Switzerland and Scandinavia. For we planted each tree in this place and watered them with the water we provided at the cost of numerous efforts. Why does a mother love her children so? Because they are her creation. Why does the Jew feel an affinity with Israel? Because everything here must still be accomplished. It depends only on him to participate in this privileged act of creation.

Ben-Gurion was buried alongside his wife Paula on the edge of a cliff overlooking a deep wadi, but, as it was pitch dark by the time we got to Sde

Boker, there was no inspiring view to contemplate. Instead, we picked our way through the bushes by the light of our iPhones. The little kibbutz at our back was home to a land-studies school, this being a natural place to establish such an institution. The gravesite, Daniel said, was a popular trysting spot for its students, although there was no one there when we reached it, and no sound beyond our breathing, which was eerily amplified by the profound desert silence. Sometimes, according to Daniel, the students made out on the gravestone itself, as though they hoped to absorb the spirit of the great man by osmosis. The ritual sounded distinctly pagan. Perhaps Ben-Gurion and the rejuvenation of this desert really were a kind of cult.

We spent the night at Mitzpe Ramon, a mountain town perched on the edge of the world's largest 'erosion cirque', a canyon-like depression 14 kilometres wide that formed when the Negev was still covered by ocean. Established in the 1950s as a camp for road builders, the town had grown into a community of 5,000, with an economy geared to ecotourism. Our hostel, called Green Backpackers, was as irritatingly pleased with itself as its name suggested. The lobby was a hippy hangout, all tie-dye floor cushions and tables made of upcycled plasma TV screens, and passive-aggressive notices about how to use the fridge; tea and coffee were paid for via an honesty box in the shape of a minion from the *Despicable Me* franchise.

The hostel showed, in its way, the direction in which the Negev is headed. It is an increasingly trendy tourist destination: *Lonely Planet* calls the Negev 'a giant greenhouse of development ... Think eco-villages, spa resorts, even wineries. In the next few years, a new international airport at Timna is scheduled to open, followed by a high-speed railway to Eilat, and more hotels.' The desert is certainly no longer the 'wilderness' described in the Old Testament. The dunes to the south-west were once home to Arabian leopards, but human encroachment on their hunting grounds has driven them to the point of extinction; none has been seen in the wild since 2007.

The next day, we drove to Kibbutz Ketura in the Arava Desert, 50 kilometres north of Eilat on the Red Sea, the southernmost point in Israel. The road wound down a steep escarpment to a desolate plain, hotter by far than the central Negev. I was below sea level once again, in another landscape guaranteed to thrill geologists. The Arava is a continuation of the Jordan

Valley, another section of the giant north-south rift in the Earth's crust caused by the 'strike-slip' separation, many millions of years ago, of the Arabian and African tectonic plates; the sunken Jordan Rift is a rare example of what geologists call a 'graben'. Strange folds in the rock strata hinted at the immense forces that are still pulling this land apart. Small earth tremors are commonplace, all along the rift; the last major earthquake, in Jericho in 1927, was powerful enough to kill hundreds.

Our destination was the Arava Institute for Environmental Studies, a modern-day version of the 1940s agricultural research station at Revivim. It is known for its date palm tree, nicknamed Methuselah, which we found flourishing in its own special enclosure by the entrance. The Institute's biologists had managed to propagate this plant, *Jurassic Park*-style, from a dried seed that was 2,000 years old; archaeologists had found the seed in a jar excavated at Masada in the 1960s.

Shira Kronich, the associate director, explained that the Institute's mission was much broader than the pursuit of clever horticulture. It was, rather, engaged in what she called 'track two diplomacy', lobbying local politicians and international organizations for greater environmental cooperation between the region's neighbours. The kibbutz's location, close to the border with Jordan, was apt.

'Nature knows no borders, so we have no choice but to cooperate across them,' she said, in a calm authoritative drawl that sounded distinctly Australian. She was born on the kibbutz, but was raised and educated in Melbourne; and now she was back, as a specialist in transboundary water management.

The Institute was established in the optimistic years after the Oslo Accords, with five separate research departments staffed by graduates from all the region's universities. Its founders dreamed that, one day, the environment ministers of Israel, Palestine and Jordan would all be alumni of the Institute. Shira was convinced – in fact, it was her core belief – that environmental cooperation, especially in the water sector, was at the 'spearhead' of political cooperation; the point of the Institute was to showcase how it could 'feed into a two-state solution'. She expounded on a model for regional water cooperation that is quite often put forward by the Israeli centre left:

the 1950s-era European Coal and Steel Community, the first iteration of the European Union.

'Maybe water is our coal,' she said. 'If the Europeans could do it, why can't we? Water is not a commodity like coal, but the effects of sharing it, prosperity and security, are the same.' She admitted, however, that the going was tough. 'We are fighting a strong tide of despair,' she said. 'The political situation has got worse, and the map is leading us away from regional cooperation.'

She was frustrated by Israel's refusal to take responsibility for the impact of their water control policies in the Occupied Territories. The dysfunction of the Oslo-era Joint Water Committee, to her, was symptomatic of that failure. 'It's weird how Israel's water people just don't see the drawbacks of their water hegemony agenda,' she said. It was unusual to find an Israeli water specialist so openly sceptical of their country's policies. I wondered if our remote location had something to do with that. We were far from the political hubbub of Jerusalem and Tel Aviv, and all the security tensions surrounding Gaza and the West Bank. Hamas's rockets seldom reach this far south-east; the relative tranquility of the region perhaps lent itself to better Israeli-Arab cooperation. Shira noted that Israel owned wells just over the Jordan border from Kibbutz Ketura, and had been able to reach and maintain them, without problem, for almost a quarter of a century.

She was much preoccupied, and frustrated, by the slow progress of the Red-to-Dead Seawater Conveyance project. I had read and heard much about this ingenious plan, a canal linking the Red and Dead Seas, which was first mooted in a different form in the mid-nineteenth century, by British officers looking for a way to circumvent the French-built Suez Canal. The idea was resurrected in the late 1960s, although forty-five years passed before the the first serious feasibility study was completed, in 2005. The plan has not much changed since then: the Dead Sea will be replenished by sea water from the Gulf of Aqaba via the Arava Valley, in Jordanian territory a few kilometres east of Kibbutz Ketura, with another pipeline sending desalinated water to Amman; the briny byproduct of the desalination process will be added to the canal water to raise its salinity to that of the Dead Sea.

Like Israel's scheme to pump desalinated seawater into the Galilee, Red-to-Dead aims to reverse decades of degradation caused by over-extraction. It is, potentially, as transformative of the environment as the NWC of the 1960s. Its appeal lies in its exploitation of gravity: apart from one natural hurdle, the water will flow down to the lowest point on earth with minimal need for expensive and energy-intensive pumps. The cost is tentatively estimated at US$10 billion: a fraction of the price, in relative terms, of the NWC that caused most of the Dead Sea's problems in the first place. Since 2005, however, the project has been almost constantly stalled by political discord on all sides. The first construction phase was supposed to begin in 2021,[9] although Shira wasn't holding her breath.[10] 'It is Jordan, not Israel, who is the main driver of the Red-to-Dead project,' Shira said. 'But why are we not driving it together, when it is in both our countries' interests that it succeeds?'

She was not alone in her frustration at the dearth of international cooperation, and Israel's peculiar blindness to the consequences of its self-serving water policies. At another agricultural research station, government-funded and an hour north of the Arava Institute, we stopped for coffee with its chief soil scientist, Effi Tripler. 'I wish we could cooperate more with the Jordanians,' he said. 'We could share their aquifer water for the next fifteen years. It would be so much cheaper than bringing in desal from Ashkelon or Aqaba.'

The northern Arava is home to some 300 farms, many of them huge, all of them intensely cultivated. Together with the western Negev, the area provides the bulk of Israel's fruit and vegetables. Unlike the western Negev, however, the northern Arava was never farmed in the past. It therefore represents the apogee of Ben-Gurion's vision, an extraordinary triumph over nature through irrigation and technology. The northern Arava is, of course, a big user of drip irrigation; its farmers are Netafim's most important customers in Israel.

Effi explained that the region, hard up against the Jordanian border, is classified as a 'peripheral' area of strategic importance, and so enjoys special government support. This meant, above all, that its water supply had long been assured. The NWC, he said, was still being extended here: a new spur reached the area in 2018, with others planned or under construction. Effi contended that the water came because the region's fruit and vegetable production was vital to national security. 'Not everyone loves Israel,' he said. 'We have to keep our food production secure.'

I had heard this doctrine expounded often before in Israel. The quest for self-sufficiency is a government policy of such long standing that it is practically a tenet of Zionism. It helps explain, and justify, why agriculture, a sector that contributes just 2.3 per cent of GDP, nevertheless uses 55 per cent of all the water available in Israel to sustain it.[11]

Just like every other country in the Middle East, Israel depends on international markets for its food. Some US$6.8 billion of foodstuffs were imported in 2019.[12] The country is self-sufficient in some agricultural sectors, such as poultry, and potentially could be in others. But while Israeli farmers do supply their internal market, they also export more than US$2 billion of foodstuffs every year: hardly the sign of a nation anxious to keep its produce for itself. Exporting agricultural produce – and with it, the 'virtual water' that is required to grow it – is, in the end, a choice made by Israel, a matter of political and economic strategy. The peripheral regions are farmed and watered not as an expedient of national security but by the requirement to keep the land occupied. 'The border will be where the farm is' was one of the earliest precepts of Zionism, a doctrine that still informs all official thinking.

Israel has always promoted its agricultural exports, and did so in the past partly for the international prestige these conferred. The seedless, easy-to-peel Jaffa orange, although no longer much grown today, was exported with such success during the Mandate years and after Israel's independence that, in the 1950s and 60s, it became an emblem of the new state. Tel Aviv is still sometimes nicknamed 'the Big Orange'; the export's legacy lives on in the consciousness of British children in the shape of the humble Jaffa Cake, first marketed by McVitie and Price in 1927. The Sharon fruit, similarly, is so well known in the US and Britain that its name has become an alternative for a persimmon – although not a correct one, because the Sharon fruit is in a fact a modern cultivar of the persimmon, developed by Yishuv farmers in the 1900s; it takes its name from the Sharon Plain, north of Tel Aviv, where it was first grown.

Palestinians have reason to be aggrieved at both export products. The Sharon Plain owes its underlying fertility to the waters of the western mountain aquifer, a resource that they have been prevented from exploiting since the Oslo Accords. The Sharon fruit symbolises this injustice; it means that the rainfall that charges the aquifer in the West Bank, where tens of thousands of people lack adequate domestic water, is exported, as virtual water, for Israeli profit. The Jaffa orange brand is no less galling, for it was originally an Arab product, a cultivar of a natural mutation found in an orchard near Jaffa in the 1840s; its first marketeers called it a Shamouti orange. By rebranding the Shamouti as a 'Jaffa orange', Israel added insult to injury by suggesting that Jaffa itself was Israeli, rather than the famous Arab port it had been for thirteen centuries until its 60,000 residents were driven out in 1948.

Effi was typically proud of the know-how that maximized productivity, the ability of Israel's farmers to experiment and innovate. Seven of the farmers in his district were holders of PhDs, he said. Foreign agronomists from as far away as Singapore and Namibia were regular visitors to his research station, on the hunt for new ideas and advice.

He was far from sanguine, though, about the general direction of his country's farming sector. It was his view that Israel could and should be more self-sufficient. 'For the last two winters there has been a vegetable deficit in Israel – not enough grapes, tomatoes, aubergines, peppers – the staples of our Mediterranean diet. The government is making up the short-fall with imports. We are even importing corn now, for the first time in Israel.'

He said there were several causes, most obviously the increased demand from the country's booming population. Yields had also been reduced by climate change. 'Every year, we are seeing one more day where temperatures top 42 degrees,' he said. 'We have had no frost here since 2013.' Meanwhile, rising production costs, caused in part by government-imposed minimum wage increases, even for foreign labourers, meant that many farmers had switched towards high-value cash crops and away from staples like corn; and the best prices for those crops were often to be found not in Israel, but abroad. Sixty per cent of that winter's Arava crop had been exported to Russia – a scandal, in Effi's view.

None of these things, however, worried him as much as the state of the land itself. Decades of intensive agriculture had raised the salinity of the soil, with dramatic negative results for many crop types. 'There is no local solution. It's like a snowball. You can flush the salts from the soil, but the deposits always come back. We could stop farming here to let the soil recover, but 60 per cent of our local people live on the land – and evacuation is politically impossible.'

Seventy years after independence, it was as though Ben-Gurion's mission to irrigate the Negev for agriculture was on autopilot. 'It is hydropolitics. In Israel, you can't separate politics and water,' Effi shrugged. His country's agricultural policies, he felt, were seriously misdirected. 'The government is doing *nothing* to maintain self-sufficiency,' he griped. More desalination was the 'quick' solution, but came with too high a cost, environmental as well as financial, and he doubted whether it could be sustained. 'As a scientist, I look thirty years ahead. But the government always wants quick fixes for our problems. If things don't change, agriculture here will not continue.'

Finally he laid his cards on the table: Effi Tripler abhorred the rightward direction in which Israel was still being led. 'The desert is still blooming – Ben-Gurion's vision was fulfilled in the 1960s or 1970s – but there are no votes in farming any more, and, with the rise of the right, a big chunk of the Ministry of Agriculture's budget keeps going to settlements in the West Bank.'

There were, in consequence, many fewer farmers in the Arava than there once had been. Declining yields and profits had driven many to give up. The public's perception of the sector's importance, based on the romantic memory of early Zionism, was laughable, and an illusion that could not be sustained. 'Farmers are really a dying breed,' he said. 'There are only 6,000 working farmers left in Israel, a country of more than 9 million. But what can I do? I speak as a liberal . . . Israel is becoming more religious and radical. It's partly why I live out here, to escape all that. There is concern for democracy in Israel now. I hope the judiciary hold the line. They are the only bulwark that stands between Israel becoming Turkey. It is a sad story.'

We went to meet Atar Shahak, a farmer at a nearby moshav called Hatseva. Daniel was proud of Atar, who turned out to be yet another relative of his, this time a cousin: a big, bluff man of few words, but with a dry sense of humour, and thus another Zionist archetype of the old school. His face and spade-like hands were nut-coloured from years of toil in the desert sun. With few preliminaries, he took us for a drive around his land, bumping along tracks in a decrepit Landcruiser that was thickly coated with dust.

His farm, which extended to 400 dunums (100 acres), was given over to aubergines, lemons, tomatoes, all growing in dozens of polytunnels, which were easily tall enough to drive a tractor down, and hundreds of metres long. His land ran right up to the border with Jordan, and was frequently patrolled by the IDF. Life in this militarized zone was not without its dangers. Many years before, when he was thirteen, Atar had stepped on an old Israeli mine that had washed down the Wadi Arava. The mine blew off half of one foot, and he still walked with a limp.

With a little prodding, Atar confirmed all that Effi had said. Increasing soil salinity was indeed a problem, as was the cost of labour. We passed a trailer-load of workers on our tour, heading back to their accommodation huts at the end of a long day in the polytunnels. All of them were Thai.

'They are good workers. They never try to think for themselves as Israelis do, they just do what they are told,' Atar said. There were, I learned, a thousand Thai workers at Hatseva, outnumbering the resident Israeli community, with whom they did not mix at all, by two to one. It sounded an awkward social dynamic, although Atar insisted the Thais were content. They were all on official short-term work visas, allocated through a programme run by the UN, and their salaries were almost more than he could afford.

A theme of complaint was emerging in the Arava. The farming community were traditionally left wing in outlook, with little patience for the religious sensibilities of the right, and they felt the government was neglecting them in favour of the voters in the cities. In 2017, Atar said, there had been big demonstrations in Tel Aviv against the high cost of living, prompting the government to open certain markets to imports. 'We are being undercut by foreigners now,' he griped. 'They're even taking veg from Gaza, even though everyone knows they irrigate their crops with raw sewage. Yet *we* are subject to the toughest regulations.'

The following day, 9 April 2019, was election day in Israel, a national poll prompted by a dispute over an extension of the exemption from military service traditionally enjoyed by the ultra-orthodox. The issue encapsulated a widening division in Israeli society. Zionism, Israel itself, was founded on the principles of labour, sacrifice and teamwork; military service was mandatory for everyone else. There was an increasing feeling, certainly in the traditional farming communities of the south, that the religious orthodox community, with their dogged and unworldly devotion to the Torah, were not pulling their weight in society. As Effi Tripler observed: 'The ultra-orthodox don't work, they just study. And I pay my taxes for this?'

It was clear that Netanyahu wouldn't be receiving much support in the rural communities of the Negev. Daniel, who had already cast his vote by post, wouldn't reveal whom he supported; but it was obvious that he was no fan of Likud.

We retraced our way westwards. There was even less traffic on the road than usual, it being a public holiday for the election, so we made rapid progress. Our next destination was a place I had been longing to see for two years, since the very start of my Israel-Palestine research project: Kadesh Barnea, in remote desert on the border with the Egyptian Sinai, the spot where, according to legend, Moses tapped water from a rock.

Daniel thought it was a wild-goose chase. The map showed there was a small moshav there – a community of perhaps 200 people – but we had no introduction; not even the name of someone we might talk to. Nevertheless, I felt compelled to at least try to visit the spot where the Zionist quest for water arguably began.

Our road traversed a hot and empty expanse of drab-coloured dunes, a rare part of the Negev where modernity had yet to properly advance. Kadesh Barnea's name – 'Holy Desert of Wanderings' in Hebrew – was appropriate. Eventually we came to Nitzana, the main border crossing for commercial truck trade with Egypt, although it was closed today. The border fence was tall and strong, and stretched out of sight in both directions in a dead straight line. Beyond was the Sinai – the home, Daniel said, of dangerous gangs of people smugglers, as well as a jihadist affiliate of Al-Qaida. In stark contrast to the easy-going Arava, the whole area was militarized. The moshav's unmanned entrance gate, just up the road from the border crossing, was firmly shut when we reached it, and impressively topped with coils of barbed wire. Daniel, however, found an intercom button by the gate, and he charmed our way in.

Inside, we had a stroke of luck: the town hall had been converted into a polling station, where half a dozen moshavniks sat yawning over the ballot boxes, happy for any distraction. It was mid-afternoon, and most of the community had already voted. Turnout this year, said one, was higher than usual, approaching 70 per cent already, double the national average. Among the group was Edina, a woman of sixty or so, who revealed she was one of the moshav's founders. She took us to a corner of the hall, and told us the Kadesh Barnea story.

The 'real', biblical Kadesh Barnea, she explained, was not here but 30 kilometres away, over the border in Egypt. This was disappointing news, because there was no possibility of my getting there without a pre-arranged visa, even when the border was open. Edina was able to tell me about it, though. She described how, as a young woman in 1977, she had set out from Jerusalem with her brother and five friends, all young men, to establish a moshav there. This was possible, then, because Israel had occupied the Sinai for a period following the 1967 war.

'We were ... *meshuggeneh*,' she sighed, smiling and misty-eyed at the memory; the word, an old Yiddish one, means 'crazy'. 'Our parents hated it. But my brother's friend had a dream to do something different ... "Start anew" lies so deep in the Israeli consciousness. Ben-Gurion said that joining a desert community was the greatest thing he ever did.'

Life in the Sinai, she recalled, was tough. They began work each day at two in the morning, and didn't stop until ten at night. With a little seed money from the Jewish Agency, they grew a few vegetables using water tankered in by the army and, eventually, brackish water drawn from a painstakingly dug shallow well.

'And was there a rock there?' I asked excitedly.

'The Moses rock? I believe so,' she said, vaguely. 'At least, there was a rock that certainly looked like it. There was a Bedouin spring there, but that was theirs, so we didn't use it.' It was, she said, coincidence that they had set up where they did; the spot's association with the Old Testament miracle played little or no part in their choice.

The tiny colony survived for two years. Under the Camp David Accords of 1978, the border with Egypt was redrawn, and the pioneers were obliged to pull back and start again in this place, officially called Nitzanei Sinai, although the moshavniks all preferred and used the venture's original name, Kadesh Barnea. Their new land was granted to them by the then agriculture minister, Ariel Sharon, who, Edina said, 'noticed some Bedouin trying to settle here, and thought our presence would stop them.'

Even so, there was little government support to begin with, and water supply remained a problem. 'We wanted to be farmers, but the aquifer here is brackish. So we selected vegetables that can tolerate salt.' In 2006, however, the moshav was granted money for a small desalination plant; and then, finally, they were connected to the NWC, via one of the longest extensions in the country. 'We thought, "the milk will come when the baby arrives" – and it did! We suddenly had all the water we wanted. That was a good time!'

Kadesh Barnea has since evolved into another southern megafarm, growing lush crops of cherry tomatoes, melon, strawberries, grapes, even truffles. They farm beef cattle, and turkeys, and produce their own bread, as well as pizzas. Nor is the land their only source of income any more. The community, Edina said, includes doctors and lawyers who commute to jobs in Beersheba. It is an improbable but prospering oasis of civilization in the mighty Wilderness of Zin, surrounded by the NWC-irrigated green fields that made it possible, their dark incongruous rectangles visible from high above via the satellites of Google Earth.

'It is a good place, and a good life here, although not easy,' Edina went on thoughtfully. 'What did Moses find here? Milk and honey? But *we* had to make what we've got. The Negev is not Europe. I am proud of what we have achieved – and I believe Moses would be too.'

The interview was over: a group of voters had turned up, and Edina had to get back to her ballot boxes. As we said goodbye, I realised I hadn't asked for her surname, for my notes. 'It's Moskovic. A Romanian name ... Funny you should ask, actually. It means "Son of Moses".' Perhaps fate had played a role in her desert adventure after all.

CHAPTER FOURTEEN

Gaza Redux

D ANIEL AND I pressed on, skirting the long south-western edge of Israel, heading straight towards Gaza, the border fence with Egypt always just to our left. The Western Negev, the first beneficiary of the NWC, was the only important agricultural area I had not yet visited. Just as interestingly, its proximity to Gaza made it a regular target for Hamas rockets, and I was curious to discover what it must be like to live with that constant threat. The immediate border area was the main drop zone for the incendiary kites and balloons that had floated over me at the Gaza fence demonstration. I was almost back where I started: the conclusion of a 1,600-kilometre circuit of Israel-Palestine that had taken many months to complete.

Yet the satisfaction I felt at closing the circle was tempered by the edginess of the region, which was perceptible even from the inside of a speeding car. The landscape altered as we re-entered the coastal zone, with more farms, and more traffic on the road, including the occasional IDF patrol. Gaza made its presence felt even from a distance; it loomed like an imaginary storm cloud, darkening the closer we came to it.

We stopped at a kibbutz called Nir Oz. The farmers here are famous specialists in long-term water conservation techniques: perhaps the closest heirs in modern Israel to the tradition of Revivim. They are major producers of asparagus, among other valuable export crops, although Nir Oz is best known for its extraordinary botanical garden, a 27-acre project begun in 1960, run in collaboration with Ben-Gurion University.

The project had been directed for years by Ran Pauker. An octogenarian, he was older than Israel itself, with the physique of a whippet and skin turned leathery by a life outdoors. He was an alumnus of the prestigious Kadoorie School of Agriculture. Founded in the lower Galilee in 1933, the Kadoorie is closely associated, in Israel, with the struggle for independence in the 1940s, because so many of its students joined the Palmach brigades, the elite units of the underground army of the Yishuv. Among Israel's agro-science community, Ran Pauker was known, inevitably, as the Wizard of Oz.

'You are now standing in a desert,' he announced, with a magisterial wave at a lawn as green as a garden in Surrey, edged by marigolds ranked in beds shaded by palm trees. 'My secret? I just copied the Nabateans. Thirty per cent of our water is trapped run-off. I'm a lazy guy, and I don't like waste, see?' He pointed to an outside wall where a system of gutters caught the drips from the back of an air-conditioning unit, and distributed them onto a flowerbed. 'I have almost discovered *perpetuum mobile*,' he smiled.

He explained how, through the careful selection of plant stock, the drought resistance of which was still constantly being monitored, the garden around us consumed precisely half as much water as any equivalent garden in the centre and north of Israel. The kibbutz doubled as an observation site for researchers from all over the country, a real-world showcase not only of the famous Netafim slogan, 'Grow more with less', but of the government's public education one, *Chaval al kol tipa*: 'Don't waste a drop'. Green fingers, Ran said, were in his family's genes: his father had been a gardener, and now his daughter was too. He called the technique he had developed 'precision gardening', based on a set of simple rules that he dubbed the 'Ten Commandments for a Waterwise Ecogarden': knowledge of the soil, the importance of matching plants to the soil type, the timing of watering and mulching, among others.

He jammed on a sunhat, and shooed us aboard an electric golf cart. A short, jerky ride later, we arrived at his first pride and joy, a pond where a fountain tinkled, blissfully shaded by an enormous fig tree in which was concealed a children's playhouse. The tour continued to his main showpiece, the botanical garden, in which 500 different species grew, all of them thriving despite, as he reminded us, three consecutive years of severe drought. The garden included sixty-five types of eucalyptus grown from seed imported from South Africa, South America, Baja California. It was a desert version of the gardens at Kew.

He freely acknowledged that he would have achieved little, if anything, without water from the NWC – an asset, I privately reflected, that had not been enjoyed by the ancient Nabateans. 'We received water from the Yarkon from 1956, and later on, from Kinneret. Today, our domestic water is all desal from Ashkelon, and our irrigation water is 100 per cent recycled, from Shafdan. It's cheap. Very good value.'

There were, however, shadows in this botanical nirvana. Gaza was just six fields away to the west – a distance of about 2 kilometres – which put Nir Oz right on the front line of that conflict. The kibbutz's antecedents were, in fact, military. It began life in 1955 as one of the very first settlements set up by the paramilitary 'Nahal' programme, an acronym for *Noar Halutzi Lohem*, the 'Fighting Pioneer Youth'. The importance of water supply to the programme's success was perhaps implicit in its name: *nahal* is also the Hebrew word for a stream. Although the goal for every Nahal settlement was to eventually become a civilian one – as Nir Oz did, in 1956 – they were designed to go on serving as a first line of defence against any future Arab invasion along the state's periphery. It was the same tactic deployed by General Allon after 1967 on Israel's eastern border along the River Jordan.

Nir Oz's secondary, military role was not one that its residents were likely to forget. The houses on the kibbutz were interspersed with self-contained bomb shelters, each weighing 67 tons. Like many Israelis, the kibbutzniks here subscribed to early warning smartphone apps with names like 'Red Alert: Israel', but Ran said that such systems were of limited use when the launch points in Gaza were so close. Israelis living along the Gaza border often have less than fifteen seconds to find cover when the rockets start flying.

In 2008, a Hamas mortar bomb hit Nir Oz's paint factory, killing one and injuring four. The IDF responded by asking the community to harvest its potatoes at night, for their own safety. In 2010, the 1950s Nahal 'heritage' building next to the community football pitch received a direct hit. The kibbutz was hit again in 2015. What, I asked Ran, was it like to live under such constant threat? 'We are used to it,' he shrugged. 'We get a lot of small stuff, incendiary kites and so on, all the time.' It was clear, nevertheless, that living here came at considerable psychological cost. In 2010, he recalled, the IDF set up an artillery battery nearby. 'The noise was incredible, and it was 24/7. Our children were afraid. But I said to them, "Imagine how scared their children must be".'

Ran's view of the conflict contained some troubling contradictions. As a self-professed 'Communist' of the old school, he was an heir to the first secular generation of Zionist settlers, the socialist *chugistim* who eschewed the eviction of Arabs in favour of neighbourly cohabitation. He naturally abhorred the conflict with the Palestinians. 'We are stupid,' he almost spat. 'I have a good friend in Gaza. We once worked together on the management of pine trees. You should *never* fight with your neighbours. We are only making the next generation of angry soldiers.'

It was evident that he had not voted for Netanyahu, the self-styled 'Mr Security' of Israeli politics. 'Our right-wing government wants a one-state solution, but what would happen to the Arabs? They cannot be evicted. So a one-state Israel would no longer be a Jewish majority state. Peace is in our interest. We *must* have a two-state solution.'

On the other hand, he also supported the military response to the Friday fence demonstrations in Gaza, as well as the IDF itself. He asserted airily that the threat of incursion implied by Hamas's name for the demonstrations, 'The Great March of Return', did not worry him in the slightest, 'because the army does an excellent job'. This was the same army, I thought to myself, that had killed children, nurses and journalists at the demonstrations, and in such numbers that the UN suggested the IDF's response 'may constitute' a war crime.[1]

It was a delicate topic; it was clear from the way Ran changed the subject that he wanted to talk about gardening, not the conflict. Yet there was no escaping the uncomfortable reality of life here. As our golf cart weaved its uncertain way back to the centre of the kibbutz, we passed a field of labourers harvesting peanuts. These labourers, Ran noted, had once all been Gazans; now, apart from 'one or two Bedouin', they were all Thai. 'We live behind fences and drawbridges like in the Middle Ages,' he sighed.

They may have water, but none of the farmers along the Gaza border have an easy life. Sderot, a 1950s development town half an hour north of Nir Oz, and the largest Israeli town in the area with a population of 25,000, is an obvious target for the militants beyond. Beit Hanoun, in the top right corner of the Strip, is barely 5 kilometres from Sderot. The town in consequence is another tainted idyll – and one of the weirdest places I have ever been.

It was a Saturday when we arrived, and the streets were deserted for Shabbat. The emptiness felt eerie, and made the town's unusual civic architecture even more obvious. Every other streetlight carries an air raid siren. All public spaces, such as the central market place, have reinforced roofs or, like the train station, are half-buried in the ground. Bus stops double as bomb shelters; the west-facing windows of all blocks of flats are accessorized with shrapnel-repellent steel sunshades.

These defence measures are not paranoid. The Qassam rockets favoured by Gaza's militants are mostly homemade affairs, fuelled by a low-tech mixture of sugar and potassium nitrate. They cannot be accurately aimed, and so can, and do, fall anywhere in the town. The region's 'Iron Dome' missile intercept system, set up by the IDF in 2011, claims to knock out 90 per cent of enemy ordnance before it reaches Sderot, but the 10 per cent that gets through is still plenty. In May 2019, Hamas and other militants launched 600 rockets at Sderot in a single week.

We found a large collection of expended rockets, 'the Qassam museum', on display outside the police station. Neatly arranged on shelves, their bent and twisted shell-casings resembled the exhaust pipe section of a well-run car breaker's yard. They came in every shape and size. Some of them had clearly been made out of sawn-up hollow lampposts. It made me wonder how the IDF's restrictions on the import of 'dual use' materials into Gaza could ever hope to succeed.

In some respects, Sderot seemed normal. It looked prosperous, and clean. Daniel explained that the cost of living was significantly less here than elsewhere, and that public services were excellent, thanks to generous government subsidies as well as donations from abroad. Around here, therefore, the people traditionally supported Netanyahu and Likud. Far from being abandoned, he said, the town was actually a popular place to move to, with long waiting lists for social housing. It was especially sought after by young families from up north looking for bigger homes to live in.

A defiant civic pride was at work, an almost perverse determination to keep calm and carry on. The ugly bomb shelter-cum-bus stops were covered not in semi-delinquent graffiti but with murals of cows in flower meadows and smiley-faced stickmen: the result, according to a sign, of a local primary school art project. This exercise in rose-tinting seemed as absurdly optimistic as the hideous Mickey Mouse gas masks that the British government issued to four-year-olds in 1942. In fact, Sderot so vividly recalled London's Blitz Spirit that I was almost unsurprised to discover direct evidence of British influence, at a roundabout generously planted with pink carnations, where a sign proclaimed: 'Together, JNF UK and the Municipality beautified the city'.

We drove on to Kibbutz Nir Am, just west of Sderot and even closer to the Gaza border. The kibbutz was home to the 'Museum of Water and Security', a name that brought together the twin themes of my research, and which promised much. The museum was, however, closed; and no amount of padlock-rattling could raise a caretaker to let us in.

Nir Am was the spot where Simcha Blass struck groundwater in 1943, and dug out a small reservoir: the first water infrastructure project in the Negev. It was from here, in 1947, that Blass laid his famous champagne pipeline to Revivim, the moment when the Yishuv's southern expansion went into overdrive. We found the reservoir close by. It was still functioning, an important collection point for water piped down the NWC, and much expanded since it was first established, to 1.5 million cubic metres, as big as a boating lake.

I was struck once again by how tiny this country is, and the extraordinary proximity, intimacy, even, of its warring inhabitants. The sprawl of Jabaliya refugee camp was easily discernible from a viewpoint on the reservoir's edge, and beyond it, the tall tower blocks of Gaza City itself. To the right hovered the IDF observation blimp over the border crossing at Erez. Beyond the blimp rose the skyline of Ashkelon city, site of the first large coastal desalination plant in Israel.

And then I looked down at the pellucid water at my feet, and thought of Sana'a Lubad, the mother of eight I had met at Jabaliya, who like many other Gazans spent two-thirds of her waking hours worrying about water supply. Water and security: security and water. The two could not be disconnected, and Israelis who lived in this part of the country, at least, had to know it; because there was no question that Gaza's water crisis, above all its inability to treat its wastewater, was a local Israeli problem, too. The overspill of rockets was mirrored, in a way, by the overflow of sewage from the Strip; rockets got there faster, but the destination was the same.

Effluent from Jabaliya, Beit Lahia and Beit Hanoun began leaking over Gaza's northern border in earnest in 2016, contaminating the water table on both sides of the line, and forcing the Israeli authorities to shut down wells and reservoirs much like this one at Nir Am. The pollution, according to a local council engineer, was 'a real danger to public health.'[2]

At Nitzan, a coastal community just north of Ashkelon, Daniel and I went to meet Yair Farjun, the former head of the Hof Ashkelon Regional Council, which had borne the brunt of the Gazan sewage overspill. Yair was another of Daniel's endless list of useful contacts: in his youth, he had served in the same Nahal unit as Daniel's father. He was now a bearded bear of a man, a famous hero of the 1973 Yom Kippur war, in which he had helped defend Tel Saki in the Golan Heights, a critical engagement in which the vastly outnumbered Israelis held off a Syrian army of 11,000, backed by 900 tanks.

Nitzan, Daniel explained, is mostly a new development, expanded to rehouse some of the 9,000 settlers who were evicted, violently protesting, from Gaza in 2005 under the terms of Israel's unilateral disengagement from the Strip. The new homes, rows and rows of semi-mobile prefabs known as caravillas, were controversial from the start. Some complained that the housing and local amenities were inadequate. The retreat from

Gaza itself still angers the ultra-Orthodox, who regard it as a betrayal of Zionism. The wellbeing of the displaced settlers thus remains a useful stick with which to beat the government.

Daniel said the community was known for its religiosity, and since today was still Shabbat, we left the car at the entrance gate and walked the road to Yair's house, despite the broiling sun. Yair turned out to be not so religiously inclined, and laughed at Daniel's sensitivity. He sat us down on his porch, a rattan-shaded bower surrounded by orange-scented flowers, while his wife brought us coffee and homemade lemonade.

He said that Gazan sewage, flowing north over the border via the Wadi Hanoun into the local Shikma river, had been a concern throughout his eleven years as head of the council. 'Locals complained about it three, five times a year, mainly about the smell, but also the mosquitoes.' The council responded with insecticide, and deployed bulldozers to dam the wadi, but the problem kept getting worse.

'By 2016, it was a catastrophe,' he recalled. 'The shit flowed in for a solid month. There was a pond of it, 400 metres across. The bulldozers couldn't cope. We asked the IDF for help, but they were only interested in checkpoints.'

The council battled on. A fleet of twenty tankers was sent to hoover up the filth and deliver it to the Sderot treatment plant, where the extra effluent so overloaded the system that a pipeline burst. The tankers operated for twenty hours a day, but still it was not enough. A local rain collection pond became polluted. One of only two aquifer recharge projects in the whole of Israel was compromised. Eventually, inspectors from the Ministry of Health arrived, and ordered the closure of four Mekorot-run wells.

'These were big wells, supplying two kibbutzim and a moshav. The farmers had to buy in extra water from Mekorot. And the wells stayed closed for the next three years. It takes a long time for nature to flush them clean again. Every pollution event adds another six months.' The well closures, Yair recalled, proved a turning point: the moment that the national media picked up the story, and began to persuade the public that 'Gaza's sewage is Israel's problem, too.'

The Israeli Water Authority finally stepped in, and provided an emergency 40-centimetre sewage pipe and pump from the Wadi Hanoun to the treatment plant at Sderot. 'We have a system in place now that should cope if it happens again. But there are limits to what it can hold,' he said. Yair was a philosophical man whose view of the sewage crisis was broader than I had expected from a retired council leader. There were moments when he reminded me of Greta Thunberg.

'Our reality is not a summer camp,' he said. 'We have to act now to protect our future. We know how to fight, but not how to live together in a single ecosystem.' The fence with Gaza, he said with disdain, was 'artificial'. The transboundary nature of the coastal aquifer – the ineluctable proximity of Israel's neighbours – demanded a more collaborative approach in every sphere. He said the Israeli section of the coastal aquifer had not yet been affected by the salinization that blighted the over-extracted Gazan section, but added: 'If nothing is done, it is absolutely inevitable.'

He had recently proposed a programme of flower-planting along the fence in order to encourage bees, and hence pollination and greater agricultural output in Gaza. Bees, he drily pointed out, did not need a passport to enter the Strip. But, he said, his project had been quashed by the new council chief who 'couldn't see the cost-benefit'. Clearly, not every regional official was as long-sighted as Yair.

'The challenges of Gaza are unquestionably Israel's problem too, irrespective of your feelings or politics,' he went on. 'Ask the water. The water doesn't respect the border.' The seaborne pollution that had floated up the coast, forcing the closure of the Ashkelon desalination plant, first in 2015, and again in 2016, was a case in point. The closures, he said, had affected the supply of 300,000 Israelis, enough to cause a level of public 'outrage' that had been very useful to his council's arguments.

'Those two closures are only the ones the public knows about. In reality, it happens more frequently. I know of at least two other occasions.'

'Is that a secret?'

'It's like the time a Qassam rocket hit an oil reservoir at Eilat,' he shrugged. 'They hush these things up to prevent panic. But Ashkelon locals all know.'

I was surprised, and heartened, to learn that water officials on both sides of the border did now work together to mitigate the damage that another seaborne pollution event could cause, by monitoring the size and movement of sewage plume, and sharing the data with the desalination plant operators to give them a chance to protect their filters. 'It's a UNESCO monitoring project,' Yair said. 'We cooperate at the level of regional NGOs, since state-to-state cooperation is impossible.'

Knowledge of the behaviour of seaborne pollution was much improved; it was well understood, now, that the sewage generally took three days to drift as far north as Ashkelon, travelling between 200 and 300 metres offshore. 'The water that Israel supplies to Gaza comes in part from Ashkelon, so in that sense, too, it is in Gaza's interest to assist us,' he added.

Yair was imbued with the no-nonsense approach of a military man, and full of practical solutions. As head of the council, he had advocated building a new treatment plant on Israeli soil specifically to handle Gaza's waste. 'We already provide them with water, so why not extend the service? We could even sell the treated water back to them.'

Like every Israeli water official I met, he was deeply frustrated by the political impasse. Talks with Palestinians, he felt, kept failing because there was no 'symmetry' between them and Israel. 'There is a power imbalance. So "talks" are always on Israel's terms; the Palestinians are constantly disadvantaged. And no one likes being talked down to.' Even so, he insisted it was the Palestinians, not the Israelis, who would have to make the first move to break the deadlock. 'Our containment policy does not work, but what choice do we have, when Hamas wants to destroy us? And we cannot destroy Hamas, because it is a mind-set – an ideology. The day Gazan ideology shifts, and starts to see Israel as a partner, then the sky's the limit. There are hard-working people in Gaza. It could benefit from Israeli prosperity and become a great entrepot again. It could be a Singapore.'

Later, on the road back to Tel Aviv with Daniel, I thought about this vision of Yair's, which did not seem so outlandish. Gaza had prospered as a port before, in Nabatean times, so why not again? It was the pipedream not only of Israelis like Yair, but also of young Gazans I had spoken to. Gaza, I had seen, is not the human rubbish dump it is so often portrayed as in the West, but a place brimming with potential. It has a young, willing and educated middle class, and a coastal location that still lends itself to international commerce. The infrastructure of a tourist industry, which was beginning to boom before 1967 – big hotels, museums, service industries – is not destroyed, but mothballed. Its beaches could perhaps be cleaned up and made beautiful again.

I also wondered if it was really still the case that Hamas wanted to 'destroy' Israel. Yair thought it was for Hamas to make the first move towards ideological compromise with their neighbours, yet there were some who argued that Hamas already *had* made such a move, in May 2017, when its then leader, Khaled Mashal, issued a new 'covenant'. This document appeared to accept, for the first time, the notion of a Palestinian state delineated by the pre-1967 borders; an acceptance that also implies recognition of Israel as a state. This was a significant departure from Hamas's founding charter of 1988, which did indeed speak of destroying Israel, in order to replace it with a unified Islamic state. The 2017 covenant, however, was ambiguously worded, and did not go far enough for most Israelis, including many progressive ones, because it still made any truce conditional on Israeli withdrawal from the West Bank and East Jerusalem; and it contained no renunciation of the goal of a 'phased liberation' of Palestine. Netanyahu accused Mashal of 'trying to fool the world';[3] and the majority of Israelis remain unconvinced by Hamas's purported change of heart.

In Tel Aviv, I went to meet Shimon Tal, who was Israel's Water Commissioner until 2006, responsible for the planning and regulation of the national water sector. Like Yair Farjun, he felt deeply frustrated by the political logjam that now impeded water sector cooperation with Palestine. As Water Commissioner, Tal was once also the co-chair of the Joint Water Committee, where Israeli and Palestinian engineers once met and cooperated in the search for solutions to water problems – though no longer.

'When I was co-chair, the JWC met every single day,' he said, sadly. He revealed that, for all its drawbacks and failures, the JWC era had spawned some surprisingly close friendships across the Arab-Israeli water engineering community. Tal's counterpart as Water Commissioner was the then head of the PWA, Nabil Sharif, one of Yasser Arafat's old comrades-in-arms.

'I remember once standing with him on the roof of the desalination plant at Ashkelon, looking southwards towards Gaza. We were talking about doubling the amount of water Israel provided. He turned to me and said, "If you and I had any brains, we could turn Gaza into the Garden of Eden".'

However, Nabil Sharif died in 2005. 'I adored Nabil,' Tal said. 'I wanted to go to his funeral in Gaza, but it was too dangerous. Even his son asked me not to come, for my own safety'. Personal relations between the two water authorities had never been so close – and nor had they recovered. It naturally became harder to make friends after 2010, when Ramallah's boycott of the JWC closed the principal forum for human interaction. Nevertheless, some sort of precedent for private cooperation had been set. If water engineers had once reached across the divide, I asked, could politicians not do the same? Perhaps their example was even the key to resuscitating the whole moribund Israel–Palestine peace process.

'The problem is that water is being treated as a political issue,' he replied, 'and not just here, but everywhere in the Middle East. I don't know why, but in my opinion the two-state dream is losing connection with reality. On *both* sides.'

He argued, even so, that it was Palestine's politicians who were most to blame for Gaza's water crisis. The ruination of the coastal aquifer, he insisted, was entirely down to mismanagement and over-extraction within Gaza; the effect on the water table of extraction on the Israeli side of the border was 'negligible'. As Water Commissioner, he recalled, he had pushed hard for the laying of a permanent power supply for NGEST, the Northern Gaza Emergency Sewage Treatment plant that I visited. Permission was obtained from both the IDF and the Israeli government, but ultimately it was Ramallah, not Israel, who had obstructed the project, for fear that Hamas would gain credit for it. Similarly, in his version of the failure to link Gaza to the NWC in the early 2000s, it was Hamas, not Israel, who had dragged their feet over construction of the final, 100-metre connection pipe to Al-Muntar reservoir. 'Why? Because Hamas gain more points by showing a girl with an empty jerry can than by putting water into the taps.'

At Oslo, he reminded me, Israel had agreed to sell Palestine a fixed amount of fresh water every year, as it still did. Indeed, he said, Israel provided more water than the Accord obliged them to. But he also acknowledged that

Palestinian population growth in the intervening twenty-five years meant that this water still wasn't enough; and that in Gaza's case, the arrangement was wholly inadequate, because the PA refused to pay Hamas's bills.

'But now that Israel has a surplus of water thanks to desalination, why doesn't Israel just supply Gaza water for free?' I asked.

'For free?' he replied. 'But that would mean going with Hamas and giving up on the Palestinian Authority. That is politically impossible for Israel.'

How will this awful gridlock ever be cleared? Can the business of water supply in Israel-Palestine ever be truly depoliticized? There are, perhaps, some grounds for hope. The fact is that Gaza's transboundary sewage crisis has for some time been pushing the two sides towards cooperation whether their political leaders like it or not.

As Yair Farjun mentioned, local Israeli and Palestinian officials are already working together, under the auspices of UNESCO, to monitor the movement of pollution off the coast. In June 2019, furthermore, it was announced that Israel was planning a new, US$4 million pipeline specifically designed to transport Gazan sewage onto its own territory.[4] Was this the beginning of the solution proposed by Yair – permanent new infrastructure on Israeli soil, built exclusively for the treatment of Gazan sewage?

No less hearteningly, Mekorot began work in June 2019 on a new cross-border fresh water pipe – the fourth, and largest yet – intended to service the crowded centre of the Strip. The construction workers were reported to be operating under heavy armed guard for fear of Palestinian snipers, a detail that implied significant dedication and courage.

'Water is a basic thing,' one unidentified worker said. 'There's an entire population in Gaza that doesn't want war with Israel, and that population is the majority that is being controlled by Hamas. It's a shame that's the situation. Most of the people in Gaza are thirsty for water, but also hungry for a normal life and a better future for their children. They're our neighbours, despite everything, and we can't ignore what's happening there.'[5]

Neighbours, despite everything: that recognition recalled what I still believe was the intended spirit of the Balfour Declaration. The Mekorot worker's altruism showed that some Israelis, at least, are willing to try to reverse the historic prejudicing of Palestinian rights, for the sake of those rights themselves.

I had observed before that water workers often regard their job as an almost noble calling, perhaps even a sacred duty to be fulfilled. Every water engineer, after all, learns at college that water, not bread, is the staff of life. The business of water provision has a humanitarian dimension that can help overcome even the most daunting political obstacles. At the height of the Iran-Iraq war in the 1980s, for instance, a total interstate war in which hundreds of thousands were killed, the regional authorities on either side of the front line secretly collaborated to maintain domestic water supply to the towns and villages in the warzone. It was the same, sometimes, in Israel-Palestine. In Gaza, I recalled, Rehby al-Sheikh told me that clean water supply was 'too important to be left to politicians', and acknowledged that at least some of his counterparts on the Israeli side thought the same way.

None of the water officials I met believed that Israeli altruism, on its own, could produce any long-term solution. But they did, often, make the case for a new approach based on the principle of 'enlightened self-interest'. The threat to desalination plant intake pipes has sharpened many Israeli minds, as has the much more serious threat of an epidemic in Gaza caused by poor sanitation, and the mass migration of its 2 million citizens that such an event could cause.

'We know from the World Health Organization that a quarter of all disease is waterborne,' said Gidon Bromberg, the director of the NGO Ecopeace, which has been warning the Israeli government for years that its policies need to change. 'Much of Gaza's supply is private and unregulated. Once disease takes hold, the genie will be out of the bottle. In Gaza, we are playing Russian roulette.'

The trigger was certainly pulled with the outbreak of Covid-19 in 2020. The Strip was spared the first ravages of the pandemic: the blockade, ironically, meant that its citizens were effectively pre-quarantined from the world, and Israel initially suffered far more. But the virus broke through in August 2020, and by late 2022, 270,000 cases had been registered in Gaza, and 2,000 deaths.[6]

Covid is not the waterborne epidemic that Gidon Bromberg warned about, although its spread is very likely linked to Gaza's poor water supply: public hygiene is harder to maintain when one in five households do not have access to sufficient water for drinking and domestic purposes.[7] Early in 2020, *Haaretz* reported that 'the scenario [of a coronavirus outbreak in Gaza] is being filed by the security establishment under the label, "God help us".'[8] The IDF's nightmare has since become a reality.

Yet, not even Covid has led the military to reboot its approach to the Strip's water problems. Instead, in May 2021, Israel and Gaza's militants went to war again, for the fourth time in thirteen years. The violence this time was prompted by clashes between police and protestors in Sheikh Jarrah, a neighbourhood of East Jerusalem, where six Palestinian families faced eviction. The following night was Qadr Night, the holiest of Ramadan, but that did not prevent the police from storming the al-Aqsa mosque compound in pursuit of stone-throwers; more than 600 people were injured.

The protests spread across Arab Israel and the West Bank. In Gaza, Hamas demanded the security forces withdraw from Sheikh Jarrah and Temple Mount. When Israel ignored them, Gaza's militants launched a vast barrage of rockets: 4,360 of them, according to one count.[9] Israel responded with airstrikes, and bombardment from land and sea.

The exchange ended eleven days later, by when at least 256 Gazans, including 66 children, were dead, as were 17 soldiers and civilians on the other side.[10] Both sides claimed victory. Among other buildings in Gaza, four high-rise blocks, forty schools and four hospitals were wholly or partially demolished. Two major water pipelines were also ruptured, cutting supply to more than 200,000 residents in Gaza City. The mayor of Gaza, Yahya Sarraj, reported that more than 6 kilometres of water pipeline had been destroyed or damaged, and accused Israel of deliberately targeting it. Sewage plants, he alleged, were also 'directly targeted', and 10 kilometres of sewage pipe destroyed.[11]

The IDF made no answer to these specific charges, but insisted, as it routinely does, that all its targets were militarily justified. 'Hamas and the other terror organizations deliberately and unlawfully embed their military assets in densely populated civilian areas, in order to make it more difficult for the IDF to attack their military assets,' a spokesman said.[12]

Whether lawful or not, the effect on Gaza's water infrastructure was the same. It is hard – above all for Gazans – to make sense of an Israeli strategy that builds pipelines with one hand, while destroying them with the other.

As so often in the past, it was left to foreigners to repair the damage: in December 2021 the state-owned German development bank, KfW, announced a €9 million project to build and connect a new drinking water reservoir, for the benefit of a million residents of the northern end of the Strip.[13] By sorry contrast, *Haaretz* reported in January 2022 that vital spare parts for the repair of bombed water and sewage systems were being held up at the border for longer than ever – sometimes for as long as five months, instead of the few weeks contractors were used to. And it wasn't only 'dual use' materials like pipes that were affected, but valves, filters, and the computer parts and specialised electronica needed to run desalination plants and reservoirs.[14]

The cycle of violence and rapprochement seems endless. And yet it must not be, because the degradation of Gaza's water supply is not cyclical, it is linear, and growing ever worse. Pipes might or might not be repaired, but the destruction of the coastal aquifer cannot be undone, and will eventually have seismic consequences that neither Israelis nor Palestinians will escape. The senseless violence of May 2021 hardened my view that, one day, both sides will have no choice but to adopt a completely different approach in their dealings with each other. That might include a political accommodation: an acceptable resolution of the Final Status talks at Oslo, for instance. But time is short for that. Nature has already fired an eloquent warning shot, in the form of a Covid outbreak, and will eventually force the politicians' hands, with or without a political settlement.

What might a different approach look like? According to Gidon Bromberg, everyone understood that Israeli water supply was a matter of national security; but not all had yet grasped that there could be no national security without *regional* water security – an 'ideological shift' that he said was 'not yet complete'. Since the 1990s, he pointed out, Israel has sold water from the Galilee to Jordan at a discount. 'Why? Because both sides understood it was in our mutual national security interests. So why do we not sell it at a discount to Gaza too?'

The solution for Israel-Palestine in the long term, he thought, was to 'decouple' water rights from the stalled Final Status talks of Oslo, and to focus on a new, genuinely regional supply settlement. Like Shira Kronich at the Arava Institute, he looked to the European Coal and Steel Community of the 1950s as a model for a new 'water and energy community'.

'We must create new interdependencies instead of always pursuing Israeli dominance. For instance, solar power could be Jordan's biggest industry, instead of Arab Potash . . . The Jordanians are already on track to produce 20 per cent of their power that way by 2020, compared to 2.5 per cent in Israel. We could take their power in exchange for our water. This is essential. Without a regional solution, the water crisis in Gaza will be repeated in the West Bank – and in Jordan, too.'

He was, I thought, right. In today's ever more crowded and resource-challenged world, regional cooperation is, perhaps, the only viable future for all of us. Israel already knows and accepts this. It is partly why the country was so keen to 'normalise' relations with the United Arab Emirates (UAE) and other Arab countries, in a deal brokered by the US in August 2020. The Gulf Arabs have various motives for cooperating with Israel, starting with the perceived need to form an alliance against their common enemy, Iran. That dangerous game of regional hegemony is still being played out.

But the deal was not only driven by fear of Iran. It is noteworthy that the first, formal ministerial-level conversation to take place between Israel and the UAE was not about defence or intelligence matters, nor even about shared commercial interests, but about something arguabuly more funda-mental to the states' wellbeing: the mutual need to improve food and water security.[15]

Israel and the UAE, after all, have much in common. Both are small, desert countries, whose governments must work ever harder to feed and water their booming populations; and both depend on desalination to meet their goals. The UAE has twenty-five desalination plants, which supply 80 per cent of its total water, including 95 per cent of its drinking water. By 2030, it is estimated that at least 20 per cent of this oil-rich nation's energy supply will be directed towards water production.[16] The UAE has invested heavily in hydroponics and vertical farming operations, while Israel leads the world in drip irrigation, wastewater recycling, and supply and demand management. Collaboration in the water technology sector is a natural fit for them.

Palestine, however, was entirely left out of the Israel–UAE negotiation, to the deep dismay of the leadership in Ramallah, who called it a 'stab in the back' for the Palestinian cause. According to the Saudi-sponsored Arab Peace Initiative of 2002, the normalisation of Arab-Israeli relations was supposed to be conditional on an end to the occupation of the West Bank. The UAE's move effectively decoupled the two issues, leaving the old principle of Arab solidarity in tatters, and Palestine more internationally isolated than ever. So, profound local obstacles remain to the fulfilment of Bromberg's enticing regionalist vision.

In Gaza, in the Jordan Valley, in the West Bank's hills, and all along the separation barrier, I saw for myself how entrenched the occupation has become, and the misery, poverty and bitterness it causes, above all the egregious injustices of the settlement programme. In the Galilee, the Golan, and in Jerusalem and Tel Aviv, I witnessed the immense prosperity of Israel, which often merely highlights the grotesque inequality between the peoples. I started out by asking where the water in the River Jordan had gone, and part of my answer was this: it had flowed into Israeli wallets.

And yet the technology that once allowed Israel to purloin Palestinian water is a double-edged sword: it has led to desalination, and the creation of a water surplus, and hence the end of resource control as a zero-sum game. I saw amazing technology in action almost everywhere I went in Israel: the reverse pipe project to refill the Galilee, the desalination plant at Ashkelon, the irrigation drippers at Netafim, the solar tower at Ashalim. Israel's water engineers are right: their ingenuity *is* a key, potentially, to peace. As Shimon Tal put it: 'Desalination can make up the shortfall, while offsetting the effects of climate change, no problem – and it is getting cheaper. It already costs $60 to $70 to produce 100 cubic metres: a year's worth of water for one person. That's less than a ticket to the opera.'

Tal added that by 2040, the Israel-Palestine region will need twice as much water as nature can provide. To him, therefore, the question of restoring Palestinian water rights is simply irrelevant.

'In the West Bank, the Palestinians know that even if they had access to all the water in the mountain aquifer, it would still not be enough for them.'

Palestinians, however, are unlikely ever to be bought off by the application of technology alone. As Shaddad Attili in Ramallah explained, the right to control natural water is a 'visceral' matter, a fundamental part of Palestinian identity and sovereignty.

'Desalination will never take away water as a source of conflict,' said Clive Lipchin, the director of the Center for Transboundary Water Management at the Arava Institute. 'While it's a fact that Israel is much more water-secure because of technologies including desalination, Israel will never relinquish its rights to the natural resources [which] are always going to be the preferred source of water, and always going to be looked at and managed as a buffer in any crisis that may arise.' He added: 'If you're talking about a viable and independent state, obviously you need to have control over your natural resources. So, what kind of state is [Palestine] going to be?'[17]

Israel, in the end, faces a choice. It can either continue to pursue its policy of dominance over the Palestinians, with all the misery it causes, and all the domestic insecurity it brings; or it can start to frame its future in terms of a genuine partnership: in other words, to get serious about the two-state solution. And a new settlement in the water sector might be an excellent place to begin. Now that Israel has enough water, thanks to desalination, the argument for retaining control of Palestine's natural water on national security grounds is much weaker. The new fact of Israel's water surplus, when their neighbours have a shortage, creates an additional humanitarian obligation to share.

Israel, not Palestine, is best placed to direct and orchestrate such a future. As Adnan Ghosheh, a senior water and sanitation specialist at the World Bank told me: 'Politicians on both sides are guilty of obstructing cooperation. But there is an asymmetry – and Israel are in the driving seat.'[18] As the dominant nation, Israel also arguably has a moral duty to try to reinvigorate the peace process. Israel has never been in such a strong position as it now finds itself vis-à-vis Palestine. The settler programme has triumphed in the West Bank; the intifadas of the past are an increasingly distant memory, even after the violent protests of May 2021; Palestine's erstwhile supporters in the Arab world are normalising relations with the Israeli government. As *Haaretz* has argued in the past, what better time to show 'magnanimity in victory'?[19]

Magnanimity, unfortunately, is not a characteristic much associated with Naftali Bennett, the hardliner who replaced Netanyahu as prime minister in June 2021. Instead, the possibility of West Bank annexation remains on the table, in line with a 'Seven Point Plan' developed by Bennett a decade ago. His approach is to 'manage' rather than try to resolve the tension in Palestinian-Israeli relations: a doubling down, in effect, on the old policy of containment. 'There are some things that we all know will never happen,' says the narrator of an explanatory video posted on Bennett's official YouTube page. '*The Sopranos* will never return for another season . . . And a peace agreement with the Palestinians will not happen.'[20]

Bennett's hand could, perhaps, be forced by foreign pressure. When Biden replaced Trump in January 2021, the way was cleared – or became clearer – for a renewal of Palestine's relationship with the US. Hanan Ashrawi, a member of the PLO executive committee, called Biden's victory a time for 'holistic and bold therapeutics'.[21] Unlike Trump, the new president 'strongly opposes' the settlement programme. Biden also asserted, before he was elected, that he would reverse 'the destructive cut-off of diplomatic ties with the Palestinian Authority, and cancellation of assistance programmes that support Israeli-Palestinian security cooperation, economic development and humanitarian aid for . . . the West Bank and Gaza'.[22] If signals from Washington have since seemed more ambivalent, an opportunity does at least exist now for the US to resume its traditional role as peace broker.

Meanwhile, although 138 nations now recognize Palestinian statehood, the US still does not. My own country, Britain, has long withheld recognition, but says it will do so 'at a time when it best serves the objective of peace' – by which it means as the result of a negotiated settlement, rather than as a prelude to one.[23] The British government, though, is under pressure to wait no longer, not least from a busy lobby organization set up by a group of clerics and academics called the Balfour Project. Its chairman, Sir Vincent Fean, a former consul general to Jerusalem, argues passionately that Britain, as the signatory of the Balfour Declaration in 1917, bears a special responsibility for the 'present injustice', and therefore a moral duty to correct it. This was precisely my thought when I saw Banksy's exhibition at the Walled-Off Hotel in Bethlehem. The Balfour Project's literature states:

> Palestinians and Israelis will share the Holy Land forever and must shape its future together. Only equality will bring safety and well-being, and essential dialogue. The two peoples, alone, have not attained peaceful coexistence. So, for the good of both, and if we truly mean what we say, we in Britain must help reverse current negative developments which only entrench separation and inequality.[24]

If change is to be sustained, however, the main impetus must come from within Israel, not from outside. As Yair Farjun observed, no one likes to be talked down to. In the meantime, Palestine's water crisis is not going away, but deepening. Nature has her own way of talking, and will not wait. Technology can achieve wonders; but those wonders may not last long if they are not underpinned by a rights-based settlement, including restitution to the Palestinians of the most important right of all, the human right to water.

Endnotes

INTRODUCTION

1. ISRAMAR, Israel Oceanographic and Limnological Research.
2. 'Securing Water for Development in West Bank and Gaza', World Bank, 2018. See Figure 3.
3. Jan Selby, *Water, Power and Politics in the Middle East: The Other Israeli–Palestinian Conflict* (Library of Modern Middle East Studies), I.B. Tauris, 2003. See also Camilla Corradin, 'Israel: Water as a Tool to Dominate Palestinians', *Al Jazeera*, 23 June 2016.
4. See for example the image at https://www.reddit.com/r/MapPorn/comments/aqjsqa/gaza_israel_border/.
5. Rowan Jacobsen, 'Israel Proves the Desalination Era is Here', *Scientific American*, 29 July 2016.
6. Author interview.
7. See https://www.youtube.com/watch?v=P_n_L1z-XJg.

1. GAZA: THE PEOPLE MUST BURST

1. Jewishvirtuallibrary.org.
2. United Nations Relief and Works Agency, 'Gaza Field Update', June 2014.
3. Hilo Glazer, '42 Knees in One Day', *Haaretz*, 6 March 2020.
4. Jack Khoury, Yaniv Kubovich and Almog Ben Zikri, 'Seven Palestinians, Including 12-year-old, Said Killed by IDF Fire in Gaza Border Clashes', *Haaretz*, 28 September 2018.
5. 'Obituary of Lord Sacks, Jonathan Sacks, Chief Rabbi of Britain', *Sunday Times*, 8 November 2020.
6. Nicholas Watt and Harriet Sherwood, 'David Cameron: Israeli Blockade has Turned Gaza into a "Prison Camp"', *Guardian*, 27 July 2010.
7. See *Palestine 2030 Demographic Change: Opportunities for Development*, United Nations Population Fund, 2016.
8. Jean-Pierre Filiu, *Gaza, A History*, Oxford University Press, 2014.

9. Jewishvirtuallibrary.org.
10. Ecopeace Middle East, 'Water Resilience', https://ecopeaceme.org/water-resilience/.
11. Ali Abunimah, 'Israeli Army Publishes Fake Image of Huge "Gaza Shopping Mall", *Electronic Intifada*, 14 August 2013.
12. 'OPT: Beit Lahia Waste Water Treatment Plant – Floods Humanitarian Situation Report #3', UN Office for the Coordination of Humanitarian Affairs, 3 April 2007.
13. 'Israel to Process Gaza Sewage with New Pipeline – Report', *Times of Israel*, 19 June 2019; and see also Chapter 13.
14. Fred de Sam Lazaro, 'Water Crisis May Make Gaza Uninhabitable by 2020', *PBS*, 1 January 2019.
15. Sandy Tolan, 'Gaza's Water Crisis is "a Ticking Time Bomb"', *Public Radio International*, 13 November 2018.
16. Author interview.
17. R.R. El Kishawi, K.L. Soo, Y.A. Abed and W.A.M.W. Muda, 'Prevalence and Associated Factors Influencing Stunting in Children Aged 2–5 Years in the Gaza Strip-Palestine: A Cross-Sectional Study', *US National Library of Medicine Archive (pubmed.gov)*, 21 December 2017; and Sandy Tolan, 'Gaza's Drinking Water Spurs Blue Baby Syndrome, Serious Illnesses', *Al Jazeera*, 29 October 2018.

2. THE DYING DEAD SEA

1. The River Jordan has two sections, with the Sea of Galilee in the middle. The 'Jordan Valley' refers only to the lower section between the Sea of Galilee and the Dead Sea, and is usually understood to mean only that part of it that delineates the West Bank. The 'Upper Jordan Valley' refers to the course north of the Sea of Galilee; it is sometimes known as the 'Hula Valley', after the lake that used to exist there.
2. Quoted in Ben Ehrenreich, 'Drip, Jordan – Israel's Water War with Palestine', *Harper's Magazine*, December 2011.
3. Watson E. Mills and Roger Aubrey Bullard, *Dictionary of the Bible*, Mercer University Press, 1990.
4. Pauli Ensio Juhani Rahkonen, '"Canaanites" or "Amorites"? A Study on Semitic Toponyms of the Second Millennium BC in the Land of Canaan', *Studia Orientalia Electronica* 4, 2016; I.J. Gelb, *Glossary of Old Akkadian*, University of Chicago Press, 1973.
5. Joshua 3:13–17 (New King James Version).
6. Haim Watzman, *A Crack in the Earth: A Journey Up Israel's Rift Valley*, Argo-Navis, 2012, p. 101.
7. 'Area C of the West Bank: Key Humanitarian Concerns', UN Office for the Coordination of Humanitarian Affairs.
8. See Greg Shapland, 'Israeli Settlements: The Position on the Ground', *Arab Digest*, 27 November 2019.
9. See for example the New International Version (1984) of Exodus 23:31: 'I will establish your borders from the Red Sea to the Mediterranean, and from the desert to the Euphrates. I will give into your hands the people who live in the land, and you will drive them out before you.'
10. See Sizer's essay 'Theology of the Land', in *The Land of Promise: Biblical, Theological and Contemporary Perspectives*, IVP, 2000.
11. Peace Now, using data from the Israeli Central Bureau of Statistics; and the pro-settler organization West Bank Population Stats, both quoted by Shapland, 'Israeli Settlements'.
12. https://www.monde-diplomatique.fr/cartes/l_atlas_un_monde_a_l_envers/a60660.
13. David M. Halbfinger, 'Netanyahu, Facing Tough Israel Election, Pledges to Annex a Third of West Bank', *New York Times*, 10 September 2019.
14. Erekat died after contracting Covid-19 in November 2020; he was buried in Jericho.

15. Halbfinger, 'Netanyahu, Facing Tough Israel Election'.
16. I later described my bunker visit in an article for *The Economist* entitled 'Batty Borders: The Benefits of a Bunker Mentality', 27 October 2018.
17. B'Tselem, Israeli Information Center for Human Rights in the Occupied Territories, www.btselem.org/.

3. THE JORDAN VALLEY: TALES FROM THE RIVERBANK

1. Genesis 13:10 (New King James Version).
2. Both are types of collective farm, the building block of Israeli expansion since the early twentieth century. The difference is slight: on a moshav, individual farm profits are not pooled and shared as they are in a traditional kibbutz community.
3. B'Teslem, www.btselem.org/, and Peace Now.
4. Dunam, an Ottoman term still in use in many parts of the Middle East, was originally defined as the amount of land that could be ploughed by a team of oxen in a day. The new metric dunam is defined as 1,000 square metres, or one-tenth of a hectare
5. Israeli Water Authority.
6. Author interview with Abdulrahman Tamimi.
7. See for example 'Israeli Dates "Misleadingly Labelled to Deceive Buyers"', *5Pillars*, 9 March 2020. Israel appears never to have responded to this specific allegation, although the government's contempt for 'boycott, divestment and sanctions' and its tactics in general are well known; Netanyahu once accused supporters of BDS of practising 'anti-semitism in a new garb' and BDS itself of attempting to 'end the Jewish state'.
8. Roy Arad, 'I Joined a Dead Sea Hippie Colony', *Haaretz*, 18 March 2017.
9. Oliver Holmes and Quique Kierszenbaum, 'Israeli Group Plan Burning Man-like Event in Occupied West Bank', *Guardian*, 16 February 2020.
10. For more on this well-known story, see 'Palestinians "Helped Settlements"', *BBC News*, 10 June 2004; Charles A. Radin, 'Palestinian Cement Sold to Israel for Barrier, Probe Finds', *Boston Globe*, 28 July 2004; Arjan El Fassed, 'Cement and Corruption', *The Electronic Intifada*, 10 June 2004; Khaled Abu Toameh, 'Palestinian Affairs: Abbas's Latest Headaches', *Jerusalem Post*, 27 March 2008; Ian Black, 'Palestine Papers: Ahmed Qureia', *Guardian*, 23 January 2011.
11. For greater detail on the water troubles of Bardala (and Umm Zuka), see the report by Rina Tzur and Yaacov Manor, 'Women for Human Rights and Against the Occupation', 20 May 2017, machsomwatch.org.
12. 'Israel's Religiously Divided Society', Pew Research Center, March 2016.
13. The Druze are followers of an ancient offshoot of Ismaili Islam. Some Israeli Druze, who number about 150,000, mostly living in the northern Golan Heights along the border with Lebanon and Syria, consider themselves to be ethnically discrete; Israel formally recognizes their community as such, even though 70 per cent of Druze self-identify as Arabs.
14. 'Benjamin Netanyahu Says Israel is "Not a State of All its Citizens"', *Guardian*/AFP, 10 March 2019.
15. Peter Beaumont, 'EU Leads Criticism after Israel Passes Jewish "Nation State" Law', *Guardian*, 19 July 2018.
16. Declan Walsh and Eric Nagourney, 'Violence on Israeli Streets Sows Fear of Lasting Rupture', *New York Times*, 13 May 2021; Harriet Sherwood, 'Israeli City of Lod Descends into "Civil War" as Violence Escalates', *Guardian*, 12 May 2021.
17. Idan Zonshine, 'Only 7% of Israeli Arabs Define Themselves as "Palestinian"', *Jerusalem Post*, 21 April 2020.
18. Jo-Ann Mort, 'The Trump–Netanyahu Plan to Force Arab Population Transfer', *New York Review*, 4 February 2020.
19. Joseph Algazy, 'Umm al-Fahm Prefers Israel', *Haaretz*, 1 August 2000.

20. Ayman Rabi, 'Water Apartheid in Palestine – A Crime Against Humanity?', *The Ecologist*, 22 March 2014.
21. Assaf Seltzer, *Mekorot: The Story of the Israel National Water Company – The First 75 Years*, Yad Ben-Zvi Press, 2011.
22. Mekorot's founders certainly thought of themselves that way, and consciously sought to promote the idea when they named the company. According to corporate legend, a board member found a verse in the Book of Psalms that says, 'the voice [Mekolot] of God is greater than water' (Psalms 93:4), but accidentally transcribed Mekolot as Mekorot. The mistake was allowed to stand because Mekorot serendipitously means 'sources': a good name for a water company.

4. RAMALLAH: WET CITY

1. Tessa Fox, 'Palestine's First Aquarium Brings Marine Life to Landlocked West Bank', *Middle East Eye*, 24 January 2019.
2. Walid Sabbah and Jad Isaac, 'An Evaluation of Water Resources Management in Ramallah District', Applied Research Institute of Jerusalem, 1996.
3. Jan Selby, *Water, Power and Politics in the Middle East*, I.B. Tauris, 2003, pp. 105–12.
4. Jan Selby, 'Co-operation, Domination and Colonisation: The Israeli-Palestinian Joint Water Committee', *Water Alternatives* 6:1, February 2013.
5. 'Troubled Waters: Palestinians Denied Fair Access to Water', Amnesty International, October 2009.
6. Norman Finkelstein, *Image and Reality of the Israel–Palestine Conflict*, Verso, 2003.
7. Orhan Niksic, Nur Nasser Eddin and Massimilio Cali, 'Area C and the Future of the Palestinian Economy', *World Bank Studies*, 2014.
8. 'Monthly Humanitarian Bulletin', UNOCHA, March 2019.
9. Ibid.
10. Selby, *Water, Power and Politics*.
11. United Nations General Assembly, Resolution 64/292, 'The Human Right to Water and Sanitation'.
12. Susan Koppelman and Zaynab Alshalalfeh, 'Our Right to Water: The Human Right to Water in Palestine', *Life Source*, March 2012.
13. palsolidarity.org.
14. For more detail on the Tamimi family's campaign, see Ben Ehrenreich's *The Way to the Spring: Life and Death in Palestine*, Penguin Books, 2016.
15. Personality of the Month, *This Week in Palestine*, June 2016.
16. Speech to the 73rd session of the General Assembly, 27 September 2018. For the full text see *Times of Israel*, 28 September 2018.
17. Bernard Lewis, 'Studies in the Ottoman Archives – 1', *Bulletin of the School of Oriental and African Studies* 16:3, 1954.
18. Yonatan Mendel, *The Creation of Israeli Arabic: Security and Politics in Arabic Studies in Israel*, Palgrave Macmillan, 2014.
19. Vincent Lemire, 'Water in Jerusalem at the End of the Ottoman Period (1850–1920)', *Bulletin du Centre de recherche français à Jérusalem*, July 2000.
20. Zvi Ron, 'Qanats and Spring Flow Tunnels in the Holy Land', Tel Aviv University, 1985, quoted by waterhistory.org. See also Oliver Miles, 'On Qanats', *London Review of Books*, 19 February 2019.
21. Melanne Andromecca Civic, 'A Comparative Analysis of the Israeli and Arab Water Law Tradition, and Insights for Modern Water Sharing Agreements', *Denver Journal of International Law & Policy* 26:3, May 2020.
22. Shlomo Guberman, 'The Development of the Law in Israel: The First Fifty Years', Israel Ministry of Foreign Affairs, 2000.
23. Gideon Levy, 'Twilight Zone/Pool of Memories', *Haaretz*, 20 August 2009.

24. Mark Twain, *The Innocents Abroad, or The New Pilgrim's Progress*, Wordsworth Classics, 2010, p. 317.
25. Thomas J. Craughwell, 'Taking the Measure of Relics of the True Cross', *National Catholic Register*, April 2011.

5. SAMARIA: WHERE THE HILLS HAVE EYES

1. Adam T. Smith, *The Political Landscape: Constellations of Authority in Early Complex Polities*, University of California Press, 2003, p. 6.
2. A *thobe* is the baggy, ankle-length garment worn throughout the Arabian Peninsula, and beyond. A *kufiya* is a headdress, and the *igal* is the twist of cord that holds it in place. All these garments have variants, with many alternative names and spellings.
3. See also Chaim Levinson and Noa Landau, 'Why is Israel's Anti-Bibi Left So Lost – and Chasing Yet Another General as Its Messiah?', *Haaretz* weekly podcast, 7 December 2020.
4. Moshe Dann, 'A Matter of Sovereignty: NGOs vs Israel', *Jerusalem Post*, 7 May 2012. It remains a thorn in the side of those in the Israeli government who would prefer the grim reality of the occupation not to be so exposed.
5. The ruling against the reoccupation of abandoned camps is controversial. As activist organizations constantly point out, the expulsion of residents of an occupied territory – 'the forcible transfer of protected persons', in legal jargon – is a contravention of international humanitarian law; arguably even a war crime. Does the Civil Administration's policy towards nomads amount to forcible transfer? The body of international law on the subject has a long tail. Article 6 of the International Military Tribunal Charter, drawn up at Nuremberg in 1945, first officially identified the 'deportation of civilians of or in occupied territory' as a 'war crime'. The fourth Geneva Convention of 1949 prohibits any 'individual or mass forcible transfers . . . of protected persons from occupied territory', a prohibition subsequently reinforced by dozens of other agreements, including the European Convention on Human Rights (1963), and the International Covenant on Civil and Political Rights (1966). Even Israel's own Nazis and Nazi Collaborators (Punishment) Law (1950) identifies 'the deportation . . . for any purpose of the civilian population of or in occupied territories' as a war crime. For more detail see *Practice Relating to Rule 129. The Act of Displacement* on ICRC's online database on Customary International Humanitarian Law.
6. For more on Uri and the allegation of IDF collusion with what is known as Uri's Farm, see Amira Hass, 'In the West Bank, the Israeli Army Works for the Settlers', *Haaretz*, 23 December 2018.
7. In fact, by ECHO, the Directorate-General for European Civil Protection and Humanitarian aid Operations.
8. Aviv Lavie, 'The Sheriff', *Haaretz*, 9 April 2003.
9. The strictly Orthodox Haredim have traditionally been exempted from military national service on faith grounds – a controversial privilege that the Israeli Supreme Court ruled was unconstitutional in 2017.
10. Corrie, a twenty-four-year-old American volunteer with the International Solidarity Movement, was crushed to death by an Israeli army bulldozer in Rafah in 2003.
11. The name references a story in the Book of Judges, Chapter 21, in which the tribe of Benjamin abducts a group of Israelite women from a dance party in a vineyard – fully 200 of them – for essential breeding purposes.
12. Aliyah, 'ascent' or 'the act of going up' in Hebrew, means the immigration of diaspora Jews to the Land of Israel, on which the Zionist project depends.
13. For a further flavour, see B'Tselem's 'Eyes Wide Open' photoblog *Defenceless Against Settler Violence*, June 2018.
14. Chaim Levinson, 'Who is Amiram Ben-Uliel, the Killer of the Dawabsheh Family?', *Haaretz*, 18 May 2020; Ilan Ben Zion, 'Israeli Gets 3 Life Sentences for Deadly

2015 Arson Attack', *AP News*, 14 September 2020; Yonah Jeremy Bob, 'Jewish Terrorist Serving Life Appeals High Court, Gets Rejected', *Jerusalem Post*, 1 September 2022.

15. There were 482 'politically motivated' crimes by West Bank settlers in 2018, compared to 140 the previous year: Amos Harel, 'Israeli "Jewish Terror" Incidents Targeting Palestinians Tripled in 2018', *Haaretz*, 6 January 2019.

6. BETHLEHEM, QALQILYA, BATTIR: BURSTING AT THE SEAM

1. State of Palestine Negotiations Affairs Department.
2. State of Palestine Negotiations Affairs Department.
3. Ilan Pappé, *The Biggest Prison on Earth: A History of the Occupied Territories*, Oneworld, 2017.
4. 'Palestinians Protest UK Invitation to Netanyahu to Join Balfour Centennial Celebrations', WAFA News Agency, 23 February 2017.
5. Resolution adopted by the UN General Assembly, Tenth Emergency Special Session, 2 August 2004. Agenda Item 5: 'Advisory opinion of the International Court of Justice on the Legal Consequences of the Construction of a Wall in the Occupied Palestinian Territory', including in and around East Jerusalem.
6. Uri Blau, 'I Have to Swallow This Poison', *Haaretz*, 4 October 2007.
7. Most notoriously, Saeed Hotari, the suicide bomber of the Dolphinarium discotheque in Tel Aviv in 2001, one of the worst acts of terrorism in Israeli history, was from Qalqilya. See Rowan Somerville, *Beat: The True Story of a Suicide Bomber and a Heart*, Lilliput Press, 2017.
8. According to the Victorian orientalist E.H. Palmer.
9. Amira Hass, 'An M16 to the Face: Israel's Violent Bureaucracy Against Palestinian Farmers', *Haaretz*, 12 May 2019.
10. See also Michal Aharony, 'Why Does Hannah Arendt's "Banality of Evil" Still Anger Israelis?', *Haaretz*, 11 May 2019.
11. Mariam Barghouti, 'By Besieging the Palestinians, Israel has Besieged Itself', *Forward*, 13 November 2018. For further reading on the architecture of the occupation, see Eyal Weizman's fascinating study *Hollow Land: Israel's Architecture of Occupation*, Verso, 2012, rev edn.
12. stopthewall.org, April 2014.
13. Diaa Hadid, 'Mahmoud Abbas Claims Rabbis Urged Israel to Poison Palestinians' Water', *New York Times*, 23 June 2016.
14. 'Abu Dis: From Land Expropriation to Landfill', The Palestinian Human Rights Monitoring Group and the Camden Abu Dis Friendship Association. See also B'Tselem's report, 'Made in Israel: Exploiting Palestinian Land for Treatment of Israeli Waste', by Adam Aloni, December 2017.
15. Joshua Davidovich, 'It Can Only Be Jared: 8 Things to Know for January 30', *Times of Israel*, 30 January 2020.
16. 'The Besieged Palestinian Agricultural Sector', United Nations Conference on Trade and Development, 2015.
17. William Booth, 'In West Bank, Palestinians Gird for Settler Attacks on Olive Trees', *Washington Post*, 22 October 2014.
18. A claim that is unlikely to be true: the oldest tree in the world is thought to be a Great Basin bristlecone pine in the White Mountains of California, which researchers at the Rocky Mountain Tree-Ring Research Group declared was 5,062 years old in 2013. Accurately dating ancient olive trees is difficult, even via radiocarbon testing, but the world's oldest olive tree is generally held to grow at Vouves in Crete, and is estimated to be a mere 3,000 years old.
19. Shimon Samuels, 'Palestinian Aggression Against Interfaith Harmony at UNESCO', *Jerusalem Post*, 10 April 2019.

7. THE ROAD TO RAWABI: AN ALTERNATIVE PALESTINE

1. William Booth and Ruth Eglash, 'Palestinians in Nablus, Once Known for Suicide Bombers, Now Seeking Better Days', *Washington Post*, 21 October 2013.
2. Raphael Ahren, 'World's Richest Palestinian, Long a Strident Peace Advocate, Slams Israel for "Giving Us Crumbs"', *Times of Israel*, 10 June 2012.
3. See for example, Oliver Wainwright, 'House of Palestine: The Architectural Wonder Built by a West Bank Oil Tycoon', *Guardian*, 6 February 2019.
4. Nir Hasson, 'Israel Tells Court Waving PLO "Terror Organization" Flag Still a Crime', *Haaretz*, 20 November 2018; Nir Hasson, 'Flying Palestinian Flags in Israel is Not Illegal, Court Confirms', *Haaretz*, 27 September 2021.

8. THE SECRET CISTERNS OF JERUSALEM

1. Isaiah 12:3 (New King James Version).
2. See Numbers 20:11 (New King James Version).
3. From the northern French region of Artois, where many such wells were exploited by Carthusian monks in the twelfth century.
4. The Gihon tunnel inscription is in fact a replica of the limestone panel original, which is on display in the Archaeology Museum of Istanbul.
5. 2 Kings 18–20, 2 Chronicles 29–32, Isaiah 36–7 (New King James Version). The story is also the subject of a poem by Byron, *The Destruction of Sennacherib*, published in 1815.
6. Rediscovered in 1847 by Austen Henry Layard, the Lachish reliefs are displayed at the British Museum in London.
7. Dwight Tucker Jnr, 'Remembering God's Gift of Water', *The Connection*, 5 June 2014.
8. Revelation 22:1 (Christian Standard Bible), my emphasis.
9. Shimon Gibson and David Jacobson, *Below the Temple Mount in Jerusalem: A Sourcebook on the Cisterns, Subterranean Chambers and Conduits of the Haram al-Sharif*, British Archaeological Reports International Series 637, 1996.
10. According to *Ussher's Chronology*, a brave attempt by the seventeenth-century Archbishop of Armagh to write a history of the world through a literal interpretation of the Old Testament, Noah's Flood occurred in 2349 BC.
11. 'Jesus Christ's Return to Earth', Pew Research Center, July 2010.
12. Twain, *The Innocents Abroad*, p. 299.
13. Alex Morris, 'Donald Trump: The End-Times President', *Rolling Stone*, 30 October 2020.
14. Jeremiah 14:2–6 (New King James Version). For more on Old Testament drought prophecy, see Douglas S. Winnail, 'Droughts and Famine Increasing', *Tomorrow's World*, July–August 2007.
15. Maoz Azaryahu, *Tel-Aviv, the First Century: Visions, Designs, Actualities*, Indiana University Press, 2012, pp. 1–12.
16. Seth M. Siegel, *Let There Be Water: Israel's Solution for a Water-Starved World*, St Martin's Press, 2015, p. 21.
17. Ibid.
18. An estimate, provided by the Palestinian Central Bureau of Statistics in 2020.
19. Author interview with Tsvika Tsuk.
20. For more detail on the early days of the Blass plan, see Siegel, *Let There Be Water*.
21. Jewishvirtuallibrary.org.

9. WATER NOT FOR DRINK: THE SEA OF GALILEE AND THE NATIONAL WATER CARRIER

1. The Sea of Galilee contains some 4 km³ of freshwater. The nearest comparable body of water is in Cappadocia in central Turkey, three countries and a thousand kilometres away. Lake Assad, 600 kilometres away in northern Syria, is larger, but that lake is artificial, created in 1974 by the closure of the Tabqah dam across the Euphrates.

2. Twain, *The Innocents Abroad*, p. 299.
3. The fish's name comes from a New Testament story relating how the apostle Peter, a fisherman from Bethsaida on Galilee's northern shore, caught a fish with a coin in its mouth (Matthew 17: 24–7). It should not be confused with a John Dory, the marine fish *Zeus faber*, which is also known as St Peter's fish, thanks to a dark spot on its side that was once held to be the apostle's thumbprint.
4. Israeli Water Authority.
5. 'Overuse, Not Climate Change, Drying Up Sea of Galilee – Researchers', *Times of Israel*, 16 September 2018.
6. Michael Price, 'Sea of Galilee Earthquakes Triggered by Excessive Water Pumping', *Science Magazinei*, 26 July 2019.
7. Alon Tal, 'Climate Change's Impact on Lake Kinneret: Letting the Data tell the Story', *Science of the Total Environment* 685, May 2019.
8. Michael L. Wine, 'Letter to Editor re Tal (2019): Climaticization of Environmental Degradation – An Anthropocene Epoch Response to Failure of Governance', *Science of the Total Environment* 685, May 2019, pp. 1269–71.
9. Selby, *Water, Power and Politics*.
10. Siegal, *Let There Be Water*.
11. United Nations Food and Agriculture Organization, Fisheries and Aquaculture Department, National Aquaculture Sector, Overview 2020.
12. Imadeddin Moh'd Albaba, 'The Aquaculture Potential in the West Bank', conference paper for the First International Congress Documenting, Analyzing and Managing Biodiversity in the Middle East, Aqaba, October 2008.
13. 'Jordan Says It Will Cancel Clauses in Peace Treaty Leasing Border Land to Israel', *Times of Israel*, 21 October 2018.
14. Damian Carrington, 'World "Gravely" Unprepared for Effects of Climate Crisis', *Guardian*, 10 September 2019.
15. 'Seven Injured as Gaza Rocket Hits Home in Central Israel', BBC News, 25 March 2019.

10. THE GOLAN HEIGHTS: WHO NEEDS ITALY?

1. The main ones are UN Resolution 242 of 1967, which speaks of the 'inadmissibility of the acquisition of territory by war'; and Resolutions 338 (1973) and 497 (1981) which reinforced the principle of Resolution 242.
2. Julian Borger, 'Trump Says US Will Recognize Israel's Sovereignty over Golan Heights', *Guardian*, 21 March 2019.
3. Ibid.
4. 'Kim Murphy, Old Feud Over Lebanese River Takes New Turn', *Los Angeles Times*, 10 August 2006.
5. Selby, *Water, Power and Politics*.
6. For more on this debate, see Lauren Risi's essay 'Beyond Water Wars', *Wilson Quarterly*, Summer 2019.
7. 'Sweden Ignites Israeli Wine Row', *Decanter Magazine*, 8 June 2006.
8. Ben Simon, 'For Maker of West Bank "Pompeo" Wine, Emphasizing Product's Legitimacy Is Key', *Times of Israel*, 19 November 2020.
9. Rami Amichay and Ali Sawafta, 'Pompeo Visits Israeli-occupied West Bank and Golan Heights', *Reuters*, 19 November 2020.
10. Joseph Krauss, 'Pompeo is 1st Top US Diplomat to Visit an Israeli Settlement', *Associated Press*, 19 November 2020.
11. 'Pompeo During Rare Golan Heights Visit: "This is Israel"', *Times of Israel*, 19 November 2020.
12. Amichay and Sawafta, 'Pompeo Visits Israeli-occupied West Bank and Golan Heights'.

11. THE BALFOUR FOREST

1. Blanche E.C. Dugdale, *Arthur James Balfour, 1848–1930: The Authorised Life, in 2 Volumes*, Hutchinson & Co., 1936, vol. II, pp. 366–7.
2. Deuteronomy 26:12.
3. See, for example, the headlines: 'Straight Outta Balfour Street', *Times of Israel*, 9 February 2018; 'The Wizard of Balfour Street', *Jerusalem Post*, 11 April 2019; 'The Enemy is on Balfour Street, Not in Umm al-Fahm', *Haaretz*, 2 March 2020.
4. Jonathan Cook, 'Britain Still Proud of Its Shameful Role as Patron of Israel's Occupation', *Middle East Eye*, 2 November 2017.
5. Theodor Herzl, *Old-New Land [Altneuland]*, translated by David Simon Blondheim, CreateSpace Independent Publishing Platform 2015 [1916], pp. 67–70.
6. Eitan Bronstein, 'Most JNF-KKL Forests and Sites are Located on the Ruins of Palestinian Villages', *Zochrot*, April 2014.
7. 'List of Villages Sold by Sursocks and Their Partners to the Zionists since British Occupation of Palestine', Exhibit 71, Evidence to the Shaw Commission, 1930.

12. TEL AVIV: MIRACLE CITY

1. The name refers to the Israelite Tribe of Dan, who originally settled here.
2. Israel Central Bureau of Statistics, 2021 figure.
3. Organisation for Economic Co-operation and Development.
4. Auja, the Arabic name for the Yarkon, is a common river name in the Middle East; the map line referred to the Yarkon and the Wadi al-Auja near Jericho that I had visited with Bassam (see Chapter 3).
5. Sharif Elmusa and Muhammad Ali Khalidi, *All That Remains: The Palestinian Villages Occupied and Depopulated by Israel in 1948*, Institute for Palestine Studies, 1992.
6. Israeli Water Authority presentation at Sorek.
7. Dana Regev, 'Israeli Kibbutz: Communal Idealism or the Privileged Few?', *Deutsche Welle*, May 2016.
8. Siegal, *Let There Be Water*, pp. 31–3.

13. THE NEGEV DESERT: HOW THE SOUTH WAS WON

1. Lawrence was well aware of the dual nature of his mission. He later wrote to his parents: 'We are obviously only meant as red herrings to give an archaeological colour to a political job.' See Jeremy Wilson, *Lawrence of Arabia: The Authorized Biography*, Heinemann, 1989.
2. Daphne Rousseau, 'In Israeli Desert, World's Highest Solar Tower Looks to Future', *Times of Israel*, 19 June 2016.
3. Abigail Klein Leichman, 'Solar-powered Desalination Cuts Energy Costs by 90%', *Israel21c.org*, 17 November 2016.
4. Between Abraham and the Philistine King Abimelech, described in Genesis 21:22–34.
5. M. Evenari, L. Shanan and N.H. Tadmor, '"Runoff Farming" in the Desert. I. Experimental Layout', *Agronomy* 60:1, January 1968, pp. 29–32.
6. Knesset Research and Information Center.
7. 'Israel Demolishes Palestinian Village of Al-Araqeeb for 209th Time', *Middle East Monitor*, 14 November 2022.
8. 'Al-Araqeeb Demolished for 130th Time', *Middle East Monitor*, 27 June 2018.
9. 'After Years of Delays, Jordan Said to Nix Red Sea-Dead Sea Canal with Israel', *Times of Israel*, 17 June 2021.
10. The project was, in fact, halted once again in June 2021, by Jordan, who reportedly complained that there was 'no real Israeli desire' for it to go ahead.
11. Knesset Research and Information Center.

12. The most recently available official figure, from International Trade Administration, US Department of Commerce.

14. GAZA REDUX

1. 'Gaza Protest Deaths: Israel May Have Committed War Crimes – UN', *BBC News*, 28 February 2019.
2. 'Israel to Process Gaza Sewage with New Pipeline', *Times of Israel*, 19 June 2019.
3. 'Israel Dismisses Purportedly "Friendlier" Hamas Principles', *Times of Israel*, 3 May 2017.
4. 'Israel to Process Gaza Sewage with New Pipeline', *Times of Israel*, 19 June 2019.
5. 'Israel Lays Fourth Water Pipeline to Gaza, The Largest Yet', *Times of Israel*, 17 June 2019.
6. Factsheet, 'Gaza in the Face of Two Viruses: COVID-19 and Occupation', *ReliefWeb* (a service provided by the United Nations Office for the Coordination of Humanitarian Affairs), 6 October 2022.
7. 'United Kingdom Government Country Policy and Information Note: The Humanitarian Situation in Gaza', July 2022.
8. Amos Harel, 'Israeli Security Officials Dread Having to Handle a Gaza Coronavirus Outbreak', *Haaretz*, 10 March 2020.
9. Arshad Mohammed, Jonathan Saul, John Irish and Parisa Hafezi, 'Israel's Gaza Challenge: Stopping Metal Tubes Turning into Rockets', *Reuters*, 23 May 2021.
10. United Nations figures from 'Protection of Civilians Report, 24–31 May 2021, UNOCHA.
11. Entsar Jahal, 'Israeli Campaign in Gaza Worsens Water Crisis', *Al-Monitor*, 28 May 2021.
12. 'Israeli Strikes on Gaza High-Rises May Be War Crimes – Human Rights Watch', *BBC News*, 23 August 2021.
13. 'Germany Announces Euro9m Drinking Water Initiative for Gaza', *The New Arab*, 17 December 2021.
14. Amira Haas, 'Israel Holds Up Vital Spare Parts for Gaza's Water and Sewage Systems', *Haaretz*, 9 January 2022.
15. 'UAE and Israel Discuss Cooperation on Food and Water Security', *Reuters*, 30 August 2020.
16. Mervyn Piesse, Future Directions International, 9 September 2020.
17. Keith Johnson, 'The Big Missing Piece of the Kushner Plan: Water', *Foreign Policy Magazine*, 4 February 2020.
18. Author interview.
19. 'Despite War, Israel Must Act with Magnanimity', *Haaretz* editorial, 19 July 2014.
20. Oliver Holmes, 'Naftali Bennett: Israel's Far-Right Prime Minister in Waiting', *Guardian*, 3 June 2021.
21. @DrHananAshwari, Twitter, 7 November 2020.
22. Linah Alsaafin, 'Joe Biden "No Saviour" of the Palestinians', *Al Jazeera*, 8 November 2020.
23. Lord Ahmad of Wimbledon, written reply in UK House of Lords (HL3850), 19 May 2020.
24. 'Conference on Jerusalem – Closing Remarks & Statement', Balfour Project, 7 December 2020.

Select Bibliography

Adams, R.J.Q., *Balfour: The Last Grandee*, Thistle Publishing, 2013.

Allan, Tony, *The Middle East Water Question: Hydropolitics and the Global Economy*, I.B. Tauris, 2012.

Assaf, Karen, Nader al Khatib, Elisha Kally and Hillel Shuval, 'A Proposal for the Development of a Regional Water Master Plan', Israel/Palestine Center for Research and Information, October 1993.

Barnosky, Anthony D. and Elizabeth A. Hadly, *End Game: Tipping Point for Planet Earth?*, William Collins, 2015.

Bauck, Petter and Mohammed Omer (eds), *The Oslo Accords: A Critical Assessment*, The American University in Cairo Press, 2016.

Bishop, Patrick, *The Reckoning: Death and Intrigue in the Promised Land*, William Collins, 2015.

Black, Ian, *Enemies and Neighbours: Arabs and Jews in Palestine and Israel, 1917–2017*, Allen Lane, 2017.

Bromberg, Gidon, 'Will the Jordan River Keep on Flowing?', *Yale Environment* 360, 2008.

Carlini, Agnese, 'The Major Role of Water in the Israeli-Palestinian Conflict', *Mediterranean Affairs Magazine*, February 2015.

de Chatel, Francesca, *Water Sheikhs and Dam Builders*, Transaction Publishers, 2007.

de Villiers, Marq, *Water Wars: Is the World's Water Running Out?*, Weidenfeld & Nicolson 1999.

Diamond, Jared, *Collapse: How Societies Choose to Fail or Succeed*, Penguin Books, 2006.

Dugdale, Blanche E.C., *Arthur James Balfour, 1848–1930: The Authorised Life, in 2 Volumes*, Hutchinson & Co., 1936.

——, *Baffy: The Diaries of Blanche Dugdale 1936–1947*, ed. N.A. Rose, Vallentine Mitchell & Co., 1973.

——, *Family Homespun*, John Murray, 1940.

Easter, K., G. Feder, G.L. Moigne, A. Duda and E. Forsyth, 'Water Resources Management: World Bank Policy Paper', World Bank, 1994.

Ehrenreich, Ben, *The Way to the Spring: Life and Death in Palestine*, Penguin Books, 2016.

Elamassi, Khalid, *Assessment of Groundwater Quality in Gaza, Palestine: Environmental Management and Monitoring*, Noor Publishing, 2016.

Elmusa, Sharif S., *Negotiating Water: Israel and the Palestinians*, Institute for Palestine Studies, 1996.

——, *Water Conflict: Economics, Politics, Law and Palestinian-Israeli Water Resources*, Institute for Palestine Studies, 1998.

Fergusson, Bernard, *The Trumpet in the Hall*, Collins, 1970.

Fields, Gary, *Enclosure: Palestinian Landscapes in a Historical Mirror*, University of California Press, 2017.

Filiu, Jean-Pierre, *Gaza, A History*, Oxford University Press, 2014.

Finkelstein, Norman G., *Image and Reality of the Israel–Palestine Conflict*, Verso, 2003.

——, *This Time We Went Too Far: Truth and Consequences of the Gaza Invasion*, OR Books, 2010.

——, *Gaza: An Inquest into Its Martyrdom*, University of California Press, 2018.

Fishman, Charles, *The Big Thirst*, Simon & Schuster, 2012.

Fletcher, Martin, *Walking Israel: A Personal Search for the Soul of a Nation*, Thomas Dunne Books, 2011.

Gibson, Shimon and David Jacobson, *Below the Temple Mount in Jerusalem: A Sourcebook on the Cisterns, Subterranean Chambers and Conduits of the Haram al-Sharif*, British Archaeological Reports International Series 637, 1996.

Goff, Chris, *Dark Waters: A Thriller*, Crooked Lane Books, 2015.

Golani, Motti, *Israel in Search of a War: The Sinai Campaign 1955–6*, Sussex Academic Press, 1998.

Halper, Jeff, *War Against the People: Israel, the Palestinians and Global Pacification*, Pluto Press, 2015.

Hass, Amira, 'The Israeli "Watergate" Scandal: The Facts About Palestinian Water', *Haaretz*, 16 February 2014.

Havrelock, Rachel, *River Jordan: The Mythology of a Dividing Line*, University of Chicago Press, 2011.

Herzl, Theodor, *Old-New Land [Altneuland]*, CreateSpace Independent Publishing Platform, 2015 [1902].

Hillel, Daniel, *The Natural History of the Bible*, Columbia University Press, 2006.

Hope, Sebastian, *Hotel Tiberias: A Tale of Two Grandfathers*, Harper Perennial, 2005.

Howe, Carrie M., 'Water Scarcity and Increased Instability – How Israel's Policies and Actions since the Creation of the National Water Carrier Have Adversely Impacted the Jordan River Basin', US Marine Corps Research Paper, 2010.

Jeffries, J.M.N., *Palestine, the Reality: The Inside Story of the Balfour Declaration 1917–38*, Olive Branch Press, 2017.

Kielburger, Craig and Marc, 'Water Can Be a Bridge to Peace in the Middle East', *Huffington Post*, 20 July 2011.

Kishawi, Yaser, 'Conceptual Multi-Objective Optimization Model for Sustainable Water Resources Management in the Gaza Strip', University of Strathclyde, MSc dissertation, August 2011.

Krieger, Barbara, *The Dead Sea and the Jordan River*, Indiana University Press, 2016.

Lazarou, Eleni, 'Water in the Israeli-Palestinian Conflict', European Parliament Briefing Paper, January 2016.

Lowdermilk, Walter Clay, *Palestine, Land of Promise*, Victor Gollancz, 1944.

Lynch, W.F., *Narrative of the United States' Expedition to the River Jordan and the Dead Sea*, Lea and Blanchard, 1849.

McDowall, David. *Palestine and Israel: The Uprising and Beyond*, I.B. Tauris, 1990.

Macgregor, John, *The Rob Roy on the Jordan, Nile, Red Sea and Gennesareth: A Canoe Cruise in Palestine and Egypt, and the Waters of Damascus*, Hanse Books, 2017 [1870].

Macintyre, Donald, *Gaza: Preparing for Dawn*, Oneworld, 2017.

Martin, Alison and Simone Klawitter, 'Treading Water: The Worsening Water Crisis and the Gaza Reconstruction Mechanism', Oxfam Briefing Paper, March 2017.

Messerschmid, Clemens, 'Hydro-Apartheid and Water Access in Israel-Palestine: Challenging the Myths of Cooperation and Scarcity', in *Decolonizing Palestinian Political Economy: De-development and Beyond*, ed. Mandy Turner and Omar Shweiki, Palgrave Macmillan, 2015.

Oz, Amos, *Judas*, Vintage, 2017.

Pappé, Ilan. *The Biggest Prison on Earth: A History of the Occupied Territories*, Oneworld, 2017.

——, *Ten Myths About Israel*, Verso, 2017.

Pearce, Fred. *When the Rivers Run Dry*, Eden Project Books, 2006.

Peled, Miko, *The General's Son: Journey of an Israeli in Palestine*, Just World Books, 2016.

Rabinyan, Dorit, *All the Rivers: Are There Borders Love Cannot Cross?*, Serpent's Tail, 2017.

Regan, Bernard, *The Balfour Declaration: Empire, the Mandate and Resistance in Palestine*, Verso, 2017.

Robinson, Daniel, Orlando Crowcroft, Virginia Maxwell and Jenny Walker, *Israel and the Palestinian Territories*, Lonely Planet, 2015.

Rouyer, Alwyn R., *Turning Water into Politics: The Water Issue in the Palestinian-Israeli Conflict*, Palgrave Macmillan, 2000.

Sabbagh, Karl, *Palestine: A Personal History*, Atlantic Books, 2006.

Schneer, Jonathan, *The Balfour Declaration: The Origins of the Arab-Israeli Conflict*, Bloomsbury, 2011.

Sebag Montefiore, Simon, *Jerusalem: The Biography*, Weidenfeld & Nicolson, 2012.

Segev, Tom, *One Palestine, Complete: Jews and Arabs under the British Mandate*, Abacus, 2001.

Selby, Jan, 'Co-operation, Domination and Colonisation: The Israeli-Palestinian Joint Water Committee', *Water Alternatives* 6:1, February 2013.

——, *Water, Power and Politics in the Middle East: The Other Israeli–Palestinian Conflict*, I.B. Tauris, 2003.

Seltzer, Assaf, *Mekorot: The Story of the Israel National Water Company – The First 75 Years*, Yad Ben-Zvi Press, 2011.

Shapland, Greg, *Rivers of Discord: International Water Disputes in the Middle East*, C. Hurst & Co., 1997.

Shehadeh, Raja, *Where the Line is Drawn: Crossing Boundaries in Occupied Palestine*, Profile Books, 2017.

Siegel, Seth, *Let There Be Water: Israel's Solution for a Water-Starved World*, St Martin's Press, 2015.

Somerville, Rowan, *Beat: The True Story of a Suicide Bomber and a Heart*, Lilliput Press, 2017.

Sosland, Jeffrey K., *Co-operating Rivals: The Riparian Politics of the Jordan River Basin*, State University of New York Press, 2007.

Sutcliffe, William, *The Wall: A Modern Fable*, Bloomsbury, 2018.

Tal, Alon, *Pollution in a Promised Land: An Environmental History of Israel*, University of California Press, 2002.

Tamari, Salim and Issam Nassar, eds, *The Storyteller of Jerusalem: The Life and Times of Wasif Jawhariyyeh, 1904–1948*, Olive Branch Press, 2014.

Tolan, Sandy, *The Lemon Tree: The True Story of a Friendship That Survives Four Decades of the World's Bitterest Conflict*, Black Swan, 2008.

Tsuk, Tsvika, *Water at the End of the Tunnel: Touring Israel's Ancient Water Systems*, Yad Ben-Zvi Press, 2011.

Twain, Mark, *The Innocents Abroad, or The New Pilgrim's Progress*, Wordsworth Classics, 2010.

Watzman, Haim, *A Crack in the Earth: A Journey Up Israel's Rift Valley*, Argo-Navis, 2012.

Weinthal, Erika, 'Water as a Basic Human Right within the Israeli-Palestinian Conflict', *American Diplomacy*, October 2017.

Weizman, Eyal, *Hollow Land: Israel's Architecture of Occupation*, Verso, 2012, rev edn.

Yousef, Mosab Hassan, *Son of Hamas: A Gripping Account of Terror, Betrayal, Political Intrigue, and Unthinkable Choices*, Tyndale House Publishers, 2010.

Zeitoun, Mark, *Power and Water in the Middle East: The Hidden Politics of the Palestinian-Israeli Water Conflict*, I.B. Tauris, 2009.

Index